D1596655

The Impossible Takes
A Little Longer

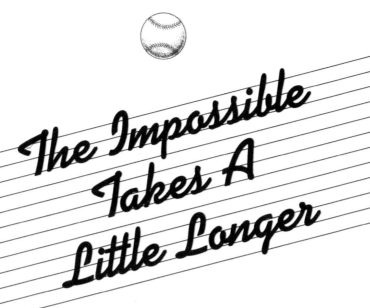

The Impossible Takes A Little Longer

THE TEXAS RANGERS
from Pretenders to Contenders

—•—

BY PHIL ROGERS

•

Foreword by Nolan Ryan

TAYLOR PUBLISHING COMPANY
Dallas, Texas

Published by
Taylor Publishing Company
1550 West Mockingbird Lane
Dallas, Texas 75235

Design by Lurelle Cheverie

Library of Congress Cataloging-in-Publication Data

Rogers, Phil.
  The impossible takes a little longer : the Texas Rangers, from
pretenders to contenders / by Phil Rogers.
     p.   cm.
   ISBN 0-87833-630-3 : $16.95
   1. Texas Rangers (Baseball team)–History.   I. Title.
GV875.T4R64 1990
796.35764'09764531–dc20   89-49192
                                                                        CIP

Printed in the United States of America

10 9 8 7 6 5 4 3 2 1

To my parents, Sid and Nelda,
and my brother Dave, who helped me
to recognize baseball as the
best of man's inventions, and to
my wife, Suzanne, who doesn't
hold it against me —
except in extra innings

Contents

Foreword

There was never any doubt that I would finish my career in Texas. It was the way things worked out, but it was also the way I would have wanted it if I had drawn things up myself. Baseball and Texas, along with my family and friends, have been my life, and have always been kind to me. It seemed natural that I would combine the two in the last years of my career.

That's what I was thinking when I made my big decision to go home—November 19, 1979. I had been pitching in the major leagues for twelve years. Being the kind of pitcher I am—a power pitcher—I figured three more years would be just about all I would hold up. That was the length of the contract I signed with the Houston Astros, and I figured when it was over, my career would be, too. It seemed like the right way to go out.

My hometown of Alvin was a thirty-minute drive from the Astrodome, so my wife Ruth, my sons, Reid and Reese, and my daughter, Wendy, could watch me pitch while leading a normal life at home. That was my plan, but there was a hitch—I stayed effective as a pitcher much longer than I thought I would. I think the explanation for this is that I always paid attention to mechanics, worked hard to be in condition, and was blessed with a strong arm.

That three-year contract led to others in Houston, and I still enjoyed pitching. I had thought about retiring after the last one ran out in 1988, but that year I led the National League in strikeouts. John McMullen, the owner who brought me to Houston, felt that I had become a risk at age forty-two, which left me with a difficult decision—quit when I could still pitch effectively, or pack up and play for another team. There were teams out there that didn't share McMullen's opinion.

Gene Autry and the California fans had been terrific when I played there from 1972-79, and the Cowboy wanted me back. That was tempting. I also received calls from San Francisco General Manager Al Rosen, who had been our general manager while I was with Houston. There were other teams who called, and when my family talked about it, they all wanted me to keep pitching. Then Dick Moss, my agent, got a call one day from Tom Grieve, who had been an outfielder with the Texas Rangers when I first came to the American

League. He was now the general manager in Texas, and he expressed interest in having me join the Rangers. This was an interesting option.

When I'd pitched for California, my starts in Arlington had always brought some friends up from home, and I had always kept up with the Rangers. Their early teams were way down, and the stands were seldom full. But they had some interesting teams in my last few years with California, making trades for older players who could win. They never won a division, but they were tough. When we won the West title in 1979, they were five games back.

Something went wrong in the '80s, but now it looked like they were on their way back. Grieve and Bobby Valentine were building with young players, and the ownership was making the kind of commitment it takes to win. They proved that before they signed me. First they traded for Rafael Palmeiro, one of the best young hitters in the National League, and then they picked up Julio Franco from Cleveland. The Rangers were trying to win, and that appealed to me. I liked their new aggressive attitude. I wouldn't be able to drive to the park from my house in Alvin, but I would be wearing "Texas" on my jersey.

It was the right decision for me. We didn't win the West in 1989, but we showed that the foundation for a future winner is in place. It was a good year for me and my teammates, even if it didn't end the way we'd hoped. Only one team every year gets to win the very last game of the season. That's our goal for next year, and we don't think it is out of reach.

Phil Rogers covered the Rangers for the *Dallas Times Herald* throughout the 1989 season, and was on the baseball beat back when Grieve and Valentine got their starts running the team. He has covered all the angles, and it's all here in his book—the long, slow climb from the dark days of 1984 and 1985 to a bright future that should make the 1990s the best decade ever for baseball fans in Texas.

Nolan Ryan, October 1989

Acknowledgments

Since it was writing that always interested me, it only figures that I was best at math. But math has served me well as a baseball writer, giving me an edge over rivals in computing earned run averages, slugging percentages, and other such necessities of the trade. It sometimes leads to idle calculations, too.

For instance, in the course of reporting on the Texas Rangers for the *Dallas Times Herald*, I have spent an estimated fifteen hundred hours per year hanging around batting cages or press boxes since 1984. I have watched Rangers pitchers throw roughly 26,250 pitches – 10,500 balls, 15,750 strikes – and heard that dreadful song, "Minnie the Moocher," about one hundred fifty times each year. The great thing is that my "work" has never really fit the definition of the word.

For that, I'd like to thank my compatriots: the *Times Herald*'s Frank Luksa, Kurt Iverson, and Louis DeLuca; Tracy Ringolsby, Randy Galloway, Blackie Sherrod, Kevin Sherrington, Gerry Fraley, and Tim Cowlishaw of *The Dallas Morning News*; and Jim Reeves, Galyn Wilkins, Tony DeMarco, and T.R. Sullivan with the *Fort Worth Star-Telegram*. Others have made me laugh before they left Dallas-Fort Worth newspapers for work in distant locales: Tim Kurkjian (now at *Sports Illustrated*), Paul Hagen (*Philadelphia Daily News*), Richard Justice (*The Washington Post*), and Tom Powers (*St. Paul Pioneer Press Dispatch*). Also, thanks to Burt Hawkins, Dick Butler, Eric Nadel, Mark Holtz, Pancho Small, and the Rangers' John Blake, Taunee Paur, and Larry Kelly.

Back in the summer of 1987 Dudley Jahnke, then with Taylor Publishing, believed that the time was right for a book about one of baseball's least successful franchises, and I thank him for that belief. The project fell to editor Jim Donovan, to whom I'm indebted for seeing it through, albeit not with the glorious conclusion that we were hoping for back in April 1989. Thanks also to Frank Luksa, again, and Carlton Stowers, who gave me direction when the book was an idea.

Finally, thanks to former Arlington mayor Tom Vandergriff, who brought the Rangers to Texas in the first place. It would have been a long commute to Washington.

A Change In the Weather

A black cloud was following the Texas Rangers. It had followed Doug Rader and his players from Arlington, Texas, where they had lost two out of three games to their counterparts in clunk, the Cleveland Indians, all the way to Detroit. There, the 1985 Rangers lost twice more in two days, leading the defending World Champions for all of one-half inning in the two-game series.

The game of Monday, May 13, set the tone for what would be among the ugliest road trips in the Texas franchise's undistinguished history. Detroit's Dan Petry retired the top of the Rangers' order without a base hit in the first inning. Lou Whitaker, the Tigers' 160-pound leadoff hitter, began the Detroit first with one of those home runs that seems even longer in recollection. His blast off Ranger pitcher Burt Hooton left not only the playing field, but also the stadium.

Whitaker's drive landed on the roof of Tiger Stadium – not far from the light tower Reggie Jackson struck in the 1971 All-Star Game – and bounded all the way over to Michigan Avenue, where someone could have picked up the unexpected souvenir simply by stumbling out of Hoot Robinson's bar at the right time. It was the twentieth home run ever to clear the roof of the historic old park. Before the Tigers finished beating the Rangers 7-4, Kirk Gibson and Lance Parrish added prodigious home runs – Gibson into the upper deck in right field; Parrish into the upper deck in left field.

Things did not go much better for the Rangers the next night, even though Rader had Charlie Hough starting. Hough had started both of the Rangers' victories in the last fourteen days, but he, too, fell victim to Whitaker. The Tigers' second baseman singled and scored in the first inning and followed with a two-run homer – this one only off the facing of the upper deck – in the second inning of what would finish as a 4-1 victory for Detroit.

Two months earlier, under the friendly Florida skies, the Rangers had counted on one thing: They could score runs. Yet this marked the eighth time in

1

the last eleven games they had either scored just one run or had been shut out completely, and it dropped their record to a numbing 9-21.

Time had run out on "The Rooster" (given name: Douglas Lee Rader), although this fact would not become official for two more exhausting days. Reports of Rader's imminent firing were being written in the Tiger Stadium press box the night of the 4-1 loss, but Rader remained with the Rangers as they headed to New York.

So did the black cloud.

When the players woke up the next morning, Wednesday, May 15, the first thing many noticed was that there was no running water in their Manhattan hotel. That was followed by a depressing notice in the New York newspapers that newspapers in Dallas and Fort Worth were saying a decision had been reached to fire Rader. It was true Rader's popularity had peaked two years before, in 1985, but no one—baseball players included—ever likes to be around when a man he has gotten to know loses his job.

"Whether it's a job or something else that's cherished, you hate to see somebody lose it," said Cliff Johnson, a former teammate of Rader's with the Houston Astros. "We understand that it's a part of the business, like paying taxes and dying. It doesn't make it any easier."

Removal of a manager was a well-rehearsed move for the Texas franchise. Rader, after all, was the twelfth manager it had employed in fourteen years. You would think experience would have taught them how to do it. But, of course, that was not the club's history.

So while Rader sat in a Yankee Stadium dugout telling a wave of suddenly interested writers from New York that he had not heard a word, oilman Eddie Chiles was in his Fort Worth office saying that not only had Rader not been fired, but it was no one's business. Chiles, a right-winger who found even the most conservative newspapers too far to the left, emphatically denied the reports, at one point saying, "I consider everything in *The Dallas Morning News* garbage."

Rader knew what was happening.

He was asked by someone who had borrowed a book from him if it was time to make a quick read of the remaining chapters. "You better get out the Evelyn Wood method," Rader answered.

Rader had been too short of admirable qualities—discretion and patience chief among them—too often during his two and a half years as the Rangers' manager. Now, as his tenure was ending, he was simply short of good fortune.

Wednesday night in the Bronx, the Rangers had every chance to end a losing streak that stood at four games. The Yankees blasted second-year left-hander Mike Mason for five runs on seven hits in the first three innings, but Greg Harris replaced Mason and threw 4⅔ hitless innings. Buddy Bell brought the Rangers to within one run with a two-run double in the fifth inning and tied the score 5-5 with a triple in the seventh, both off Yankee ace Ron Guidry.

In the ninth, #9 hitter Curtis Wilkerson collected his third hit of the game, a double. Toby Harrah followed with a single, but left fielder Ken Griffey cut down Wilkerson with a strong throw to the plate. Second baseman Willie Randolph then made a good catch on a line drive by Bell to end the inning with Texas runners on second and third.

Johnson's leadoff double led only to more frustration in the Texas half of the tenth inning, and the Yankees used Dave Schmidt's leadoff walk of Dave Winfield to start a rally in the bottom of the inning. With two on and one out, an error by first baseman Pete O'Brien – his first in 315 chances – allowed Winfield to score the winning run. "We wanted the ball hit on the ground . . . and it was," Rader said. Nevertheless, the losing streak hit five.

After the game, the tactless Chiles continued to attack the Dallas-Fort Worth media, when he would have been better served by simply answering reporters' questions. He could have ducked the phone calls, or simply said he had no comment. What Chiles wound up saying was that he could run the Rangers exactly as he pleased, the same way he had always run his oil-supply business, the Western Company of North America.

"The Rangers operation, a baseball club, is a privately owned business. It is not operating under any sunshine laws," Chiles said. "We don't have to tell the public everything we do . . . and we're not going to. What difference does it make to me how people think we handle something? It doesn't have anything to do with what I do. I'm not playing to an audience. I'm not on stage."

Chiles felt strongly he was doing nothing wrong. "You newshawks are the ones making a mess," he said.

Chiles continued the charade the next afternoon, while the streak went to six with a second consecutive 6-5 loss to the Yankees. This day the Rangers left four men on base in the eighth and ninth innings and then watched a bad-hop single, balk, and sacrifice bunt put Rickey Henderson on third base as the winning run with one out in the New York ninth.

Enter the Rader factor. Facing the trio of Randolph, Don Mattingly, and Winfield, Rader played the percentages. Randolph and Mattingly were intentionally walked to load the bases. Rader then told Wilkerson to play medium-deep at shortstop, leaving open the possibility of a double play rather than playing in for Winfield. No one was surprised at the result. The powerful Winfield topped a soft chopper to short. Wilkerson had neither a play at the plate nor a chance at a double play, and the Rangers were headed to Chicago with a 9-23 record.

"If I'm playing up, I think I have a play at the plate," Wilkerson said. "It's the only shot I have. It would have been close."

Rader insisted once again that he had heard nothing from Chiles. But that changed when the Rangers reached their hotel in downtown Chicago. Mike Stone, the corporate achiever whom Chiles had moved over from the Western Company to serve as his point man with the baseball franchise, was waiting, along with the team's thirty-seven-year-old general manager, Tom Grieve.

Rader, a man referred to as a "cancer" by *Dallas Times Herald* sports columnist Skip Bayless the previous September, was sent back to Florida, taking a contractual guarantee of about $400,000 with him. (With a year remaining on his contract, Stone had given him a good-faith extension of two years as the 1984 Rangers were wrapping up a 69-92 season. Great move, huh?)

Now Rader was being fired with 454 games remaining on his contract. Of course. That was the way this team had always done business.

Stone admitted the awkward spectacle of Rader twisting in the New York breeze was caused by a search for his replacement. "We felt it was a benefit to the ball club to make the move without wholesale confusion," Stone said. "We thought this would be a more orderly change as opposed to (hiring an interim managor)."

There were lengthy conversations with Earl Weaver, the manager who brought four pennants to Baltimore and was now in brief retirement on the golf courses of South Florida. Weaver decided that a man his age did not need this kind of a challenge.

Grieve quickly turned to Bobby Valentine, who had never managed a baseball game—anywhere. Not in the major leagues. Not in the minor leagues. Not in the Dominican Republic. Not in Mexico. Not in the Stamford, Connecticut, Little League. At thirty-five, he was younger than six of the players he would inherit.

Valentine, a third-base coach for the New York Mets, had been among the three finalists when Rader was hired before the 1983 season. Jim Leyland (then a coach for the Chicago White Sox and later a manager in Pittsburgh) Valentine, and Rader had all been brought in for a round of final interviews. Valentine, in fact, had been interviewed three times.

He had impressed Joe Klein, Grieve's predecessor, with his self-confidence. A man with Frankie Avalon's good looks and an outgoing personality to match, Valentine had been preparing himself to become a major-league manager ever since an unexpected rendevous with the Anaheim Stadium outfield fence had robbed him of his speed. That tremendous speed was Valentine's most valuable asset as a player; without it he had become expendable, his playing days over at the age of twenty-nine.

"Why I think I'm the best man is not necessarily that I think I'm the best man in this race, but I think I can and will be a really good big-league manager some day," Valentine told the *Fort Worth Star-Telegram*'s Jim Reeves. "Obviously it's not because of any experience I have, but because of the things I feel go into making a good manager."

When he listed those qualities, it became clear that he felt he fit the mold perfectly. "I think I could go head to head with anyone who is managing now," Valentine said that October day in 1982. "And I'm anxiously awaiting an opportunity to prove it."

It was asking too much to be hired to manage in the big leagues at age thirty-two. But three years later with a good friend and former Mets teammate now the Rangers' general manager, Valentine was given his chance.

The Rader-Valentine switch was well received in the clubhouse. "Any kind of change would be for the better," Hough said.

Added center fielder George Wright, "Things have been going so bad for us we needed something. The same things kept happening over and over again, so they had to make a change."

But the players had seen how the firing had been handled; it had given Rader the aura of a Greek tragic hero. And this did not increase their confidence in Chiles and Stone. "If a decision had to be made, fine, but it was a little sloppy in New York, don't you think?" Hough said. "I didn't particularly care for it. I know if I was Doug, I would have probably been more upset than he let on. There is a professional way to handle that business, and that was not it."

On Friday, May 17, Valentine flew from Houston to Chicago to join the Rangers. He was full of himself. So much so, in fact, that he told reporters he could turn around this sick puppy of a team that had been gasping for air since Eddie Murray's game-winning home run off Dave Rozema on Opening Day in Baltimore, that had played six games before it won one, and that thirty-two games into the season had already endured losing streaks of at least five games on three different occasions.

At this point attendance was lagging behind even that of the previous season, when the Rangers had drawn their smallest full-season gate since 1973, their second season in Arlington. Every empty seat represented more money Chiles was throwing down this dry hole of a franchise.

Valentine admitted he had seen the Rangers play only occasionally since 1979–when Valentine was finishing his playing career with Seattle and the excitable Brad Corbett was the Rangers' owner–but claimed to have done his homework.

"I've read the box scores, and I've been amazed to see the numbers mount in the loss column," Valentine said, meeting with Texas sportswriters in the cramped visiting manager's quarters at Comiskey Park on Friday afternoon. "I don't understand why this team hasn't been able to win."

He soon would.

The long road trip wasn't over. Two more telling events happened that May weekend in Chicago.

In the seventh inning of Valentine's first game as a manager, rookie outfielder Tommy Dunbar, whom Rader had kept at the expense of popular veteran Mickey Rivers, sprained an ankle trying to beat out a double play. The injury was bad enough to put Dunbar on the disabled list. In his place, the Rangers promoted twenty-two-year-old Oddibe McDowell, a 1984 Olympian who had been the organization's #1 draft choice the previous June. He had played only thirty-one games in the minor leagues, hitting .400 with 18 RBIs and 12 stolen bases at Oklahoma City.

George Wright, whose center-field job McDowell would soon claim, was among those warmly greeting the quiet rookie. After all, Wright had been in West Palm Beach the day McDowell both hit a grand slam and bunted his way on base in an exhibition against Montreal–his first game as a professional player. "That league couldn't hold you," Wright told McDowell, referring to the American Association. "I knew it couldn't."

McDowell was the ghost of the Rangers' future.

Buddy Bell was the ghost of the Rangers' past. After his first game under Valentine, a 4-2 loss to the White Sox, Bell headed for a Division Street club, The Lodge, to unwind with some drinks and the best jukebox in America. Who could blame him?

But Bell unwound to such a liquid degree that he was more than hoarse the next day. When he returned to his hotel room, most likely after a 4 A.M. last call, he managed to shut the door on his thumb. The Rangers' blond-haired poster boy was unable to play the next night because of the mysterious injury.

Burt Hooton gave Valentine his first victory that night–without Bell.

2

"Dogs On the Field and Off"

It was the kind of scene Bob Short had envisioned when he uprooted the Washington Senators. One of the country's booming areas—full of high-stakes businesses, sports-minded citizens, and comfortable suburbs—had focused its attention on what two years before had been Turnpike Stadium, home of the Texas League's Dallas-Fort Worth Spurs.

On this day, June 27, 1973, the Old Turnpike Stadium was the place to be. From every direction, cars headed to the renamed Arlington Stadium, still more a nice little ballpark than a major-league arena. In a preview to rush hour on Dallas' freeways a few years later, ticket holders faced gridlock on the Dallas-Fort Worth Turnpike as they approached from Dallas to the east and Fort Worth to the west. From the north, Highway 157 was a mess. Those on the way to their first game must have thought it would be this way every time the Rangers played.

Hardly.

But even those who had been coming since, in April the year before, Frank Howard had hit a home run in the local opener, were stumped. Back roads like Randol Mill were bumper-to-bumper, and already announcer Dick Risenhoover was on the air.

Although the start of the game was pushed back fifteen minutes—during which the Rangers wrapped up a P.T. Barnum-style spectacle complete with lion cubs and Polynesian dancers—a lot of the people who wanted to witness David Clyde's first pitch, heard the call from Risenhoover as Minnesota's Jerry Terrell stepped in to face the schoolboy legend from Houston.

"Ball one."

Clyde, fresh from leading his Westchester High School team to the state 4-A championship game, had been the first pick in the annual amateur draft. Twenty days after the last of his twenty-nine consecutive victories at Westchester (senior year: 18-0 with a 0.18 earned run average, 14 shutouts, 5 no-hitters, and 328 strikeouts in 148⅓ innings) and a week after receiving a bonus reported to be a whopping $125,000, Clyde was facing the Minnesota Twins. The Twins' batting order that night would include lifetime .300 hitters Rod Carew and Tony Oliva.

(Clyde told the *Times Herald*'s Joe Rhodes in a 1983 interview that his bonus was actually $65,000. "If I'd held out for [a six-figure bonus]," he said, "I'd have priced myself right out of the Rangers' organization.")

Many wanted Clyde to mow them down, but only the truly naive believed he could. Exposing Clyde to such a potentially demoralizing situation never would have happened in Detroit or Boston, where baseball had firm roots dating back to Ty Cobb and Babe Ruth. But this was Arlington, Texas, in 1973.

Not many people cared about the kind of baseball played by the Rangers in those years, but everyone loves a good show. By the time the traffic cleared, 35,698 beer-swilling, hot dog-eating fans had made their way into Arlington Stadium—almost sixteen thousand more than had attended its formal christening in 1972. As many as ten thousand others were turned away at the gates. It was the first sellout in Ranger history.

It was "one of the most amazing spectacles I've ever seen," remembers Arlington Mayor Tom Vandergriff. "The crowd buzzed as if the seventh game of the World Series was unfolding before their very eyes."

For those who watched, Clyde's debut was too good to be true. Wearing #32, which he had borrowed from idol Sandy Koufax, the eighteen-year-old left-hander struck out the side in the first inning. True, he walked Terrell and Carew before catching his breath, but what everybody would remember was his coming back to strike out Bobby Darwin, George Mitterwald, and Joe Lis.

Minnesota pushed the kid to the edge in the second inning, when he walked four and allowed a two-run home run by #8 hitter Mike Adams, a rookie outfielder who would finish his major-league career with only three home runs. Clyde escaped the inning trailing only 2-0, thanks partly to catcher Piggy Suarez, who threw out Steve Braun as he tried to steal second base. The crowd sighed with relief when Clyde got out of that inning and peeked through its collective hands when he came out to start the next. By that time he was working with a 2-2 tie via Ranger Dave Nelson's two-run single. Reasonable people expected the worst.

What Clyde gave them was scoreless work in the third, fourth, and fifth innings. He had thrown 112 pitches in the five innings, walking seven while striking out eight. Rookie manager Whitey Herzog felt Clyde had gone far enough. Clyde left the game with a 4-2 lead. Bill Gogolewski pitched the final four innings of a 4-3 victory, earning one of his ten career saves and preserving the image of Clyde's having won his professional debut. "If I hadn't saved that win for Clyde, they would have ridden me out of town on a rail," Gogolewski said a few years later.

Herzog was thrilled, although he was not among those who kept a telephone line open for the call from Cooperstown. "Considering the press and the buildup he's had, frankly he did better than I thought he would," Herzog told reporters after the game. "As mature as he is, I'm sure he realizes already that one win doesn't make a season."

How about a career? Clyde's developmental path would become one of the least forgivable chapters in the volumes of Ranger bad judgment. Rushed to the big leagues, then subjected both to the indelicate handling of Billy Martin and to the major-league lifestyles of madmen like Bill Sudakis, Clyde had no chance to grow up. He finished his career 18-33, never winning more than eight games in a year.

When the Rangers decided Clyde was used up, they had to pair him with veteran slugger Willie Horton even to get outfielder John Lowenstein and a minor-leaguer from the Cleveland Indians. By 1985, when Clyde should have been at the peak of his career at the age of thirty, he was working at his father-in-law's lumberyard in Tomball, Texas. He had been out of baseball six years.

But David Clyde had served his purpose for the young franchise. When he pitched, people came to watch. In his rookie season of 1973, when he went 4-8 with a telling 5.03 ERA, he attracted six crowds in excess of 21,000, including four over 25,000, and two of more than 30,000. Before his unveiling in 1973, the woeful Rangers had drawn only four 20,000-plus crowds, with the largest one being 24,222.

Some say Clyde saved the franchise. He may have. He definitely saved owner Bob Short's shrinking bank balance. The twelve times Clyde pitched at Arlington Stadium in 1973, the Rangers drew 218,240. But those were the only times most people went to a game. For the year, the Rangers finished 57-105. They drew 686,085, an average of 9,271. It broke down like this: with Clyde pitching, 18,187; without Clyde pitching, 7,546. Clyde was a sideshow.

But never underestimate good sideshows. They were the only things that distinguished the Rangers in their first decade.

Writing about a typical Texas Ranger front-office screw-up in the spring of 1981, the *Dallas Times Herald*'s Peter Pascarelli concluded: "Again, the Rangers appeared to be a team born under a bad sign."

That describes the Rangers perfectly.

When the subject is futility, the baseball reference is generally to Casey Stengel's 1962 New York Mets. That team, led by Marv Throneberry, Felix Mantilla, and Roger Craig, may have been bad enough to lose 120 games and finish 60½ games behind Willie Mays and the Giants, but at least it had the good fortune to set its own direction. When Mayor Vandergriff's aggressive efforts brought a franchise to North Texas, it was in much the same shape as Bob Irsay's Baltimore Colts when they, too, fled Washington, D.C. a decade later.

In their own way, Bob Short's Washington Senators were the same lovable losers as the 1960s Mets. Although the original Senators—a franchise that had boasted of Walter Johnson when it had last won a World Series, in 1924—had bolted to Minnesota after 1960, they were immediately replaced with an expansion team of Senators. Under Mickey Vernon, that team tied the Kansas City A's for last place in the American League in 1961. They never got much better. Before the league split into two divisions in 1969, the Senators had never finished higher than sixth in the ten-team league.

In 1969, the first year of divisional play, the Senators won eighty-six games and finished fourth in the American League East behind six-foot-seven-inch slugger Frank Howard. But they fell to sixth in the six-team division the next two years, giving the expansion franchise five last-place finishes and a collective record that was 292 games below .500 in eleven years in Washington. Not only that, but the nearby Baltimore Orioles seduced what fan base the Senators had built up, as the Orioles won four American League pennants between 1966 and '71.

Short, who purchased the Senators in 1969, felt on top of the world when 918,106 watched Howard and the Senators that year. It was an especially impressive total, considering that the Orioles were in the process of winning 109 games. But the Senators' attendance dropped to 824,789 in 1970 and 655,156 in '71. Their radio-TV package netted Short only about 30 percent of the lucrative package held by the Orioles.

Short estimated his losses at $2.6 million for the three years—almost one-third of his $9.4 million purchase price. He was primed for Vandergriff's wooing and agreed to shift the team to Texas for the 1972 season. "If I had been forced to stay [in Washington]," he said, "it could have bankrupted me."

Before they became Rangers, the players who would accompany manager Ted Williams to Texas were accustomed to losing. Washington had lost 92 games in 1970 and 96 in '71. Would the change of scenery break their fall?

It wasn't going to be that easy. The Rangers were scheduled to open in their new home in 1972. But baseball's first players' strike, over a $450,000 difference in the owners' contributions to the players' pension pool, delayed the start of the season. While Howard, the highest-paid Ranger, was missing his $665 a day, Short had to issue rain checks for the entire first homestand. When the season did open, it was on the road.

In Anaheim, California, on April 15, 1972, the Rangers suffered their first loss. It was the kind of loss that would bedevil them and their new fans for years to come. Ranger Dick Bosman pitched heroically, carrying a shutout into the ninth inning. But Texas failed to score. In the ninth inning the game was decided by a wild pitch from the Rangers' left-handed reliever, Paul Lindblad. It was a 1-0 loss that had been ten days in the making.

It was also a sign of things to come.

That year the Rangers' leading home-run hitter, Ted Ford, hit fourteen home runs, and its winningest pitcher, Rich Hand, went 10-14. The transplanted club recorded 54 wins and an even 100 losses.

Thus began a long history of deficit spending that would not slow until 1986. Short estimated his break-even point for 1972 at 800,000 fans; the Rangers drew 662,974. The result was a cash-flow drain that eventually sent Short to a Dallas bank for loans to help him meet operating expenses.

Bob Short was a Minneapolis businessman who owned two freight lines and six hotels, including the Leamington in Minneapolis that continued to house baseball teams until Short's death in 1985. Short had made much of his fortune with the $200,000 purchase of the National Basketball Association's Minneapolis Lakers in 1955. Ten years later, after the franchise had been shifted to Los Angeles, he sold his eighty-percent share for over $5 million.

But after his costly experiences with baseball, first in Washington and now in Texas, Short was more akin to Calvin Griffith than George Steinbrenner. Short needed his baseball team to make money. It didn't take the business acumen of an H. Ross Perot to understand what was going on when the Rangers kept trotting out David Clyde every fourth or fifth day in 1973.

Ted Williams, a baseball legend whom Short dared not fire, left voluntarily after the 1972 season. Short then surprised the two Dallas papers, both of which had predicted that Dick Howser would be the new choice, by naming the little-known Whitey Herzog to replace Williams.

This was the first of what would be a flurry of managerial changes for the Texas franchise. But, like most of these changes, it did little to reverse the direction of the club. In fact, the 1973 Rangers set a club record that still stands, losing 105 games. It was that team which elicited this admission from Short, as quoted by *Times Herald* columnist Blackie Sherrod.

"There have been many nights when I didn't want to go watch them," Short said, "and I get a free seat."

Apart from the move to Arlington, Short's five years as owner in Washington and Texas is memorable mostly for an incredible spasm of stupidity.

Short took the blame for the 1970 trade that sent talented pitcher Joe Coleman and infielders Aurelio Rodriquez and Ed Brinkman to Detroit in exchange for a washed-up Denny McLain, who had won 111 games in the previous six years but won only 14 more after coming to Washington. But that deal pales next to the move he made on Friday, September 7, 1973.

Short fired Whitey Herzog.

Watching Herzog succeed elsewhere, winning seven division titles with Kansas City and St. Louis in twelve years from 1976 to 1987, has been painful for those who follow the Rangers. Barroom brawls have broken out over speculation about what would have happened to the franchise had Short not jettisoned Herzog for Billy Martin.

Short had acted on the recommendations of General Manager Joe Burke in hiring Herzog, then age forty-one. A lifetime .257 hitter during a forgettable eight seasons in the major leagues, Herzog had worked as a scout, major-league coach, minor-league manager, and farm director before getting his chance with the Rangers.

Herzog then walked into a team that had lost big with its share of veterans—Howard was far past his prime at age thirty-six—and was committed to waiting for prospects like Pete Broberg and Jeff Burroughs to develop. At least that was the philosophy as Herzog had understood it.

At the news conference announcing his hiring, Herzog offered a blunt assessment of his new team, calling the Rangers "one of the worst I've ever seen, when they played a series (I saw) with Kansas City."

He amended that statement only slightly when pressed. "I guess they weren't any worse than the Mets used to be," he said. "The Rangers have a lot of players with potential. The job is to develop them, and that's what appeals to me. It's what I've been doing, on a different level, for five years. I intend to put the stress on teaching."

If there were any delusions of grandeur about that 1973 team, they weren't spawned by Herzog. He knew a bad team when he managed it. He was looking forward to a time when the team would change its doormat image. He believed that he had been hired to develop a team, not to win immediately.

Short, as it turned out, did not have the patience to take the long road. He wanted a shortcut, and on September 2 he found Billy Martin. Martin, who had won the American League East with Detroit the year before, had just been fired by the Tigers.

Herzog's Rangers were floundering, a 47-91 record illustrating their futility. He had been around long enough to know what was coming. When the Rangers' schedule called for two consecutive days off, September 5 and 6, he headed to his home in Independence, Missouri, to prepare his wife and family.

"I did not know how soon it would be," he told the *Times Herald*'s David Fink, "but I knew I was finished."

Short made it official on a Friday, citing increasing financial pressures as his reason for firing Herzog in the first year of a two-year contract.

"I'm not sure that anybody could have done better than Herzog did," Short said at the news conference, from his seat beside Herzog. "But this franchise is in financial trouble because we are not drawing. There is no way we could draw any worse than we are now. If we don't produce a winner here fast, chances for baseball's success in this area are very slim."

Herzog said he misunderstood the demands of Short, thinking the development of young players was as important as immediately correcting a losing record. "I was wrong," he said. "And when you guess wrong with a 47-91 record, you get fired.

"I was under the impression that since I had a two-year contract, I could take the first year and devote my energy to building a solid nucleus for the future. I think I've done that. We kept our young players down in [triple-A] Spokane and didn't run a shuttle back and forth. Most of them got the seasoning they'll need.

"As far as this club goes, I think I could have made a move here and there and won sixty games. But that didn't seem to be of importance to Bob. Every indication I had from him was to build for the future. Bob would come into that dressing room after most of the games, and he was all smiles."

It was clear at the news conference that Martin would succeed Herzog. "If my mother were managing the Rangers and I had the opportunity to hire Billy

Martin, I'd fire my mother," Short said. "I owe it to the fans to give them my best shot, and I am hoping that in time people will be able to say that this was an excellent decision."

In a parting aside, Herzog offered this advice: "Right now, I'd like to see (David) Clyde sent home for the winter. His arm is dead, but there is no way Short would allow that to occur. And I don't blame him because this franchise apparently needs every extra thousand fans it can draw. But I did what Short wanted without making an issue of it with him, and I still got fired. That's baseball."

Clyde did continue to pitch, although not even the boy wonder could salvage the Rangers' vanishing gate once North Texas got its first whiff of football fever. When the dead-armed Clyde faced California on Friday, September 21, the official Arlington Stadium attendance (including paid no-shows) was listed as 2,513. Dozens of area high-school football games outdrew major-league baseball that night.

When that dreadful season ended, Short tallied up the plusses and minuses of the woeful franchise, consulted his bankers, and decided to sell the franchise. A Houston group, led by financier R.W. Askanase, was considered the leading contender for the purchase, although continued absentee ownership did not excite those interested in keeping the franchise in Arlington.

Short sold the team on April 2, 1984, to a Dallas-Fort Worth group headed by a transplanted New Yorker: Brad Corbett. The price was $9.5 million, with the group agreeing to take over $1 million in debts from Short. Corbett's group was impressive. It included Fort Worth publisher Amon Carter, Jr.; Dallas developer Raymond Nasher, who designed NorthPark, a prototype shopping mall; Fort Worth heart specialist Bobby Brown, who would later serve as American League president; Dallas insurance executive Bill Seay; and Dallas socialite Sharon Simons.

Short estimated his losses in Texas at $1 million over the two years, bringing his total operating losses to $3.6 million in five years. Selling the club for $100,000 more than he purchased it for did not defray those losses, but he did think he was leaving the franchise in good shape.

"My problem was that if I lost a million I had to absorb the burden," Short said, "and I just didn't have that kind of money year after year, debt after debt. The job was fun until the debts mounted and the financial strings pulled too tight.

"These people will never feel that kind of pain," he added. "If they lose a million, it will be split so many ways none of those rich Texans will feel it at all."

Bradford G. Corbett, age thirty-six when he bought controlling interest in the Rangers in 1984, walks and talks with a swagger. His transparent confidence at the time of the Ranger purchase was the result of his success in the business world. Corbett had taken a $300,000 loan from the Small Business Administra-

tion and turned his Fort Worth-based business, Robintech, Inc., into a stagger-
ing success. When he purchased the Rangers from Short, Robintech had eighteen
manufacturing plants scattered over eight states. Thirteen of them turned out
plastic pipe for industrial use, two produced resin for use in printing record
albums, two produced copper tubing, and another manufactured printed circuits.

At the initial news conference of his turbulent six-year ownership, Corbett
said, "I wouldn't call myself the honcho," he said, when asked about his group,
"but the catalyst."

He tried to deny his appearance, that of a rich young man buying himself
an expensive toy. "I look at this as a business transaction. I think this can be a
good business venture. With a good solid foundation and with the right kind of
team, money can be made."

Corbett's first real move with the Rangers appeared sound. He pursuaded
Brown to take a leave of absence from his medical practice and serve as the
Rangers' president. Brown had a strong baseball background, having played
third base in four World Series with the New York Yankees before pursuing his
medical career. His addition to the front office was taken as a signal that Corbett would not meddle in the daily operation of the team.

Alas, that was not true.

By the time Corbett's ownership had run its course, he was a laughingstock among baseball owners and executives. Corbett made his mistakes in
ways that directed as much attention to him as to his baseball team. For a
while, he signed top-dollar free agents to long-term contracts—the kind derided
by owners a decade later. When that didn't achieve the desired results, he mort-
gaged the franchise's future with ill-conceived trades for veteran players.

"The guy is crazy," long-time baseball executive Frank Lane told the *Times
Herald*'s Paul Hagen at the winter meetings in 1978. "Having him run a baseball
team is like giving a three-year-old a handful of razor blades."

During the six seasons Corbett controlled the team, the Rangers played
under six different managers—four of them in one bizarre stretch of eight days
in 1977. Jim Sundberg, a catcher who wore #59 to spring training in 1974, was
the only major-league player or coach to survive all six seasons. No one was
safe from Corbett's involvement.

It always seemed that the Rangers were just one player away from success, and Corbett was always willing to try to acquire that player. In the
process, he traded away talents like Len Barker, who at age twenty-five threw
a perfect game for the Cleveland Indians, and Dave Righetti, who at age
twenty-four threw a no-hitter for the New York Yankees.

Corbett seemed never to get over Billy Martin's 1974 teasing. Due in part to
Herzog's patience and in larger part to a tomorrow-for-today trade to get right-
handed pitcher Ferguson Jenkins, with some simple good fortune thrown in,
Corbett walked into the most amazing season in franchise history.

The team publicist Burton Hawkins dubbed the "Turn-Around Gang" improved by an incredible twenty-seven victories in the standings, going from a

57-105 season in 1976 to an 84-76 finish in 1977. It even put some September heat on the Oakland A's, who were in the process of defending their world championship a second consecutive time. Anything seemed possible. In fact:

• Mike Hargrove, who had disdained high school baseball in the Texas Panhandle town of Perryton and had never before played above Class A ball, won the American League's Rookie of the Year award by hitting .323.

• Sundberg, who went to spring training as a non-roster player with one year's experience in the minors, went to the All-Star Game.

• Jeff Burroughs, a second-year outfielder who was the Senators' #1 pick in the 1969 draft, hit 25 home runs, drove in 118 runs and was named the American League's Most Valuable Player, joining Stan Musial and Vida Blue as the only second-year players ever to receive the award.

• And Jenkins did his part, too, winning twenty-five games and losing only twelve, with a 2.83 earned run average. He finished twenty-nine of his forty-one starts, including four 1-0 victories and two 2-0 victories.

Jenkins' record was a nice short-term reward for a trade that cost the Rangers minor-league infielder Bill Madlock, who would win four National League batting titles with Chicago and Pittsburgh.

Texas won thirteen of twenty-one games in April to take an early, completely unexpected lead in the West. The lead was gone by May 8, but Jenkins and Burroughs kept the Rangers within sight of first place until mid-July, when the A's began to pull away. A 2-7 stretch from July 8 to July 16 caused Texas' deficit to stretch from four and a half games to nine. Martin could get them no closer than 7½ games in August, but a surprising thing happened in September.

The Rangers made a real run at first. Seven games remained against Reggie Jackson, Catfish Hunter, Gene Tenace, Joe Rudi, and the rest of the A's when the Rangers flew west for a four-game series in Oakland beginning September 5. Texas had just finished a 6-3 homestand in which Jenkins beat Baltimore 2-1, Cleveland 2-0, and Minnesota 1-0, but still the Rangers trailed Oakland by 7½ games.

When Hunter beat the Rangers' Jackie Brown 3-0 in the series opener, the A's lead grew to 8½. But Texas reeled off three straight victories at the Oakland Coliseum, moving within 5½ games on September 8 when Jenkins won for the sixth time in six starts, beating the A's Ken Holtzman 5-1.

After winning two of three games against California and Chicago, the Rangers returned home to open a ten-game homestand six games out of the lead. The first three games were scheduled against Oakland, meaning a sweep would leave the remarkable Rangers three out with fourteen games to play.

Jenkins faced Hunter in the opener. As a crowd of 21,411 saluted every out, Jenkins held off the A's 3-1. With Brown, the "Oklahoma curveballer," facing the A's Vida Blue the next night, 28,140 people found their way to Arlington. Oakland went down, 8-3, leaving the Rangers only four games out. Reality returned the next night, however, as the A's beat Jim Bibby 4-1. Martin's "Turn-Around

Gang" never got back within four games of first, finishing the year in second place, five games behind Oakland.

A season attendance of 1,193,902 left Short feeling he had sold out too soon, if not for too little. Four years later, he told Frank Luksa of the *Times Herald*, "If I hadn't sold, we would have won the Western Division. I would have made a few changes Corbett couldn't in his first year because of unfamiliarity. But I was beat before I got to Texas."

That may have been the only time Corbett was ever criticized for moves he did not make. His free-wheeling style erupted in 1975. Half-expecting a pennant, he either approved or orchestrated off-season trades that brought his team veteran outfielder Willie Davis, whose one big move in Texas was a spring training sit-down strike in center field, and left-handed pitcher Clyde Wright, who had lost twenty games the year before with Milwaukee. In return, Corbett parted with a collection of one-time top prospects, including shortstop Pete Mackanin and pitchers Pete Broberg and Don Stanhouse.

Then, after a slow start by his team, Corbett approved another deal made by General Manager Dan O'Brien. This one was a three-for-one swap of pitchers, sending Bibby, Brown, and left-hander Rick Waits to Cleveland in exchange for Gaylord Perry. The Rangers were 28-29 when they acquired Perry, who failed to provide a one-man cure.

What the Perry trade did do was signify Corbett's early willingness to spend heavily. At a time when baseball's average salary was less than $45,000, the Rangers were paying a combined $335,000 to their top two pitchers: $175,000 to Jenkins and $160,000 to Perry .

They didn't pitch well enough to save Martin, who was fired on July 21, with the Rangers' record at 44-51. Frank Lucchesi, Martin's animated third-base coach, was named to replace him. Lucchesi had a track record as a manager—a bad one. He had compiled a 166-233 record with Philadelphia from 1970 until he was fired in 1972.

Under Lucchesi, the Rangers finished 79-83 in 1975. They followed that with another forgettable season in 1976 after an unusually busy off-season. Following the disappointment of 1975, the Rangers dealt Jenkins to Boston for center fielder Juan Beniquez and two undistinguished pitchers, Steve Barr and Craig Skok. They also obtained outfielder Gene Clines, a World Series veteran with Pittsburgh, for another faded prospect, Joe Lovitto. Pitcher Bill Singer and catcher John Ellis, who like Clines were veterans near the end of the line, were acquired in separate deals mostly put together by Corbett.

None made much of an impact, except perhaps Ellis. And his contribution was largely visual. Both Ellis and the Rangers got off to good starts, but on May 9, with his new club in first place with a 15-6 record, Ellis broke his leg in grotesque fashion sliding into second base at Boston's Fenway Park. Ellis was through for the year, but the memory of his pained expression lingered on.

Singer was gone June 1, traded to Minnesota along with prospects Jim Gideon (a #1 draft choice in 1975), Roy Smalley, and Mike Cubbage for twenty-five-year-old pitcher Bert Blyleven, who had already won ninety-nine games for the Minnesota Twins. Corbett also traded for Fritz Peterson simply because Peterson, at the urging of former teammate Ellis, had written Corbett a nice letter. Peterson had been used sparingly in Cleveland, so the Indians were more than happy to accept the Rangers' offer of pitcher Stan Perzanowski.

Finally, after making no major move for three months, Corbett restructured the Rangers' front office in September of the 1976 season. Without relieving anyone, he brought in recently fired Braves' executive vice-president Eddie Robinson to the same post with the Rangers.

Robinson's hiring created a confusing chain of command that included Corbett, Robinson, O'Brien, and Lucchesi. Corbett attempted to simplify the formula by removing himself from the equation. At the news conference held to announce Robinson's hiring, Corbett said he no longer planned to be involved in the day-to-day operations of the club "because the daily operation of a baseball club is not something that can be done on a part-time basis."

Corbett added, "It takes a 100 percent effort and my business demands prevent that. The only other alternative was to sell the business. I didn't want to do that."

Corbett did leave himself an "out" clause. "There're only two things I'd like to be involved with," he said. "One would be the signing of free-agent players this winter because of the tremendous amount of money that it's going to take. The other thing would be if there's a trade working for any one of about five players on the team. You know, our five key young players."

In less than five months, Corbett not only signed the club's first significant free agents, shortstop Dagoberto Campaneris and pitcher Doyle Alexander, but also worked out the biggest trade in the club's history.

The primary player was Texas' leading hitter, Jeff Burroughs. Frustrated by the prevailing south wind that turned many of his drives into fly balls that fell in front of the right-field warning track at Arlington Stadium, Burroughs was ready for a change. He had led Texas with 86 RBIs on 18 homers and 22 doubles in 1976. Three years after his MVP season, and five years into his major-league career, the twenty-five-year-old outfielder should have commanded strong value in trade.

But the best the Rangers could get was grab bag from Atlanta that included pitchers Carl Morton, Roger Moret, and Adrian Devine, and outfielders Dave May and Ken Henderson. Corbett also received $250,000.

The cash was worth more than the players. Morton, who had won seventeen games two years before, hurt himself before spring training and never threw a pitch for the Rangers. Devine won 11 games and saved 15 more in 1977, but was involved in a no-help trade for Willie Montanez the next winter. Henderson and May played one year in Texas before moving on. And Moret left his own sad legacy by lapsing into a catatonic trance in front of his locker one April night in 1978.

Corbett's continuing influence on all items big and small was made obvious to O'Brien during a late-night phone call in February 1977.

Corbett awakened the general manager to say, "Guess who I got for you?"

O'Brien was afraid to ask.

He was relieved to learn that Corbett had acquired utility infielder Sandy Alomar, giving up only young minor-league infielders Brian Doyle and Greg Pryor. It didn't make much sense, but it could have been worse.

Corbett was riding high. He also went above both Robinson and O'Brien that winter to buy relief pitcher Paul Lindblad from the Oakland A's. At $400,000, Lindblad was no bargain.

Corbett also had the final say in one of the many decisions from that era that would haunt the Ranger franchise in the next decade. He had developed a strong bond with John Ellis, the double-tough catcher who had gone to the Florida Instructional League to prove he could come back from his broken leg. Corbett insisted that Ellis be protected in the expansion draft. Consequently, right-handed pitching prospect Jim Clancy wasn't protected and was taken by the Toronto Blue Jays. He quickly developed into one of the Jays' most consistent starters.

With that chain of command, which left local reporters guessing, began one of the strangest years in any franchise's history. Some of the highlights from 1977:

• *March 28, Orlando:* Lucchesi is talking quietly to second baseman Lenny Randle before an exhibition game, when Randle suddenly punches the forty-eight-year-old manager in the face. Randle lands a right-left combination that decks Lucchesi, then scores on another combination as Lucchesi is falling to the ground. Randle, who had lost his starting job the week before to rookie Bump Wills, continues to flail away at Lucchesi on the ground until Campaneris intervenes.

While Lucchesi is rushed to a hospital, bleeding profusely from the mouth and nose, Randle moves to the outfield to run some solitary wind sprints. The diagnosis on Lucchesi's condition includes a broken cheekbone, a lacerated lip, and a concussion. Randle says only that Lucchesi called him a punk during their discussion, a charge Lucchesi later denies from his hospital bed.

Randle, quickly traded to the New York Mets, eventually is fined $1,050 by the courts for the incident. Lucchesi had the line that would be remembered. "My only wish," he told *The Dallas Morning News'* Randy Galloway from his bedside, "is that I was ten years younger so I could handle this situation myself."

• *June 21, Minneapolis:* Following a 31-31 start, Lucchesi is fired in ugly fashion. Like Doug Rader eight years later, Lucchesi learns of his firing from reporters. He gamely answers their questions, saying only that he hasn't heard from his bosses, then manages a 9-5 loss. After the game, Lucchesi hears that Eddie Stanky, then manager of the University of South Alabama baseball team, is on his way from Mobile, Alabama.

Lucchesi breaks down. "I've heard from people all over the country, but not the Ranger people in Arlington," Lucchesi says. "If someone would just pick up the phone and give me a vote of confidence, tell me things are going bad and they might have to make a change, anything. Let's do this in a professional way. The way this is being done is affecting my family, and that's not right."

• *June 22, Minneapolis:* Stanky, indeed, is hired by the Rangers. He bubbles over at a news conference called before he manages his new team to a 10-8 victory over the Twins. "I don't think a baseball man ever gets it out of his system," says Stanky, who had managed both St. Louis and the Chicago White Sox after a playing career that ended in 1953. For the last nine years he had managed at South Alabama.

"I wanted back," he says, then later adds, "I haven't lost my zest. Damn! I haven't lost that." The money's not bad either–his contract calls for $250,000 spread over three years, with a $50,000 bonus if the team wins a divisional title.

• *June 23, Minneapolis:* At 6:10 A.M., Stanky picks up the phone in his hotel room at the Leamington to call his wife, Dickie, in Alabama. He is homesick and has decided he made the wrong decision when Corbett offered him the job.

Dickie tells him, "Now Eddie, you just do what you think is right."

Stanky packs three months' worth of clothing and catches a cab to the Bloomington airport. From there he calls Robinson back at the hotel to resign.

Robinson says, "Wait, I'll come to the airport."

Stanky says, "No, that won't be necessary," and hangs up.

Stanky then places quick calls to coach Connie Ryan (who would be named interim manager later in the day) and to players Mike Marshall and Toby Harrah. Stanky is in the process of dialing Willie Horton's number with Bert Campaneris next when it's time to board the plane that will take him home.

Stanky leaves the Rangers with an undefeated, 1-0 record. In Mobile he is greeted by South Alabama's athletic director and president, who presents him with his old uniform while the school band plays.

Twenty-six hours after leaving, Stanky is back at his Spring Hill Avenue home, drinking champagne and watching his wife play with a toy poodle. "This is the reason that I am back," Stanky tells the *Times Herald*'s Jim Dent, one of the reporters hastily dispatched from Dallas. "I want the people of Texas to know the real and exact reason. God, I wanted that team. But I had to weigh my contract against my family."

• *June 27, Oakland:* Billy Hunter, a Baltimore Orioles coach dubbed "Little Hitler" by Frank Robinson, arrives to manage Texas, ending a procession that has brought the franchise much ridicule. Hunter is the fourth Texas manager in six days. He brings with him a no-nonsense reputation and a telegram from Stanky. Says Eddie Robinson: "I think Billy is the type of guy who will jerk (players) up if they need it."

Hunter was not the Rangers' second choice. He was their fourth choice. The interim manager, coach Ryan, reveals that he was offered the job on a permanent basis. And there had been a long talk with former Minnesota Twins slugger Harmon Killebrew on June 25 at the Beverly Hills Motel. Killebrew told the Associated Press that he also had been offered the job.

"Not being the first choice doesn't make me feel bad at all," Billy Hunter says. "I'm the fella who has the job." He also had a team that was 33-35 and in fifth place. The day before, it had managed to lose twice to California reliever Paul Hartzell, who would win only twenty-seven games in his entire career. "I expect to give 100 percent and I'm sure most of the players (will), too," says Hunter. "The ones that don't will hear about it."

• *July 4, Arlington:* Fireworks in Arlington. Corbett, possibly inebriated and definitely crestfallen, stumbles out of his suite after a 1-0 loss to Kansas City and tells reporters that he has had all he can take. Not only are the Rangers languishing in fifth place with a 37-40 record, but in a recent editorial the *Fort Worth Star-Telegram* blamed his handling for making the Rangers the "laughingstock of the nation."

He levels a blast at his big-money players and says he is selling the team. "Some of them are dogs on the field and off the field. It's not worth it anymore. It's killing me. I've never been in public life before, and I guess maybe I didn't understand all the ramifications."

• *August 11, Arlington:* After being promised a five thousand-seat expansion at Arlington Stadium as well as control of the team's radio-TV rights from the city of Arlington, Corbett takes the team off the market. And why not? Two days after Corbett's Fourth of July demonstration of spontaneous combustion, the Rangers began a six-game winning streak.

They finished July at 19-8, went 6-2 on a road trip to Detroit and Chicago, and opened a homestand with a doubleheader sweep of Oakland, a once-great team sold out by owner Charlie Finley. Billy Hunter had transformed Corbett's kennel into the hottest team in baseball. When Corbett's decision became public knowledge in a story broken by *The Dallas Morning News*, the Rangers were three games out of first, and assured of sellout crowds for a weekend series against the White Sox. Everything was beautiful.

Texas stayed hot, finishing the season 94-68 by winning twenty-one of its last thirty-one games. Unfortunately, that wasn't good enough to catch the Kansas City Royals, who won 102 games. The late-starting Rangers were finally reduced to scoreboard watching, playing the Royals only four times after July 5 due to the quirky post-expansion schedule in the American League.

Hunter seldom showed more personality than a resin bag. But he had won more games than any of his predecessors, and Corbett was committed to putting the Rangers over the hump in 1978. As usual in Texas, that meant more new faces.

Everyone knew that the nucleus of the team was its starting pitching, with Alexander (17-11), Perry (15-12), Blyleven (14-12), and Dock Ellis (12-12) all having had successful years in 1977. Corbett's goals were to improve an offense that had been outscored by three of its divisional rivals and to take some of the load off the starters with a proven stopper in the bullpen.

As always, brash Brad did things in a Texas-sized way. During three days in November 1977, he signed as free agents Richie Zisk, the powerful outfielder who had given the White Sox thirty homers and 101 RBIs the previous year, and pitcher Doc Medich. For Zisk, Corbett put together an eight-year, $2.8 million package that angered many in baseball.

"The Rangers ought to have to put that money right in escrow, right in the commissioner's office," Whitey Herzog, now with the Royals, told Hagen. "That would stop this crap. You have to wonder. They sign Zisk for ten years. He's twenty-eight and has bad knees. Campaneris was thirty-four when they signed him for five years. People tell me that Brad's business, Polytech or whatever, isn't going so good. You have to wonder if these people are ever going to get paid."

(Zisk did get paid through 1985, although he was out of baseball after 1983. The Rangers paid only slightly more than $1 million, and the Seattle Mariners were stuck for the rest.)

But adding one bat to the lineup did not satisfy Corbett. In one wild day during the winter meetings in Honolulu, Corbett put together deals involving three different National League clubs. The biggest was a trade sending Bert Blyleven and outfielder John Milner, acquired earlier in the day from the Mets, to Pittsburgh for line-drive hitter Al Oliver and shortstop prospect Nelson Norman. In addition, the Rangers went home with left-handed pitcher Jon Matlack. They parted with future general manager, Tom Grieve; the club's save leader, Adrian Devine; and minor-leaguers Tommy Boggs (a former #1 draft choice), and Eddie Miller, as well as Willie Montanez, who was sent to the Mets after being included in the trade with Atlanta.

Not even that trading orgy satisfied Corbett. Less than a week later, he reacquired Ferguson Jenkins from Boston, giving up pitching prospect John Poloni and $20,000. Just to make sure Hunter had what he needed to win a pennant, Corbett signed the versatile Mike Jorgensen as a free agent. Under baseball's new rules for free-agent compensation, that signing cost the club its first-round choice in the next June's draft. But this was not a club worried about the future.

The present was the issue – a management philosophy that looked great on Opening Day 1978. With a national television audience watching, Matlack pitched his heart out, and Zisk pulled a home run just inside the left-field foul pole to give Texas a 1-0 victory over Billy Martin and the Yankees, the defending world champions.

Just when it looked as if the Rangers had arrived, they followed a split of the opening series with eight consecutive losses. One-run losses to Detroit and Boston caused Hunter to remind the front office that it had traded away the team's save leader, Devine, without replacing him. The best Corbett and Robinson could do on such short notice was to sign Reggie Cleveland. He blew his first decision, dropping the team to three wins and ten losses.

With Oliver (batting .324, with 35 doubles and 89 RBIs) and Zisk (22 homers, 85 RBIs) both producing, and the nomadic Bobby Bonds hitting 29 homers and stealing 37 bases after the May trade that brought him from the White Sox (the cost was twenty-three-year-old Claudell Washington and outfielder Rusty Torres), the Rangers began to play well. They went 84-65 after April 24, but finished the year five games behind Herzog's Royals.

Hunter was fired just before the final 1978 game, leaving few friends behind in the clubhouse. His authoritarian rule had not set well with the veteran Rangers, who had only two regular players and two starting pitchers below the age of twenty-eight. His antiquated rule that banned drinking on team flights, and at the bars of hotels where the team stayed, led to one of the more memorable arguments in the franchise's history.

On the team bus from the airport in Minneapolis one day in May, the unpredictable Dock Ellis had instigated a confrontation with Hunter by loudly encouraging his teammates to ignore the drinking ban at the hotel. Hunter then told Ellis (believed to be the first major-league player to wear hair curlers onto the field) to "sit down and shut up."

Responded Ellis, "He may be Hitler, but he's not going to make a lampshade out of me." Ellis, another player who had grown close to Corbett, remained after Hunter had gone.

Pat Corrales, a former roommate of Johnny Bench's and known for his toughness, replaced Hunter. Corrales quickly received help in the one area where Hunter had been forsaken: the bullpen. Two days after the '78 season ended, the Rangers dealt Bonds and twenty-three-year-old Len Barker to Cleveland for Jim Kern, who had saved forty-six games in the previous three seasons.

Corbett should have quit there. But he had the itch, so three weeks later he sent former Rookie of the Year Mike Hargrove, infielder Kurt Bevacqua, and catcher Bill Fahey to San Diego for slugger Oscar Gamble, catcher Dave Roberts, and an estimated $300,000.

As Herzog had noted the year before, Corbett's business, Robintech, was struggling and his plastic-pipe business was going under.

The Gamble deal was one of six Corbett made to bring cash into the Rangers' treasury between August and December of 1978. In return, as usual, he helped stock rival teams. Corbett and his front office sank to all-time depths on the November day they satisfied his quest for reliever Sparky Lyle. It took much maneuvering to put together a five-for-five swap in which the Rangers would get Lyle, pitchers Larry McCall and Dave Rajsich, catcher Mike Heath, infielder Domingo Ramos, and, of course, cash (reported at $400,000). Yankees owner George Steinbrenner set the cost at Juan Beniquez, left-hander Paul Mirabella, and minor-leaguers Dave Righetti, Greg Jemison, and Mike Griffin.

Righetti, of course, was the kicker. At nineteen, he was considered the Rangers' best minor-league pitching prospect, having just gone 5-5 with a 3.16 ERA at double-A Tulsa. "He is another Guidry," said Yankee scout Jerry Walker.

Corrales defended the deal. "The biggest thing we considered when we talked about trading Righetti was that he has a history of arm problems," he told the *Times Herald*'s Hagen. "He might turn out to be a helluva pitcher. But I feel, like Mr. Corbett does, that he (Corbett) wants to win a pennant for the area. And I think a guy like Lyle can help us do that next year."

(A footnote to the trade: Ranger insiders later said Corbett had been instructed to try and get talented minor-league second baseman Damaso Garcia from Steinbrenner; instead, a confused Corbett asked for Domingo Ramos.)

In sacrificing the future (Righetti) for the present (Lyle), Corrales illustrated a delusion that would haunt the Rangers for a full decade, from 1975 through 1985. The belief that this was a team just a player or two short of a division title, a team that would go out and get that player, no matter what the cost.

It would be a long ten years.

3

Mad Eddie's New Bidness

Eddie Chiles always was a believer in the human capacity for success. His Fort Worth-based oil-field service business, the Western Company, once blitzed the Southwest with an advertising campaign featuring the slogan, "If you don't own an oil well, get one."

And Chiles' personal philosophy would have added, "Get it now, dammit!"

Perhaps that attitude explains why Chiles assumed control of the Rangers when the bills got to be too much for Brad Corbett. The club always had been something of a local embarrassment; Eddie Chiles felt he could change that image. But he doesn't want anyone to think he was overly eager for the opportunity.

"I got an opportunity to buy an interest with Brad in his team. I intended it to be just an interest, a non-management type of interest," Chiles said in 1984. "But knowing baseball like I know it now, it's a very hungry monster. It just eats up dollars, and eats them up faster than they can be provided. So after I bought in with Brad, I bought a little more and a little more in order to funnel money into the team.

"Later on, one day Brad came to me and said, 'I've got to get out. I need my money for other purposes. Could I sell my stock to you?' And I said, 'Sure, Brad, I'll buy it,' not intending ever to take over the ownership or the manager's job or whatever position that is."

Chiles was seventy years old when he took over the Rangers in the first month of the 1980 season, but he was hardly slowing down. The little fireball with the Henry Fonda hairline and the weathered face had been on the move since he'd hitchhiked from his family home in Itasca, Texas, to the oil fields near Houston as a teenager. Back then his responsibilities were simple.

"All I had to do," he once told the *Morning News'* Steve Pate, "was earn enough money to eat on everyday—or I didn't eat."

Chiles kicked around for a few years, once earning $29.50 a month working on a freight boat that hauled grain between the Gulf Coast and Europe. He returned to Texas, then hitchhiked to Norman, Oklahoma. By 1934, Chiles had earned a petroleum engineering degree from the University of Oklahoma.

With the help of a cousin whose brother-in-law was a Dallas banker, Chiles took out a loan in 1939 to start the Western Company. He began with a pickup truck and a small tin building in the West Texas town of Seagraves. Chiles slept in a bedroom in the back of the building, but almost every waking hour he could be found in the nearby oil fields, drilling. The hours were long.

"There wasn't anybody falling into fortunes," Chiles says. "People were making a living, but I don't have any knowledge of people getting rich quick."

Chiles eventually succeeded, of course, building the little Western Company into a Fortune 500 organization that employed more than five thousand people worldwide at its height. "I am just like many thousands of other Americans. I am a product of the free enterprise system," he says. "I saw an opportunity to start my own business and I did."

Chiles has never seemed comfortable as a public figure, but he made himself one with a conservative advertising campaign he financed in the late 1970s. He began many radio tirades against government involvement by saying, "I'm Eddie Chiles and I'm mad." Bumper stickers soon followed. ("I'm mad, too, Eddie.") Chiles stated his philosophy in one full-page newspaper ad: "There are only three things the government should do—defend her shores, deliver her mail, and leave her alone."

Given his aggressive nature, Chiles was surprisingly passive in his first two seasons as the Rangers' controlling owner. Oh, there was the familiar firing of a manager, but not too much clamor over it. Few questioned the decision to replace Pat Corrales with Don Zimmer after the Rangers slipped from eighty-three victories in 1979 to seventy-six victories in 1980.

Much of Chiles' attention during those years was directed toward an examination of the game's economics. The more he learned, the more he wondered what he was doing owning a major-league team. After all, this was the golden age of player salaries. Free agency and binding salary arbitration were in full bloom; both forced a dizzying climb in salaries.

In 1976, the year before Andy Messersmith and Dave McNally precipitated the free-agent issue, baseball's average salary was $51,501. In 1979, the year before Chiles agreed to take the Rangers from Corbett, the average salary was $113,558. At the end of 1982, less than three years after the Rangers had become Chiles' main responsibility, the average salary had more than doubled again, to $241,497. Chiles was on the wrong end of this case study in free enterprise.

By then, he was also openly questioning his involvement. "Yeah, I've asked myself what the hell am I doing here," he said at a 1982 news conference. "I guess I'm about like the mouse who said I'm not after the cheese anymore, I'm just trying to get my head out of the trap."

In 1981 the Rangers' average salary of $178,131 had ranked them seventeenth among the major leagues' twenty-six teams. Texas' average grew to $186,424 in 1982, but despite the 5-percent increase, the Rangers' ranking slipped from seventeenth to twenty-first. By 1984, the Rangers' average of $247,081 ranked twenty-third in baseball, ahead of only frugal Calvin Griffith's Minnesota Twins, the Seattle Mariners, and the Cleveland Indians. Chiles was unable, as well as unwilling, to keep up with free-spending owners like the Yankees' George Steinbrenner, the Braves' Ted Turner, and the Angels' Gene Autry. He wasn't even matching the Brewers' Bud Selig, for that matter.

In 1982 the *Times Herald*'s Randy Youngman asked Chiles about the meaning of the salary trend. "It means baseball people are crazy," he responded.

Chiles, while fighting a running war with Commissioner Bowie Kuhn, was among the owners willing to sit out the rest of the season before yielding to the demands of the players' association and its leader, Marvin Miller, during the 1981 strike. When the strike was settled after fifty days, Chiles voiced bitter disappointment.

"Baseball would have been better off to have closed its season and finally worked out a livable arrangement with the union," he told Paul Hagen. "We do not have a satisfactory arrangement with the union. In my opinion, under the Basic Agreement we now have, baseball will probably self-destruct."

Chiles' Rangers, of course, were imitating Inspector Jacques Clouseau of the *Pink Panther* films, particularly the scene in which the bumbling policeman has been handed a bomb.

"A boooomb . . . a boooomb . . . a boooomb!" Clouseau says, in his inimitable French accent.

You know the punch line. The bomb explodes, sending Clouseau flying through the air. That was what Chiles and the Rangers were doing in the early 1980s.

One quirk of the 1981 strike season was a solid showing by the Rangers. In fact, although they did not know it at the time, they came closer to post-season play that year than the combined Washington-Texas franchise would in its first twenty-nine seasons.

On June 8, left-hander Rick Honeycutt pitched the Rangers to a victory over Detroit. It was the Rangers' sixth win in seven games, propelling Zimmer's team to a 32-20 record and first place in the American League West. There was no way of knowing it at the time but, had the club maintained its division lead over Oakland for three more days, it would have been given the chance to play Kansas City in a best-of-five "mini-series" for a spot in the American League Championship Series. Teams leading their division when Miller called the player strike—a strike that would last fifty days—were declared first-half champions as part of the strike settlement.

Texas dropped two of its last three games in the first half, finishing 1½ games behind Oakland. The Rangers never quite got things rolling after the season resumed on August 10, 1981, when they opened against eventual pennant winner New York in Yankee Stadium. The Rangers scored one run in the first two games against Tommy John and Dave Righetti, the erstwhile farmhand they had traded away to get Sparky Lyle three years before. But even with a 24-26 performance in the second half of the split season, Zimmer and his players went home enthused. After all, Oakland was the only Western Division team with a better overall record than the Rangers' 57-48.

Who could have known it was a house of cards?

Certainly not General Manager Eddie Robinson, who decided Lee Mazzilli was just the ticket to push the Rangers over the hump in 1982. Never mind that the flashy native New Yorker had not driven in as many as eighty runs in four full seasons with the Mets, or that the asking price was extremely steep. Robinson had to have Mazzilli; he consummated the deal, appropriately enough, on April Fool's Day.

While Robinson was telling writers that Mazzilli was "the final piece of the puzzle," farm director Joe Klein was reduced to swearing when he learned about the trade: Minor-league pitchers Ron Darling and Walt Terrell were the price for Mazzilli.

Darling, a Yale graduate, had been the Rangers' #1 draft pick in 1981, costing them a reported $100,000 signing bonus. By contrast, Terrell had climbed from an obscure thirty-third-round draft choice in 1983 to a top prospect by winning a Texas League-high fifteen games in 1981.

"I know how disappointed Joe Klein is," Robinson said. "I can appreciate the problem an organization has getting talent and then developing it. But this is a calculated move. It wasn't thought of one moment and done the next. We're trading young talent for a twenty-seven-year-old who's going to play for us for a long time, a player that we all agree could be a big key for this team."

No trade in the Rangers' fire-sale history would prove as poor. It didn't take long to find this out, either.

Mazzilli had played center field in New York, but was switched to left to make room for rookie George Wright, who had used a spring-training injury to Mickey Rivers as a springboard to jump from Tulsa to the major leagues. Mazzilli rebelled, calling left field "an idiot's position." He never adapted to Texas. His play wasn't much to write home to Brooklyn about, as now he was hitting only .241 with four homers and 17 RBIs when Paul Richards, now running the front office, pulled the plug. He sent Mazzilli to the New York Yankees for aging shortstop Bucky Dent on August 8.

Meanwhile, Terrell was with the Mets by year's end. It took Darling until 1983 to make it there. Both became fixtures in the major leagues; Darling as the #2 starter on the Mets' world championship team in 1986 and Terrell as the scourge of Tiger Stadium. Between them, they went 146-109 between 1983 and 1988.

It didn't help Robinson's long-term security that the 1982 Rangers broke from the gate running like Mr. Ed on Valium. A twelve-game losing streak that included four one-run losses left them ten games under .500 (6-16) by May 6. They kept slipping further into the night until Chiles could no longer sit by and watch his investment wither.

When the Rangers came home after a 1-5 road trip to Chicago and Kansas City, Chiles called an off-day summit at Arlington Stadium. He scheduled separate meetings with the front office, coaching staff, and players, and asked Zimmer to attend all three of them. He advised interlopers, especially those with pads and pens, to stay away. "I've put a news blackout on the whole situation," Chiles told the *Times Herald's* Youngman. "I feel like I've got a job to do, and I don't need any help."

The daily press corps (Youngman, the *Fort Worth Star-Telegram's* Jim Reeves, and *The Dallas Morning News'* Tim Kurkjian) and a couple of camera crews arrived the next day to find guards at every stadium gate. They were all carrying guns. "Sure it's loaded," one guard said of his weapon. "It wouldn't be any good if it wasn't."

Fort Arlington?

Despite the sinister aura around the meetings, little happened in them except that club president-to-be Mike Stone was introduced to the players. Stone's management seminar, stressing personal and group goals, was received warily by such veterans as Buddy Bell and Mickey Rivers.

Considering the team's twenty-one losses in twenty-six games, it is surprising that no one was fired—at least not immediately.

"It's never been my style to wave my arms and rave and have heads fall," Chiles said at a news conference following a second day of meetings. "I don't think that's the way you motivate people and accomplish what you want to accomplish. I'm aware of the standard operating procedure of a baseball team, or any team not performing up to proper standards. You walk in and fire somebody. It seems like the sports world thinks the cure of any difficulty is to fire somebody. In industry, that's not true. Probably the poor guy who got you in trouble has got to sit there and get you out of trouble. But getting mad . . . is the poorest solution you can make."

Thirteen days after Chiles spoke, Robinson was gone, replaced supposedly by Chiles himself. On July 28, Robinson was joined in unemployment by Zimmer. And, as usual, the firing of Zimmer was handled as skillfully as the Watergate burglary.

On Monday, July 26, Chiles told Zimmer he would be fired. He also asked him to keep that fact to himself, and to remain as manager until a replacement had been lined up. By Tuesday, the *Star-Telegram's* Reeves knew of the meeting and reported it for Wednesday's edition. It finally became official late Wednesday night, after a 3-2 loss to Milwaukee.

In the interim, Zimmer managed a three-game series a lame duck. The final announcement made everyone angry.

Zimmer felt he had been put through a needless ordeal. "You don't fire people and tell 'em to go to work," said Zimmer, who attended the news conference officially announcing the change. "This is something I never heard of in baseball. I was fired Monday and asked to work Monday, Tuesday, and Wednesday night. That's a very strange thing in baseball."

Buddy Bell, the fair-haired boy of the organization, voiced the feelings of his teammates. "It's a shabbily run organization right now," Bell said. "I'm afraid things aren't going forward anymore. They're going backwards. It's just like we're an expansion team now."

Chiles was steaming because the press had aggressively reported the situation. "It would not have been handled this way if the press hadn't gotten itself involved in a way it wasn't entitled or supposed to get involved," Chiles said. "I think the press and the media still have some of the old Watergate syndrome, where they dig in and make something negative always . . . find something bad or wrong that's been done or at least state that it is. It seems the press and the media spend a great deal of their time on negatives and seldom report anything that's good."

Zimmer had been asked to resign before he was fired. He declined. His explanation: "This place is a mess and quitting would be the easy way out."

While still on the job, he never heard first-hand that he was being replaced, but virtually the whole ugly mess was repeated three years later with Doug Rader. When Rader was canned on the 1985 magical misery tour through Detroit, New York, and Chicago, there was the same deception by Chiles, followed by an almost identical bombast aimed at nosy reporters.

Like Zimmer, Rader had received a two-year contract extension the year before his firing. While the team's payroll remained among the lowest in either league, once more a manager would be paid long after his job was terminated.

For a while, it appeared that the Rangers were making progress under the stewardship of Rader and long-time organization man Joe Klein. Klein had been promoted from farm director to fill the vacant general manager's job at the end of the 1982 season. Klein's first big move—and the one on which he would eventually be judged—was to hire Rader as the successor to interim manager Darrell Johnson.

Johnson might have had the job himself, but the Rangers won only 26 of 66 games after he took over for Zimmer, finishing the miserable 1982 season 64-98 —the club's worst record since 1973. Instead of getting better, things were getting worse. Buddy Bell was right. These guys still looked like an expansion team.

But for awhile Rader did an amazing job of hiding that fact. His kick-the-door-in personality had a lot to do with the Rangers fooling themselves and the rest of the American League for the first three months of 1983.

As a player, the red-haired Rader probably figured more prominently in the Houston Astros clubhouse than anyone before or since. He played a large part in Jim Bouton's infamous *Ball Four,* most notably for his imaginative desecration of a birthday cake.

Rader stories are a dime a dozen. In college, he and some friends left a dead horse in the bathtub of a fraternity house. He once sped a motorcycle into a brick wall just because, he said, "It was there." Disgusted with his play one day on the golf course, he drove his cart into a lake. During his first spring training with Texas, he ritualistically drove his car into the same tree outside the park every day.

At the 1982 winter meetings in Honolulu, six weeks after he had been hired to manage the Rangers, Rader made quite an impression with his "Creature from the Black Lagoon" imitation. Late one moonlit night, Rader popped up on shore after some snorkeling. Wearing only shorts, fins, and a mask, he walked into a nearby hotel bar, plopped down on a stool, and ordered a drink. Never mind that some general managers and their wives were in the bar at the time.

Welcome to management, Doug.

This was the irreverent side of Rader which Bouton had portrayed so well in *Ball Four.* Bouton wrote of one airplane conversation while both were playing for the Astros. "In the dark of the airplane, Doug Rader was saying that he feels he's living out of time and out of place," Bouton wrote. "He thinks he would have been much happier as a Tahitian war lord, or even a pirate."

Another thing about Rader: It is a wonder he was never arrested for indecent exposure, since he considered the shock value of a penis funny. As a player, he would sometimes invite another player and his wife over to his house, and then greet them at the door naked. In his first year with the Rangers, he once returned from the bathroom of a bar frequented by players, coaches, and reporters with his pride hanging out of his pants.

He was also proud of a picture taken of him and some of his Florida running buddies. At first glance, it seemed to be just a picture of some guys on a golf course. But the reason Rader hung it over his desk was because—you guessed it—his genitals were hanging out of his pants. It was a private joke he played on everybody who came into his Arlington Stadium office, particularly those intending to conduct serious business. He got a huge kick from an unknowing visitor's reaction. "The bottom line," Rader told Reeves, "is that this world was meant to enjoy."

Rader also brought a hint of Bruce Lee with him for his first spring at the Pompano Beach, Florida, winter home of the Rangers. A black belt who at 6 feet 3 inches and 230 pounds needed few tricks, Rader demanded respect from his players. He often told of how he handled San Diego farmhand Alan Wiggins while managing the Padres' Pacific Coast League team in Hawaii.

Feeling Wiggins was trying to do some unlicensed managing one night in Spokane, Rader invited the little infielder into what he called "a very small room." He handed Wiggins a bat and told him he could run the team if he was the last one breathing. "And if he failed, he would comply with the overall program." Wiggins didn't try his luck at Rader—or at any more managing.

Rader inherited almost the same team that had lost ninety-eight games the year before. He gave young players like Pete O'Brien, Wayne Tolleson, Mike Smithson, John Butcher, and Odell Jones opportunities, and rekindled the hopes of his corps of veterans. Something clicked.

For a change, the Rangers were ready when they left Florida. They swept the Chicago White Sox in a three-game series to open the season, then took two out of three games from Boston. Rader's record as a major-league manager was a smooth 5-1.

Dave Hostetler's home run off Cleveland's Bert Blyleven gave them a 2-1 victory in the road opener, raising their record to 6-1. But they struggled to score runs the rest of the month, finishing April 12-9 and in third place. A stretch playing eighteen of twenty-four games on the road hurt the young team in May, dropping it below .500 after a 2-8 road trip to Detroit, Kansas City, and Chicago.

But even then Rader had his team doing some good things. Tolleson, a feisty utility infielder, became the regular second baseman after Baltimore's Dan Ford crushed Mike Richardt's left knee in a collision at second base on April 21. Tolleson had only hit .128 in 52 games with Texas in 1981 and 1982, but this time he responded to the chance. His twelve-game hitting streak in May kept the month from being worse for Texas. And left-hander Rick Honeycutt, acquired two years earlier in an eleven-player trade that sent Richie Zisk to Seattle, stunned everyone by rebounding from a 5-17 season to become the staff ace.

Honeycutt earned eight of the Rangers' first twenty-five victories, including three in May in which Texas supported him with a total of nine runs. He wasn't the only unexpected pitching bonanza. Jones, a ten-year minor leaguer taken by Texas when Pittsburgh left him unprotected in the December 1982 draft, anchored an anonymous bullpen. He delivered a five-inning performance that allowed the Rangers to win a fourteen-inning game 1-0 at Boston's Fenway Park—another Honeycutt start—and showed some guts by striking out Robin Yount with the bases loaded in the ninth inning to preserve a victory in May.

Everything clicked for Rader and the Rangers when their offense awoke on a West Coast road trip at the beginning of June. They began the Dome tour of Seattle and Minnesota with a 10-0 victory over Seattle—a shutout for Honeycutt—and continued it when Smithson beat the Mariners 1-0. Danny Darwin got into the act in Minnesota, blanking the Twins 11-0. Texas finished the trip 5-1, having scored 32 runs. Its record was back above .500 (29-27) and it was only three games out of first. Best of all, it was coming home for fourteen games in Arlington.

It was a magic time for the team and its new manager. A crowd of 31,238 welcomed them home, and Smithson beat the Mariners 5-2. By the time the homestand ended, Rader had the Rangers in first place. A doubleheader sweep of Oakland vaulted them into the lead in the American League West, and they finished the homestand 10-4.

Remarkable things continued on the road. A day before the team was to disperse for the All-Star game, the Rangers put together the most incredible inning in team history. Tied 4-4 after 14 innings in Oakland, Texas sent up 16 batters and scored 12 runs in the top of the fifteenth. There were eight hits off Oakland's Dave Beard and Ben Callahan, a six-foot-seven inch rookie right-hander who would get to pitch in only three other major-league games and would finish his career with a 12.54 ERA. Bobby Jones doubled off both Beard and Callahan in the fifteenth. Although Smithson lost the next day, the Rangers went home with a 44-34 record and a two-game lead at the All-Star break.

But this was to be the year of the Chicago White Sox. Reality set in after the break, beginning with a three-game sweep by Toronto at Exhibition Stadium, a place Rader dubbed the "Voodoo Palace." It didn't take long for Texas to backslide to .500. The Rangers did it in nineteen days, winning only five of their first twenty games back. Rader's offense died. The final straw was a three-game sweep by the Yankees at Arlington Stadium, including a nationally televised 6-5 loss at the hands of Dave Winfield.

Chicago went ahead of Texas for good that night, and eight days later had put six games between itself and the Rangers. It was only August 19 when Texas unofficially conceded. That day, with Honeycutt rested and scheduled to pitch in a doubleheader against the White Sox, Klein traded him to Los Angeles for two pitching prospects, Dave Stewart and Ricky Wright. Although Honeycutt would finish as the AL leader with a 2.42 ERA, he was unsigned for 1984. In fourth place, eight games behind Chicago, the Rangers' management began thinking of next year.

September would be like so many others in Texas, with the Rangers playing out the string. The night of September 5, as the Dallas Cowboys were opening their season against Washington on "Monday Night Football," only 1,843 showed up for a game against Minnesota. Larry Parrish drove in six runs that night, but the eerie quietness of Arlington Stadium was more memorable.

"For the first time ever," Rader said, "I heard the bullpen phone ring." Said Bell, "I heard the typewriters in the pressbox."

There wasn't much left for Rader to do that season.

Except lose control of his team.

The Reign of the Tahitian Warlord

By the end of the 1983 season, which deserved a happy ending, Doug Rader was a walking collection of frayed nerves. The season seemed to last two months longer than his sanity.

For those close to the team, the first clear sign came on a hot August night in Kansas City. It was a week after the poorly timed trade of Rick Honeycutt, and the Rangers were losing touch with the .500 mark, not to mention the white-hot White Sox. Yet nothing about this loss could explain Rader's reaction to a confrontation between the Rangers' Danny Darwin and Kansas City's U. L. Washington.

Darwin, an old-school hardball player from the Texas outback, threw a fastball in the vicinity of the toothpick that always stuck out of Washington's clenched teeth. Washington hit the dirt, then jumped up and began screaming at Darwin. As Darwin motioned Washington to the mound, Rader began shaking the padded railing in front of the visitor's dugout. "Go on, go out there," Rader shouted at Washington. He continued cursing Washington while the Royals infielder allowed discretion to win out over valor, remaining near home plate. Order was restored; only words were exchanged.

This was the kind of scene that once happened nightly in the major leagues, but for some reason it stuck to Rader. This became clear when a reporter asked him about Washington after the game.

Rader went berserk. He slammed a shoe against the door to his office and screamed, then smashed the clothes rack, sending hangars and parts of his wardrobe flying across the little room. His pants landed on the head of Jim

Reeves. "I wish he would have gone out there," Rader snarled of Washington. "I would have broken his —ing back."

Reeves calmly removed the pants and continued the interview. It had been a comical sight, but no one dared snicker. This was not a man behaving rationally.

In September, as the White Sox ran away to a final twenty-game margin over the rest of the West, Rader became obsessed with the idea of finishing second. It was not exactly a novelty to his players. Veteran catcher Jim Sundberg, for instance, had played on four second-place teams in Texas, most recently in 1981. The season was over for the players, but Rader kept pushing them hard.

Some veteran players thought it would be good for Rader to relax. Buddy Bell expressed that feeling to pitching coach Dick Such on one team flight, and Such later summoned his courage to get the message across to Rader. Such remembers their meeting clearly. Rader got angrier and angrier as Such talked, until Such thought he might actually punch him. It was another sign of Rader's frayed nerves.

But perhaps the most telling incident occured on a Sunday in September. Rader and some of his coaches were having breakfast in the coffee shop at the Seattle Sheraton when Larry Parrish, Bucky Dent, Bell, and some other players had the poor fortune to wander in. They had obviously been out all night. A game was scheduled that afternoon.

An irate Rader called a team meeting before the game in the Kingdome outfield. He blasted the veteran players in front of their younger teammates. Worse, he criticized them the next afternoon in Oakland, this time to reporters. Until then, the night out had been the team's secret. But Rader did not own kid gloves.

"A number of guys are just trying to play out the string, and they don't want me to say anything," he told the *Star-Telegram*'s Reeves. "They want me to make it easy on them to fail. I won't do that. If somebody makes them play, makes them dedicate themselves, then they just get upset. That's just too bad . . . I'm not going to look the other way for them, like other managers may have had in the past. I'm not going to let this perpetuate itself. I was hoping we'd have a little more character than we evidently have."

Rader had not said anything radical, but it was enough to alienate the players he wanted loyalty from.

"No one has ever said anything like that to me in my career," Bell told the *Morning News*' Tim Kurkjian. "This team doesn't have an attitude problem. It has a talent problem."

A season that had started with such freshness and promise ended like many before in Texas—none too soon. With Bell and Parrish still sulking and Rader looking at young players like Tommy Dunbar and Curtis Wilkerson, the Rangers were shut out four times in their last eight games, by the likes of journeymen Mike Moore, Pete Filson, Ken Schrom, and Steve Brown. They attracted three crowds over 10,000 after September 1, and finished the season 77-85. As the song goes, *Welcome back, baby, to the poor side of town.*

Once darkness had fallen, there was no sign of dawn for the Rangers under Rader. He managed them for 193 more games in 1984 and 1985, but all he accomplished was to alienate the spending public and destroy the confidence of youngsters like Jeff Kunkel, George Wright, and Tom Henke. It wasn't much of a legacy.

Rader committed one public-relations blunder after another. In the spring of 1984, one *Dallas Morning News* sports editor made a trip to Florida to discuss Rader's treatment of the media. After listening to his pitch, Rader succinctly replied, "Eat me." One night that season, he called a group of season-ticket holders seated behind the first-base dugout "assholes" when they questioned a pitching change.

His image had already suffered a beating with his handling of a trade that sent Sundberg, a local landmark, to Milwaukee for the unfortunate Ned Yost. Certainly, a case could have been made for trading Sundberg. His once deadly throwing arm looked worn during the 1983 season. His batting average had dropped from .251 in 1982 to .201 in '83. He had driven in twenty-eight runs in almost four hundred at bats. He was on the slide.

But Rader failed to grant Sundberg the dignity he had earned during his decade as a team leader and a local civic leader. Sundberg's steady play had often been the only thread of credibility for the franchise. Wrote Reeves: "He was, in fact, something of a life preserver for Ranger fans, a hope to hold onto when there was no other." *Times Herald* columnist Skip Bayless paid him the ultimate compliment for Dallas in the early 1980s: "Jim Sundberg should have been a Cowboy. He is Bob Breunig in shinguards, Danny White in mask. Sunny was Roger Staubach before it was fashionable."

Maybe Rader perceived Sundberg as a threat. Maybe he just wanted to make Sundberg think twice before again exercising his veto power over a trade, as he had at the Honolulu winter meetings in 1982 when Joe Klein had him headed to Los Angeles in a trade that would have brought the Rangers Orel Hershiser, Burt Hooton, Dave Stewart, and outfielder Mark Bradley. Rader may never have forgiven Sundberg for blocking the deal, even though Sundberg claimed the Dodgers were trying to renege on some deferred money in his contract with Texas.

In any case, Rader was questioning the popular catcher before Sundberg ever played a game for him. In February 1983, he said, "I've heard that Sunny doesn't always go hard into first base or that he doesn't always round first hard. I'm going to expect players to go hard at all times."

In April, Rader exploded over a base-running error by Sundberg. In June, Rader briefly gave the starting catcher's job to rookie Bobby Johnson. In July, Sundberg responded to Rickey Henderson's stealing ten bases in a series by explaining that he had been taking medication for a sore shoulder. Responded

Rader, "You can't go out on the field and not hurt. That's part of your job description." Throughout the season he muttered about Sundberg's reluctance to block home plate.

After the season ended, Rader directed blame at Sundberg. "I don't think we can go much farther with Jim Sundberg," he said. "I think we need a different kind of human being. . . . We need a little more offense out of that position and a little more overt get-up-and-go."

Rader succeeded in dragging Sundberg into a battle of words. "He just works through intimidation," Sundberg told Kurkjian. "He's the intimidator; he wants to be totally in control. He wants to be the top dog."

Rader kept barking even after Sundberg was sent to Milwaukee for Yost and Class A pitcher Dan Scarpetta. "We made the deal because Yost is a better player. Period. That's it," Rader said. "I would have traded him even up."

Dallas Morning News columnist Randy Galloway correctly assessed the damage to Rader in a column written shortly after the trade. "His comments made the trade a much bigger deal than it would have been," Galloway wrote. "Worse yet for Rader, other players saw and heard his treatment of Sundberg. And when Rader goes into spring training, he will have lost some believers. Believe that. His respect in the clubhouse slipped over this situation."

Yost's performance destroyed what was left of Rader's credibility. A twenty-eight-year-old backup to Milwaukee's Ted Simmons at the time of the trade, he was released by the Rangers after one season—he finished it second in the league to teammate Donnie Scott with 12 passed balls, and hit .182, never getting his batting average above .200 after April 6—and by 1986 was catching Atlanta's double-A pitchers.

Rader suffered even more because he tried so hard to make the trade for Yost work out. When Yost's struggles forced the organization to promote Scott from Oklahoma City at the start of June, Rader—who had scoffed at Sundberg's shoulder injury—said that Yost had been having trouble with his contact lens due to "excessive lid tension." He said the problem would be treated "like a knee injury."

It was a similar quirk that put Jeff Kunkel in Rader's path.

While Rader's Rangers were getting off to a quick start in 1983, Kunkel, son of the late major-league umpire Bill Kunkel, was finishing an All-American career as a shortstop at tiny Rider College in Lawrenceville, New Jersey. He was the third player picked in the 1983 June draft, and quickly showed he could play at a top level. After signing with Texas, Kunkel finished his first pro season at Tulsa in the Texas League, hitting .285 with five homers and twenty-five doubles in thirty-seven games. His future looked bright, particularly in an organization that in the past five years had used a string of shortstops that included Nelson Norman, Bud Harrelson, Pepe Frias, Dave Roberts, Mario Mendoza, Mark Wagner, and Bucky Dent.

Kunkel earned an invitation to camp in the spring of 1984. "If he develops power, he'll be a Robin Yount," GM Joe Klein said after one impressive display. "I've got to get him out of here before Doug gets attached to him."

Kunkel was sent back to double-A Tulsa to open the season, but was never far from Rader's mind. It must have been better to think of the future than of what was happening to the current Rangers. They started slow, losing seven of their first ten games, and by the All-Star break were securely in last place with a 38-49 record. Attendance was down. Something had to be done.

At a meeting, the staff decided to bench second baseman Wayne Tolleson, who was hitting .226 and had driven in only eight runs in almost 300 at bats. Parties to the meeting remember leaving with the knowledge that twenty-three-year-old Stanford grad Steve Buechele would be promoted from Oklahoma City to replace Tolleson.

The next day, July 23, the media was summoned to an afternoon news conference at the stadium, ostensibly to announce the signing of #1 draft choice Oddibe McDowell. All the brass was there: Eddie Chiles, Joe Klein, Doug Rader, Tom Grieve. Moments after McDowell had been introduced, Klein said he had a surprise. Kunkel stepped out from behind a curtain.

Eighteen days earlier, Klein had said this about Kunkel: "We want him to have a nice quiet year." In the words of that erudite scholar Gomer Pyle, "Shazam!"

Wilkerson, a rookie whose development triggered Dent's release in the spring, was shifted from shortstop to second base to clear a space for the twenty-two-year-old Kunkel, whose minor-league resumé included only 115 games. "He's here for one reason," Rader said. "He and Curtis are the best short-stop and second baseman the organization can put out there. Period."

Riding the high, Kunkel had the kind of debut of which he and his father had dreamed. Kunkel took a called third strike from Baltimore's Mike Boddicker in his first at bat, but then lined a single up the middle. He beat out a slow roller his third time up and finished his three-for-four night with a soft single to left field. He was flawless in the field, leaving only the Rangers' sixth consecutive loss to mar the evening. "He did everything you could possibly ask for," Rader said afterward.

The compliments ended there.

Kunkel made the first of what would be 17 errors in his forty-eight games the next night, and it would be a long time before he had another multiple-hit game. What Rader got when he called up Kunkel was an underdeveloped player who blanched in the major-league spotlight.

Kunkel's struggle in the field was surprising (his .922 fielding percentage was the lowest in the majors for a shortstop playing forty games since 1977), but the Rangers should have known his lack of discipline at the plate would be found out by major-league pitchers. He didn't draw a walk in his first 132 plate appearances, and finished the season hitting .204 with an on-base percentage of .218. He was overmatched at the major-league level.

Emotionally, he was no better prepared. At least one tongue-lashing by Rader left Kunkel in tears in the dugout, and others forced him to fight back more tears. Here was the major-league dream gone bad.

It never really got better for Kunkel, hard though he kept chasing that dream. His father died from cancer of the colon in May 1985, and his batting average fell all the way to .195 that season at Oklahoma City. Then, in a September promotion to the majors, as he chased a pop fly he collided with center fielder George Wright and destroyed his left knee. In the spring of 1987, with a chance to make the team as a utility man, he separated his shoulder trying for a diving catch in an exhibition game. Later that year he needed an appendectomy. He toyed with trying to make it as a pitcher before eventually sticking in the majors as a valuable utility man in April 1989. By then he was not much more than a survivor.

Other players, too, came in contact with Rador's Midas-in-reverse touch: George Wright, Tom Henke, Dave Hostetler, and Dave Stewart, to name a few. All were young, talented, and unable to deal with the man outfielder Billy Sample called Uncle Doug.

Wright's athleticism was the talk of the American League in 1982 and 1983. At the age of twenty-four, he played in every one of the Rangers' games in Rader's first season, hitting .276 (his highest average since leaving Oklahoma City's Capitol High) with 18 home runs and 80 RBIs. Combine that with his uncanny ability to play the shallowest center field in baseball yet make catches at the wall, and he looked like a force in the game. "He is outstanding, and he will develop to be a premium player," Rader said.

Wright's stock took a nosedive after he ran into the outfield fence at Chicago's Comiskey Park on May 11, 1984. It was the most serious of a series of injuries that contributed to a monumental loss of confidence for Wright. His pride was also hurting. The biggest blow to it came after the All-Star break in '84. Shortly after returning from an Oklahoma City rehab stint caused by a strained knee, Wright was told that he was no longer a center fielder. Rader had decided that Gary Ward should play center, with Wright moved to right. Rader said his strong arm made him "a prototype right fielder."

But Wright grew up idolizing Willie Mays, not Roberto Clemente. He saw himself as a center fielder, and went into a funk over the change. The playfulness was gone from his face, and his standard reply to any question became, "I only work here."

One year later, McDowell replaced Wright as the regular center fielder. Two years later, Wright was traded to make room for Ruben Sierra. Now, he is remembered mostly for dropping a ninth-inning fly ball to help turn a no-hit bid by Charlie Hough into a 2-1 loss in Anaheim. New manager Bobby Valentine called him "my biggest disappointment since I've been a manager or a coach."

The winter before his June 1986 trade to Montreal, the Rangers couldn't even get Houston left-hander Mike Madden for Wright. "I think we've shown as much patience as he deserves," Grieve said after the eventual trade. "You can't just keep hoping."

Rader experienced the same frustration with Hostetler, a strapping (six-four, 215 pounds) first baseman acquired with Larry Parrish in the 1982 trade for Al Oliver. He flashed his potential with 10 home runs in June that year—a

Dallas Times Herald headline from July 1 proclaimed "Hoss rides into Arlington and baseballs look for cover"–and finished his rookie season with 22 home runs and 67 RBIs in 113 games. Here was a man about to hit the big time.

The length of Hostetler's home runs drew as much attention as their number even if Hostetler himself seemed not to notice. "Little guys remember home runs because they don't hit that many," Hostetler said. "I'm not a little guy."

Hossmania swept through Arlington as a team that had been 12-27 when he was called up won sixteen of its first twenty-nine games with Hostetler aboard. A local sportscast showed a medley of Hostetler home runs set to the theme from "Bonanza." Newspapers compared his start in the major leagues to that of some other home-run hitters–Hank Aaron, Mickey Mantle, Babe Ruth, Harmon Killebrew, and Willie Mays.

"Strength-wise, I'd put him in a category with Jim Rice, Frank Howard, Dave Kingman, and George Foster," Don Zimmer said. "I'm not saying he is as good a ballplayer as those guys, but he has a chance to be." Jim Fanning, who had managed Hostetler with Montreal, agreed with Zimmer. "Dave Hostetler won't just make it with the Rangers," he said. "He'll be a star."

Under Rader, it didn't happen.

Rookie Pete O'Brien won the first-base job with flashy defense in the spring of 1983, leaving Hostetler to platoon with Mickey Rivers as the team's designated hitter. Hostetler's home run production fell off to eleven that season as he struck out once every three at bats. Rader himself later diagnosed the problem as overcoaching. "He started doing so many things, we had to correct so many things, he changed every day," Rader said in 1984. "But we couldn't let him keep going that way. We'll give him less (instruction this year). He won't be as confused."

It was not that easy. Hostetler was a defensive liability, and the off-season acquisition of Ward moved Parrish from right field to the designated hitter spot, leaving Hostetler with little opportunity to work out his stroke. He never really got it back, and was sent down to Oklahoma City in June and then traded back to Montreal for fringe left-hander Chris Welsh after the 1984 season. His major-league career was practically over, his home run total stopped at thirty-seven, only 718 short of Aaron's.

Henke, the original country boy, had experienced some success in the Texas organization before Rader's arrival. His wicked sidearm delivery made him a terror in the minor leagues (412 strikeouts in 416 innings), and he was equally successful in a trial with Texas at the end of 1982. He was 1-0 with a 1.15 ERA in eight outings.

With Rader around, however, Henke seemed to freeze up. He was sensitive to criticism, particularly when it was delivered in a loud voice. He pitched in Oklahoma City in '83, joining the Rangers only as things were crumbling around Rader in August and September. Still, he struck out seventeen in 16 innings, whetting appetites for the next season.

Henke broke camp with the Rangers, but was sent back to Oklahoma City April 26. He came up again June 30, but lasted only until July 4. The next time he was back was August 9. He had a 6.35 ERA in three stints with Texas, walking twenty men in 28 innings. At Oklahoma City, his ERA was 2.64, and he walked only twenty-five in 65 innings. There was no way around the conclusion: in Rader's glare, he wilted.

"I'd walk a guy and he would start kicking trash cans," Henke said later. "He had me intimidated, you know."

Henke didn't have to worry about Rader after 1984. Because the Rangers had signed Type A free agent Cliff Johnson, they could only protect twenty-four players, not twenty-six, in the since-abolished compensation draft. Henke was one of two players taken off the protected list (Rivers, released the next spring anyway, was protected) and was selected by Toronto. There, away from Rader, he developed into one of baseball's most dominant relievers.

"Toronto saw something in me Texas didn't," Henke says. "It's been a breath of fresh air for me."

Dave Stewart is another who got away, although there were no tearful farewells by the time he was traded to Philadelphia in September of 1985. Stewart failed every way a person can fail in his two years in Texas.

Like Henke, he created anticipation with a strong close to the 1983 season, going 5-2 with a 2.14 ERA in eight starts after coming over from Los Angeles in the Rick Honeycutt trade. He was a large man (six-two, 200 pounds) who could throw a baseball very hard. He was friendly and well liked, traits which came back to hurt the Rangers.

Two days before he was to accept the club's "Good Guy" award, he was found in a compromising position with a woman named Lucille in the back seat of a car parked in an East Los Angeles alley. At least, according to police reports, he thought it was a woman. It turned out to be a transvestite prostitute named Elson Tyler. Stewart eventually pleaded "no contest" to a charge of participating in prostitution and was sentenced to twelve months probation and a $150 fine.

That did not keep him away from the Rangers' midwinter banquet. He shocked club officials by coming to Dallas two days after his arrest to accept his "Good Guy" award, then turned his acceptance speech into a public apology. His judgment could be questioned, but not his guts.

Stewart never sold himself short. Before the '84 season, he told the *Morning News'* Kurkjian he felt capable of winning "twenty to thirty" games. Rader's #2 starter, he was 0-6 in April and finished 7-14. Rader tried him as a short man in the bullpen the next year, but with equally poor results. He made forty-two appearances without a victory.

Stewart never developed a pitch to go with his fastball while he was with Texas, but with a newly successful forkball he won twenty games for Oakland in 1987.

Stewart had decided in the winter of 1984 to work on the forkball. But Rader could not stand to see the Baltimore Orioles punish Stewart in an exhibition game in Pompano Beach. The capper came when minor-league infielder Kelly Paris belted a fat forkball for a home run.

"I kept throwing forkball after forkball and they kept hitting it," Stewart said. "Rader came out to the mound and said he didn't like my mound appearance, that I needed to change my act. He bawled me out on the mound, and anybody could see what was going on. He told me, 'Quit throwing the pitch. Work on your fastball, work on your breaking ball. Just don't throw that pitch.' "

Three years and two teams later, Toronto's Lloyd Moseby said the pitch Stewart was forced to shelve in Texas had become unhittable. "You've got to tip your hat to him," Moseby said after a game in 1987. "It's no secret what he's going to throw. He's not cutting the ball, he's not throwing a spitter. The forkball is his pitch. We knew what he was going to throw. We just couldn't hit it."

Try telling that to Doug Rader.

Under Rader, Texas fell to the bottom of the American League West in 1984, a position it had avoided since Whitey Herzog's time eleven years earlier. The Rangers finished the season in grand style, once again unoffically punching out before closing time.

On the next-to-last day of the season, thirty-eight-year-old junk-baller Geoff Zahn beat Texas with an eight-hit shutout. Zahn did not allow a baserunner after Wright singled with one out in the sixth. As it happened, Wright was the last baserunner of the season for the Rangers.

The next day Mike Witt threw a perfect game for California, the thirteenth in major-league history. About five thousand people sat in the Arlington Stadium stands on a sun-soaked Sunday and watched the angular Witt beat Charlie Hough 1-0. Witt struck out ten and second baseman Rob Wilfong fielded eight ground balls. Third baseman Doug DeCinces made the defensive play of the day, perhaps taking a hit away from Larry Parrish in the fifth inning.

Mickey Rivers said afterward that the Rangers "had packed our tent" beforehand, but a sign of just how deep the franchise had sunk into the bottom of the barrel could be found in Rader's choice of ninth-inning hitters. Faced with the ignominy of ending the season with thirty-eight Rangers up and thirty-eight Rangers down, Rader could do no better than to let Witt face the left-handed trio of Tommy Dunbar, pinch-hitter Bobby Jones (for Scott), and pinch-hitter Marvis Foley (for Wilkerson).

It created a good trivia question—whose last career at bat was the final out in a perfect game?—but underscored the desperation Rader took home to Florida. Eddie Chiles shared the feeling, having watched attendance drop from 1.4 million in 1983 to 1.1 million, but still approved a major expenditure for free agents recommended by Rader.

That winter, with Rader calling the shots for Grieve, who replaced Klein as general manager in September, the Rangers spent $4 million to sign Cliff Johnson, Burt Hooton, and Dave Rozema. None made a difference, and all three would be gone by May 5, 1986. Rozema, the last member of the trio still in Texas, lasted almost a year longer than Rader.

He was fired after that 9-23 start in 1985, getting the word in Chicago at the end of the pathetic trip that began in Detroit and continued into New York. Maybe Rader was right. Maybe he was meant to be a Tahitian war lord or a pirate.

He sure wasn't cut out to manage the Texas Rangers.

Opportunity Calls—and Tom Grieve Answers

In the summer of 1949, seven-year-old Tom Grieve took a break from watching Mickey Mantle on television to break some news to his mother.

"I'm going to be a major-leaguer."

Polly Grieve looked at her son and smiled. "It's great to play and have fun," she said. "Baseball's a good game, but you have to be real good to play in the major leagues. Really good."

"But, Mom, somebody's got to make it."

She had to admit the kid had a point.

Ten years later, Grieve was on the verge of living every boy's dream. He was the best athlete at his high school in Pittsfield, Massachusetts. He played every sport in season: football, basketball, and baseball. He dated a cheerleader. He had the world on a string.

A guidance counselor asked the teenage Grieve about his career goals. Grieve gave him the same answer he had once given his mother. "I want to play major-league baseball," he said. "It's all I've ever wanted to do."

"I know, Tom, I know," the counselor said, "but what do you want to *be* in life?"

When are they going to understand, Grieve would ask himself.

He had always liked baseball best, even if the local climate made its pursuit difficult. The season was short, yet by his senior year in high school he had captured the attention of scouts from colleges as well as major-league teams. The Washington Senators drafted Grieve with their first-round pick in 1966.

Grieve was thrilled, at least until it was time to talk money. He and the Senators clearly had a different idea of what a first-round draft choice should earn. Grieve carefully studied his alternatives–which, as a National Merit Scholar, included enrolling at Dartmouth–before arriving at the decision to play baseball for the University of Michigan.

His answer to the Senators: No thanks.

But that was before he spent the summer playing in the nearby Cape Cod League, which showcases top college players for pro scouts. It is a good measure of amateur talent. The more Grieve looked around, the fewer players he saw whose talents matched his. Eventually he decided that he was the best in the league.

Then why wasn't he willing to test himself against professionals? That question nagged him for some time. Three days before the fall semester was to begin at Michigan, he called up the Senators' scout who had tried to sign him.

"I've changed my mind," Grieve said. "I'm ready to take what you offered me." Later, he remembered, "No one was more surprised than the Senators."

Grieve was by no means the instant big-leaguer he would one day make of Pete Incaviglia. He came up the hard way, with minor-league stops at Burlington, Geneva, Salisbury, Buffalo, and Denver before getting a chance with the Senators in 1970, the same year he married Kathy, a former Pittsfield cheerleader.

Those were the Vietnam years. Having passed on a student deferment, Grieve did the only thing he could to avoid the draft–he joined the Army Reserves. His obligation was one weekend a month and two weeks every summer.

It wasn't the best situation for a ballplayer, but it definitely beat the career choice made by Bobby "Ace" Jones, one of his teammates at Geneva and Salisbury. When Grieve was making his major-league debut at Yankee Stadium, Jones was with an artillery group, shelling the Viet Cong daily with howitzers. He returned from a fourteen-month tour of duty deaf in his right ear.

Grieve was in on the ground floor with the Rangers, making the move to Arlington along with Bob Short's Washington franchise in the first months of 1972. He wasn't excited about moving, having lived almost all of his life on the Eastern seaboard. But North Texas grew on him, and for the first time in his career he stuck with a team. The Rangers' charter season was Grieve's first full season in the major leagues.

Grieve was never a top-of-the-line outfielder, playing in more than a hundred games only twice in nine big-league seasons. He was never an All-Star, although he did hit .309 one year. Too often, he finished with averages like .204 or .225. But like most players, he found satisfaction in both the lifestyle and the feeling of acceptance by other major-league players. In his own words, "There's no better feeling than to be one of the regular guys on the team."

Despite his merit-scholar intelligence, Grieve–known in the clubhouse as "Tag," the result of his full name, Thomas Alan Grieve–was in many ways a stereotypical baseball player. He certainly tried to fit the role. His answers to a *Dallas Morning News* questionnaire seemed appropriately old-school:

Favorite all-time television show: " 'The Beverly Hillbillies' and 'The Honeymooners.' "

Favorite magazine: "*Sports Illustrated.*"

Favorite fashion designer: "Levi Strauss."

More often than not, Grieve's recollections about his playing days involve incidents rather than games. There was the time in Venezuela when he watched as two people were killed in a ballpark argument, and another time in Venezuela when fans attacked the team bus, starting a fight that, he said, ended with Toby Harrah booting someone "just like a kickoff." There was the home-run-hitting contest in Milwaukee that matched him against Hank Aaron. This was in the twilight of Aaron's career, and Grieve was the victor–by a shutout. "When it was over," Grieve said, "I would have given anything for me to be the one that hadn't hit any home runs."

With the Rangers, Grieve played for managers Ted Williams, Whitey Herzog, Billy Martin, Frank Lucchesi, Eddie Stanky, and Billy Hunter–an impressive list for six seasons, particularly since it omits interim managers Del Wilbur and Connie Ryan. Then came a Brad Corbett trade after the 1977 season, sending him to a New York Mets team managed by Joe Torre. He lasted only one season there, getting a meager 101 at bats–only fifty-nine less than teammate Bobby Valentine–before joining St. Louis in 1979. The late Ken Boyer was managing the Cardinals, and apparently saw enough of Grieve in the nine games he played before his May release.

By then, Grieve knew plenty about losing teams. With the exception of his brief stay in St. Louis, the 1974 and 1977 Rangers were the only winning teams he knew. His love for the game never faded, but he did begin to question his position in it after spending the last four months of the 1979 season as a thirty-one-year-old playing triple-A ball for the Rangers' Pacific Coast League team at Tucson. At that point, he had only one viable alternative as a player–Japan.

It was tempting.

But after talking it over with Kathy, and considering his family responsibilities, Grieve decided to look for a new way to stay in baseball.

"I had three children, my wife had been to Venezuela five times, two kids were in school," Grieve says. "I couldn't see how I could justify going to Japan."

Corbett, always a kind-hearted owner, came to the aid of the former player, offering him a job in group ticket sales and promotions with the Rangers. "It's not much," Corbett told him, "but it's all I've got. You can make it what you want."

Grieve accepted the job, happy to be living in Arlington and working in baseball. He had his foot in the door of a major-league front office, and vowed to make the most of the opportunity. He had no regrets about his playing career.

"You play till you know in your own heart that it's time to quit," he later said. "In a lot of cases, guys play until they take the uniform away. I quit a little before that. I knew it was time."

It didn't take long for Grieve to experience almost every situation possible in the front office. He moved steadily from job to job, never really spending enough time to master any of them. Once he left the ticket office after one season, his job concentrated primarily on the development of younger players. He was both a scout and an assistant to farm director Joe Klein in 1981 and 1982, then moved into Klein's job as farm director when Eddie Chiles promoted Klein to general manager, replacing Eddie Robinson. As farm director, he was an almost invisible executive, spending the spring at the Rangers' minor-league complex in Plant City, Florida, and the season in places like Burlington, Iowa, Sarasota, Tulsa, and Oklahoma City.

Grieve didn't attract much attention until September 1, 1984. Chiles called another news conference, this time to announce that Klein was "resigning," a human sacrifice to another numbing season. Mike Stone, the Western Company executive turned club president, had picked the thirty-six-year-old Grieve to replace him.

Grieve had wanted a general manager's job since he had taken Corbett's offer of a job selling tickets five years earlier. But he did not expect it so soon and he felt unprepared.

"Wow . . . I don't think I'm ready," Grieve said to Stone.

"It's not beyond you," Stone countered.

"I'll think about it."

Grieve did just that. There were compelling reasons to continue his education for a few years before putting his neck on the line. This was not exactly a sweetheart of a job he was being offered. Just ask Klein.

"I had some reservations about it," Grieve later admitted. "The mechanics of the waiver rules, handling the front office, whether I would be accepted by the other general managers, whether people would slough me off because I had not been involved in baseball a long time."

They all seemed legitimate concerns. But then Grieve asked himself a question: If I don't take the job, who will? Fear of the unknown eventually convinced Grieve to take perhaps the biggest risk of his life. The chance for embarrassment seemed high.

"I knew if I didn't accept it, they would offer it to somebody else and that person would come from outside the organization," Grieve said. "I knew the scouts. I knew Doug and the coaches. I figured I would rather take a chance I could do it and work hard and learn the ropes than take a chance of not being too thrilled with the person that came in.

"It was important to keep the continuity going from the standpoint of knowing that we wanted to be successful in the minor leagues, in scouting and developing players."

Randy Galloway, a columnist for the *Morning News* who had covered the Rangers daily during Grieve's tenure as a player, publicly pleaded with Grieve after the announcement. Don't do this to yourself, Tom, he wrote. Association with the Rangers will destroy a promising front-office career, he reasoned. There are better jobs than being head man at a funhouse.

Grieve did not have much time to fill the gaps in his working knowledge of his new job before it was time to use that knowledge. Two months after he took the job, baseball executives descended on the Hyatt Regency hotel in downtown Houston for the annual winter meetings–Grieve's first test of strength.

The annual winter meetings are to baseball's sharpest executives what feeding time is to Sea World sharks. Skilled traders like Jack McKeon, Hugh Alexander, Pat Gillick, and Joe McIlvaine go to each meeting to prey on the weaker teams and less experienced general managers. Both leagues conduct official business during the week, but the real action happens in the lobby, at the bar or in the private suites of the ball clubs. General managers play a game of human baseball cards, seeking the trades or free-agent signings that will either pull them up to respectability or put them over the top.

It was at meetings like these that the Texas Rangers had shot themselves in the foot so many times, always leaving with smiles on their faces only to later discover that their pockets had been picked.

Grieve's situation was made even more difficult by the quirky power structure that had been set upon his hiring. Doug Rader, unlike most managers, did not report to the general manager. He answered directly to Stone, making him Grieve's organizational equal. But it was the experienced Rader who appeared to run the show. And it was Rader who impatiently demanded major changes in his team, more than once trying the patience of everyone concerned.

During one long meeting in the Rangers' seventeenth-floor suite, Rader lay on a couch, drinking beer and trying to be funny. His attention span could not handle mundane matters like the reading of scouting reports. He was bored, and clearly showed it. On the way out the door, veteran scout Joe Marchese shook his head and muttered what would soon be an epitaph for the Rader era. "The manager," Marchese said, "is a jackoff."

Welcome to the big leagues, Tom Grieve.

Grieve's main man at the meetings was Sandy Johnson, his newly hired director of player personnel and scouting. Johnson had the experience Grieve lacked, and in many ways represented the future of the organization. While the general manager, Klein had headed the scouting operations personally; many thought he had spread himself too thin in the process. But when Grieve met with Stone to discuss the general manager's job, Grieve negotiated a commitment to hire a scouting director and to strengthen the department.

Grieve did not know Johnson, then the San Diego Padres' scouting director, but others did. "Every time I heard his name mentioned," Grieve said, "it was in glowing terms." Grieve courted Johnson during the 1984 World Series between the Padres and the Detroit Tigers, and eventually won him over by telling him he could set his own budget and have authority over farm director Marty Scott.

That chain of command gave Johnson unusual control over the players he brought into the organization. "In most situations, a scouting director signs them and that's the last he sees of them," Grieve said.

Johnson, forty-four at the time he was hired, had been among the men responsible for getting the Major League Scouting Bureau off the ground. A former minor-league player, he had tried managing minor-league teams for the Seattle Pilots-Milwaukee Brewers organization before commiting himself to scouting in 1972. Scouting amateur prospects had become his love – so much so that two years after the Rangers hired him, Johnson declined a chance to become the Chicago White Sox's general manager.

"I was flattered," he said, "but I never had the desire to be a general manager. I had never really thought about it. My first love is scouting, and the days of the general manager going out and watching high school players are over."

Johnson's only rule in the quest of players was not to be bound by any rules at all. "I'll do anything to get a ballplayer," he said. "Maybe you better not write that, but that's the way I am . . . We're not in business to win a popularity contest."

Johnson proved that on the first day of the winter meetings. Before moving to the Texas organization, he had been asked by the Padres to sign an agreement saying he would leave their farm system alone, but had refused. Thus the Rangers used the third pick of the major-league draft (a draft of minor leaguers with at least three years' experience who are not on a team's forty-man major-league roster) to spend $25,000 on a twenty-year-old left-handed pitcher named Mitch Williams.

Williams had a million-dollar arm but had thus far produced results worth about $1.25. Never pitching above the Class A level, Williams had a composite professional record of 20-25 with a 5.18 earned run average. He had averaged 8.8 strikeouts and 7.6 walks for every nine innings.

Johnson left the Padres organization thinking Williams was the best pitching prospect it had, but also knowing that differences with farm director Tom Romenesko had left Williams frustrated and with little future in his own organization. "He's had control problems, but he has excellent stuff," Johnson said. "We'll see if he can get his arm under control. We felt he was the best prospect of the draft. Three or four years from now, we might be talking about a 17- or 18-game winner. His tools are that good."

It was blessed relief for Williams, who badly wanted out of the Padres' organization. His senior year in high school at West Lynn, Oregon, Williams broke all of his brother Bruce's pitching records. He was 17-0 with 190 strikeouts, and was clocked throwing ninety-three miles per hour. San Diego had selected him in the seventh round of the 1982 June draft. To hear Williams tell it, that was the last thing they did for him.

"When Texas drafted me, they (the Padres) insinuated I had drug problems, which is totally false," Williams says. "I heard from different people they thought I had a drug problem. They came out in the paper and said that I had a good arm but there were questions about my makeup."

Williams departed the Padres with this image of GM Jack McKeon: "He's a man who walked around spring training in a sweat suit zipped down to his waist, with a big belly hanging out, smoking a cigar . . . and I'm supposed to have respect for him?"

Williams found Grieve—who took long runs at dawn—much more to his liking. But that was yet to come. At the time, after the brief high that came with adding a prospect like Williams to the system, Grieve had his own problems. He and Rader had made little secret of the availability of designated hitter-right fielder Larry Parrish. Parrish was coming off a season in which he had been the Rangers' bright light, driving in 101 runs with 22 homers, 42 doubles and a .285 batting average. At thirty-one he was not at the end of his career. With that in mind, Grieve set a high asking price.

He and Rader had marked the Pittsburgh Pirates as their primary target, noting that while the Pirates finished last in the National League East their pitchers had the lowest staff ERA in the league. Grieve knew the Rangers needed pitching. They also needed a second baseman or shortstop—having soured on Wayne Tolleson and knowing Jeff Kunkel needed time to recover from his disastrous late-season trial—and a leadoff hitter. Pittsburgh had just the person to fill those needs, Johnny Ray.

Pittsburgh GM Harding Peterson bit when offered Parrish as bait, but balked when he found out what Grieve wanted—Ray and left-hander John Tudor, a twelve-game winner in 1984. Talks were going nowhere, but Peterson kept returning Grieve's calls. Here were two teams desperate to do something.

Meanwhile, the New York Mets got into the act. They, too, wanted Parrish, and were offering a three-for-one package of Walt Terrell (the former Ranger farmhand who went along with Ron Darling in the Lee Mazzilli trade two years earlier), shortstop Ron Gardenhire, and catcher Mike Fitzgerald. Grieve countered with these names: Parrish for Darling, right-hander Floyd Youmans, catcher John Gibbons, and Gardenhire. End of discussion.

Perhaps feeling pressure to complete a major trade before leaving Houston, Grieve went back to Peterson with this offer: Parrish for Ray and Mike Bielecki, the minor-league pitcher of the year that season at Class AAA Hawaii.

"We'll consider it," Peterson said.

Later, the phone rang in the seventeenth-floor suite. Peterson was summoning the Ranger brass to a meeting. He had his answer.

"I got the impression when I left the room (after making the offer) that they were close to doing it," Grieve said later. "When I walked back into the room, I thought they were going to say yes."

Instead, Peterson said no.

Grieve did not go home empty-handed. In addition to drafting Williams, he also signed free-agent designated hitter Cliff Johnson to an incredible three-year, $2.1-million contract—a move he would regret within the year. He had an empty feeling en route back to Dallas-Fort Worth Airport.

* * *

Grieve put together two deals in the six weeks following the winter meetings. The first was blocked when Bill Stein's back problems were found in a physical given him by the Pittsburgh Pirates. The other was a dandy, a four-team swap-o-rama.

It brought the Rangers the catcher they badly needed in Don Slaught, at a cost of home-grown Danny Darwin and an obscure minor-leaguer. Darwin went to Milwaukee, Jim Sundberg went from Milwaukee to Kansas City (where he would catch Bret Saberhagen as the Royals won the seventh game of the 1985 World Series), Tim Leary went from the New York Mets to Milwaukee and Frank Willo went from Kansas City to the Mets.

Kansas City GM John Schuerholz orchestrated the trade, knowing he could not single-handedly satisfy Brewer General Manager Harry Dalton's demands for Sundberg. Since they were getting a quality catcher in Sundberg, the Royals were willing to give up Slaught, a twenty-six-year-old UCLA graduate who had caught 124 games in 1984.

"Obviously, that's a stiff price to pay," Grieve said. "We're giving up a starting pitcher who will pitch 225 innings for Milwaukee this year. But with our catchers' performance last year, we felt we had to make the deal."

Darwin departed the organization in traditional style. That is, he said the Ranger front office should look in a mirror the next time it tried to decipher the franchise's sorry history. "The only thing I'd like to see 'em do is get some stability in the front office and with the players," Darwin said. "That's something we've lacked every year I've been here. You're not going to win many ball games today when you put a new team out there every year."

Grieve could not have agreed more. He dreamed of the day someone would accuse him of growing complacent. But for now, he took satisfaction in the reaction of rival general managers.

Said Peterson: "I could not say enough good things about Tom Grieve. He conducted himself like a gentleman. Whatever he told me, I would believe . . . [and] . . . I think he will do a good job. Not only does he have a good head on his shoulders, he knows what he wants, what the team needs, and he's going about filling those needs."

And Dalton: "I have been impressed. He's very forthright and candid. He's aggressive and he works hard in what he's doing. I've enjoyed my dealings with him because he makes common sense about baseball."

Grieve allowed himself a brief daydream in January, shortly after completing his first major trade.

"The image of the team is bad," he told the *Morning News'* Tim Kurkjian. "It's a fact. Nothing can change that perception. The people with that perception are pretty vocal, so it appears to be the majority . . . A pretty good season is not going to change that, if in fact it can be changed. But three or four or five years from now when we've gradually gotten better, we will be respected throughout baseball, not just here."

Why Is This Man Smiling?

Tom Grieve answers the telephone, talks for a moment, then returns the receiver to its hook. Suddenly, he looks much older than twenty-nine.

It is December 8, 1977, and Grieve has just been told that he has been traded from the Rangers to the New York Mets. Dismay is too mild a description of his reaction. Downright, belly-grabbing shock is more like it.

Grieve has been in the organization for more than a decade. He had moved from Washington with the Senators and had adopted Texas as his home. Two months before, in fact, he had bought a new house in Arlington. Sure, he knew baseball players get uprooted by trades all the time; but it had never before happened to him.

Questions flash through his mind: How would he tell Kathy, his wife? What about the kids? Could they all pack up again? And just how does a person who learned to enjoy the drawling pace of Texas survive the slam-dancing that is life in New York City? Was this really happening?

Forget that he was leaving perhaps Texas' best-ever team, a team that came together under Billy Hunter to win ninety-four games, to join a team that had itself finished in last place in 1977. Forget that two-thirds of the Mets' outfield was set with Lee Mazzilli and Steve Henderson, and that the traditional rules of the National League did not include a spot for a designated hitter. Forget the difference between a Dallas-Fort Worth dollar and a Manhattan dollar.

Forget everything except the comfortable feeling of acceptance, and its importance to Grieve. He once called it the best feeling a person could experience in baseball. And now he was going from being one of the guys to, in his own words, "an outsider" with the Mets.

Because of the gnawing feeling that his life-support system had been stripped away, Grieve dreaded that spring. Enjoying his family, he counted down the days until he had to report to the Mets' spring-training camp in St. Petersburg.

"It was unbelievably traumatic," he remembers. "I wasn't prepared for it. I had been with the organization for ten, twelve years. Our family knew the other families. I was going to a different league, and very few people knew much about me. I didn't know one single person on the team."

But Grieve had always made friends easily, and this would be no different. He found himself especially drawn to another man on the fringe of the team, another who waited until the starters have taken batting practice to take their rounds in the cage. Of course, it was easy to be drawn to Bobby Valentine. He seldom stopped talking.

Valentine, like Grieve, was on his way down as a player. His life had changed four years before when he shattered his dreams of becoming a dominant player, as well as his right leg, in a collision with the outfield fence at Anaheim Stadium. Now he tried to hide a limp, and find a way to stay in the major leagues without the speed that had gotten him there. It was not going well. The year before, Valentine had hit a mind-boggling .133 after coming to the Mets from San Diego, where he had been hitting .179.

Valentine needed friends, too.

Grieve and Valentine began spending all their time together. At the ballpark, they encouraged each other. Away from the ballpark, they shared a cottage near the beach. They often went down to the water to sit and talk about baseball. They rode to the ballpark together each day, as always talking about baseball.

Just before camp broke, Grieve made a decision: his wife and children would remain in Texas while he went to New York. There was no reason to disrupt more than one person's life, he said to himself. He still had not worked up much enthusiasm for a season in which he figured to spend most of his time on a bad team's bench.

Valentine had an idea. "When we break camp," he said, "there's no reason for you to live all alone in an apartment in New York. Come live with Mary and me. We've got a big house and plenty of room."

Grieve balked.

"I can't do that," he said. "We barely know each other, and I don't know your wife at all. Thanks just the same."

Mary Valentine joined the chorus after she arrived in Florida. "There's plenty of room," she said. "If your family is going to remain in Texas, you won't know anyone in New York. Believe me, staying with us will be better than living alone."

Grieve relented. And so began a friendship that one day provided a down-on-its-luck franchise in Texas with the youngest manager and general manager in the major leagues.

* * *

That summer, while sharing the bench with him in New York, Valentine convinced Grieve that he would one day manage in the major leagues. The Mets stayed in the National League East cellar, losing ninety-six games instead of the ninety-eight they had lost the previous year. Valentine occasionally spelled Doug Flynn at second base; Grieve was no more than a pinch hitter and fifth outfielder. Between the two of them, they contributed three home runs and twenty-six runs batted in. The one thing they did really well was talk about baseball.

"I'll take what he knows about baseball, coupled with his communication skills with people, and put it up against anyone," Grieve said. "I know he comes across as cocky, but it's confidence. He has been planning to be a big-league manager ever since he was twenty."

Indeed, Valentine had gained an invaluable ally. "I never had any aspirations to be a big-league manager or coach," Grieve said. "The front office was more intriguing to me. But I knew Bobby wanted to manage. Every big-league game he ever saw, Bobby managed in his mind. I always said to myself, 'If I was ever in a position to either recommend or hire a big-league manager, it would be Bobby Valentine.' "

Grieve did just that when Joe Klein began a managerial search at the end of the 1982 season. He steered Klein to him, and Klein got in touch with Valentine. This was no token contact, either. Klein interviewed Valentine three times before giving the job to Doug Rader.

Valentine, thirty-two when he made that first run at a managerial job, eventually found himself on Davey Johnson's coaching staff with the Mets. He was coaching third for the Mets when the Rangers broke from the gate so poorly in 1985. Grieve was never especially enamored of Rader, but he didn't want a power struggle in his first year on the job. He bided his time and, by May, Rader had lost the support he needed. Eddie Chiles was ready for a change. Mike Stone instructed Grieve to find a replacement.

No one doubted that the Rangers needed a new image, and the new manager would be expected to provide one. Stone's eye was on the bottom line as well as the American League standings.

Attendance at Arlington Stadium had dropped 250,000 in 1984, and it appeared on its way to a further nosedive. Since the home opener against Milwaukee, the Rangers had failed to draw a single crowd of as many as nineteen thousand. Eleven of the first seventeen home dates drew crowds below fifteen thousand. Despite the addition of $4.7 million in free agents (albeit the Moe, Larry, and Curly trio of Cliff Johnson, Dave Rozema, and Burt Hooton), attendance was already running below the pace that had attracted only 1.1 million the year before.

Here was a franchise that needed instant credibility, and there was one man around who could provide it—Earl Weaver. The chain-smoking, hard-driving former manager of the Baltimore Orioles was in early retirement in Florida. Chiles liked the idea of bringing Weaver to Arlington.

Grieve called Weaver in Florida, but, he said, "It was very apparent getting back in baseball at this time was something he (Weaver) was not interested in." Maybe not, but later that year Weaver resumed his career in Baltimore. He simply had not wanted the kind of challenge presented by the Rangers.

Who would? Grieve thought he knew one man. But not even Valentine knew whether he wanted to be the one to do the dirty work.

When Grieve offered the job to Valentine on a Wednesday night, with Rader and the Rangers in New York, Valentine turned him down. Grieve persisted, making another pitch in person Thursday morning.

Chiles, Stone, and Grieve flew to Houston to meet with Valentine. Although the Hobby Airport summit lasted five hours, Grieve's pitch was simple, and Valentine was an easy target. He had stayed up the entire night, weighing his instincts against the advice of those who knew more about the Rangers' Sad Sack history.

Grieve practically dared him to take the job. "Anybody can stay with the Mets," he told Valentine. "I don't blame you, because the Mets have got a chance to go to the World Series. Coaching third base for the Mets is a good situation. It would take a special man to take on the job we are offering—to turn around the Texas Rangers."

Grieve had hit a nerve. Valentine wanted a chance to manage in the major leagues too much to turn down a challenge others would know about. Valentine began searching for flights to Chicago.

"It was the toughest situation of my life, going from the most stable and positive situation I have ever been in to one that is less stable and possibly less positive," Valentine said a few days later. "The last forty-eight hours have just been very unique and an awkward situation."

He laughed when someone asked if he was more qualified to manage now than he would have been in 1983 at age thirty-two. "See those gray hairs?" he asked reporters in Houston, taking off his cap to reveal a full head of dark hair. "The only difference this time is that there's a different general manager."

Friendship aside, Grieve was confident he had found a tough man for tough times. "Based on his qualifications, what I know about him, he is without a doubt the best available person for that job," Grieve said. "I know him very well. He compares very favorably in baseball knowledge, baseball savvy, with anybody I've ever met. . . . I have absolutely no doubt a lack of managerial experience will not play any role in his ability to manage."

In a post-season interview with the *Star-Telegram*'s Jim Reeves, Valentine said, "I took the job because of the challenge it presented. I don't think I'll ever have as great a challenge again. I might manage for another thirty years and never have another situation where Tom Grieve is the general manager, in need of me as a manager. Or where the community and the team were so down. It's going to be tough to find a team as down as the Texas Rangers. But I'm obsessed with the challenge."

Randy Galloway, the ranking oracle of the Arlington Stadium press box, summed up the situation in an article for *Sport* magazine.

"The Rangers and Senators have trashed thirteen managers in fifteen seasons. Manager Bobby Valentine obviously needs your prayers. Tom Grieve, the third general manager in four years, also needs your prayers. Pray for the entire franchise. Pray for rain."

Culture shock for a new manager in baseball is leaving behind young stallions like Dwight Gooden and Ron Darling for backsliding veterans Dickie Noles and Burt Hooton. That's exactly what Bobby Valentine faced when he went from the New York Mets to the Rangers.

Valentine must have gotten quite a surprise when he opened the morning papers on his way from Houston to Chicago to join the Rangers. There, in living black and white, was the news that Dickie Noles would start his first game as manager. It was as if every man who had ever previously managed the Rangers – all twelve of them – was welcoming him aboard the fraternity of losers. This was *cruel*.

It was also a 4-2 loss and an easy excuse to get a look at the future. Outfielder Tommy Dunbar turned an ankle running across first base during Valentine's managerial debut. Quick as that, Tom Grieve put in a call to the minor leagues for Oddibe McDowell, former leadoff hitter for the U.S. Olympic team and the club's #1 draft choice from 1984. More than just the manager was changing.

Relieved of Doug Rader's need to win, Grieve was willing to admit just how bad this team had become. The distance it had yet to cover was briefly obscured when the team took five of seven games during Valentine's first homestand, including a fairly incredible four-game sweep of a Boston team that was one year away from the World Series.

Valentine, as is his style, did not act as if he were in awe of either his new status or his new contemporaries. In fact, he angered the first two managers he faced, Chicago's Tony La Russa and Kansas City's Dick Howser.

After a drawn-out victory in Chicago, Valentine asked if the White Sox were getting paid by the hour. Back in Arlington two nights later, Valentine helped win his home debut by rattling Kansas City reliever Joe Beckwith with some well-chosen words from the dugout. Beckwith's wild pitch finished off an 8-7 victory in which the Rangers had once trailed 7-0 to a team that would go on and win the World Series. No wonder Howser was steaming. He was especially upset that Valentine had been swearing at Beckwith. "Nobody else does that," said Howser, "and he's not going to be able to get away with it. I don't mean just getting on a guy, but staying on a guy. That stuff is for the players involved in the game."

But such distractions could not hide the fact that the Rangers were overmatched most nights. After the four-game sweep against Boston, Texas lost ten of seventeen games, falling fifteen games under .500 after only fifty-nine games. Grieve was ready to officially declare this a lost season.

He did just that on June 20.

Frank Tanana, a veteran left hander making the difficult conversion from power to finesse pitcher, had taken his family to the Six Flags Over Texas amusement park the day he learned of his trade from the Rangers to the Detroit Tigers. It was a fitting place to say farewell to the franchise he had pitched for since 1982. Only a circus might have been better.

In exchange for Tanana, who would eventually pitch the 1-0 victory that put Detroit into the playoffs in 1987, the Rangers received minor-league right-hander Duane James. He was said to have potential (although while Tanana was clinching the AL East title for Detroit in '87, James was resting from a season spent with San Luis Potosi in the Mexican League), but that wasn't really the point. Tanana was being moved to clear a spot in the starting rotation for a young pitcher, Glen Cook. It would have been nice to have gotten more of a return for Tanana, but Grieve did not gnash his teeth when James was released in the spring of 1988.

"We scouted the best game he (James) ever pitched," Grieve said. Neither of the scouts who recommended James were still in the organization when he was released.

Cook would eventually beget Bob Sebra, who would beget Jose Guzman. It was a chain reaction that could only take place on a club committed to its young players, and for the first time since Whitey Herzog's brief tenure in 1973, that is exactly what the Rangers had become.

"We're not taking the safe way," said Valentine. "We're trying to do what's the right thing—now and for the future of this organization."

Later, Grieve remembered the trade like this: "Tanana was still a good pitcher, but he was not pitching good for us. He was 1-7. We had to get on with the future."

The day following the Tanana-for-James trade, Skip Bayless's column in the *Times Herald* carried this headline: "*One more trade: Set Buddy free.*" It was a doozy of a column. Some excerpts:

- "It's time for the Rangers to quit putting used Band-Aids on old wounds. Time to chop away the deadwood. Start fresh. Stick the kids out there and let 'em learn the hard—and best—way."

- "Some of us are tired of watching Toby Harrah, thirty-six, and Cliff Johnson, nearing thirty-eight, and what looks more like a slow-pitch softball team."

- "Bell hit .315 last season with 83 RBIs, and he was one Rangers baseball card that kids everywhere didn't make a face at. Yet only in Bell's first Ranger season did the team finish above .500 (83-79 in 1979). And the long losing summers have beaten Bell into a rather lifeless lump who tends to get by just on talent."

- "Buddy Bell has lost some concentration and lots of heart for his current job. Financially, owner (Eddie) Chiles has treated him like a grandson, and it's almost as if Bell has semi-retired."

After the Bayless column, Bell became known in the press box as "the lifeless lump." It wasn't a bad description. Nor was it hyperbole to call Bell the best pure player the Rangers had ever had. He had won six Gold Gloves (one of which he had given to Chiles for display in his Western Company offices) and played in five All-Star games. He was on his way to consideration for the Hall of Fame.

Certainly, he was a popular player. Blond hair, blue eyes, and a boy's enthusiasm for a game. That was the way he looked when he came to the Rangers in a 1979 trade for Toby Harrah.

It was a good trade for Bell. Not only had he been freed from Cleveland, but he was going to a place that fit his pace. He and Texas looked like a good marriage. But try as the partners did, they could not get past a string of frustrations followed by disappointments.

After an 8-3 victory over Cleveland on Opening Day in 1982, Bell called the Rangers "the best team I've ever played on." This, remember, was a team that went on to lose ninety-eight games. "The hour before and after a ballgame was the toughest," Bell remembered about that season. "I remember sitting in the clubhouse thinking, 'If we win today and California loses, we'll be only twenty-one games out.'"

In 1983, after Rader insinuated that Bell was not the leader the Rangers needed him to be, Bell bristled. "I don't know what a leader is. I really don't," he said. "I try to take charge and know what's going on. I don't think this team needs any more leaders. It needs some more talent."

That became a familiar refrain with Bell. He repeated it again in 1984, this time incredibly blowing up only a few days after Rader had gone to the unusual lengths of naming him team captain. Again, it was choice words from Rader about the team's level of effort that ignited the explosion.

"I'm sick and tired of hearing about how we don't do this and don't do that," Bell said. "We're —ing short. We need to have a better team. We don't have a good enough team, that's all. If they want to put a good team out there, let 'em —ing pay some money and make the right moves."

Take that.

Bell put himself in a Catch-22 when he pleaded for a better team. To improve the depth would take a major trade, and for most of his tenure in Texas he was the only player with a high market value. He was in the middle of trade rumors each season, but general managers Eddie Robinson and Joe Klein could never pull the trigger.

Can you blame them? Mess up a trade that took away your team's most valuable player and you could be doing some advance scouting for another organization the next year.

But by June of 1985 it seemed that Bayless had posed a good question: What purpose did Bell serve on a team that was going nowhere?

Grieve asked himself that question lots of times, but he no doubt felt just as vulnerable as Robinson and Klein before him. Any trade of Bell would have to be done with kid gloves. At least that was the way it looked until Bell got greedy. He decided he needed more money to get through the 1985 season, so he asked Grieve to renegotiate the three years remaining on his contract (Bell later said that club president Mike Stone had reneged on a promise). Never mind that a renegotiation before the 1984 season had brought Bell a $999,999 signing bonus. It was time to talk contract again.

Grieve didn't think so.

He saw Bell's request as the opening he needed to give young third baseman Steve Buechele a chance. "The Texas Rangers were better off without Buddy Bell," Grieve said later. "Buddy Bell felt that way, too. It was not that the trade fit into our big philosophy. The trade was made out of necessity. It turned out to get Steve Buechele a chance in the big leagues. It turned out to be a positive step toward the future of the Texas Rangers."

Just one day after the All-Star break, Bell was traded to his home town, Cincinnati, for outfielder Duane Walker and right-hander Jeff Russell, an eighteen-game loser with Cincinnati in 1984. Grieve originally asked about right-hander Jay Tibbs, but settled on Russell to complete the trade.

Walker (who would not last through the spring of 1986 with Texas) and Russell seemed little return for a five-time All-Star. "That's all?" catcher Don Slaught asked. "I would have thought we would have got more for Buddy."

"We weren't going to get (more)," Valentine said. "There was no market for it." Valentine said he began to understand Bell's fading value in a talk with his former boss, Mets manager Davey Johnson. "I said, 'Davey, you're talking about an All-Star third baseman,' " Valentine said.

"No," replied Johnson, "I'm talking about a guy who hits .260 and drives in sixty runs."

Valentine said Baltimore would not discuss trading outfielder Mike Young or pitcher Storm Davis for Bell, and found it significant that the Los Angeles Dodgers opted to sign Enos Cabell to play third rather than continuing their long-time pursuit of Bell. Bell was more than a little surprised to hear how far his stock had dropped.

"I must have a disease," he said.

Valentine summed up the trade. "It's a new era," he said. "One player in the clubhouse called it A.B. It's going to give a lot of guys the opportunity to take on more responsibility. Because of the mental condition of Buddy and the other guys, this might be addition by subtraction."

Just like that, the franchise's poster boy was gone.

While he was on a roll, Grieve also wanted to rid himself of nuisance Cliff Johnson, whom he had been pushed into signing by Rader the previous winter.

Johnson had been productive as a player. He may have been on his way to the All-Star game in Minneapolis before undergoing arthroscopic knee surgery in mid-June. He was hitting .257 with twelve homers and had driven in fifty-six runs in only eighty-two games as the September 1 deadline for freezing postseason rosters approached.

That was the good side of Johnson. The flip side was that he considered himself the clubhouse authority figure, and in less than three months had worn out his welcome with Valentine. One night in Baltimore, for example, he backed out of the batter's box in disgust when third-base coach Art Howe flashed him a take sign. Valentine worked himself up into a nice little rage after that game and his voice echoed through the corridors of Memorial Stadium. Later, that would be remembered as the night Valentine formally took charge of his team.

"That was new to me," said Buechele, the rookie third baseman. "It was the first time Bobby was showing, 'Hey, I'm the one in charge here. If we're going to go down, we're going to go down because of my mistakes.' "

Valentine conceded years later that he had put on a show intended mostly for youngsters like Buechele and McDowell. "I didn't think it was going to affect Cliff Johnson," he said. "It was a territorial definition. A line was drawn, my breaking point was established."

Johnson had alienated some of his teammates by tactless stunts like demanding the same shower head after every game and distributing a flyer requesting funds for his daughter's scholarship fund. Some thought his $1.5-million contract with the Rangers should have given her a sufficient start toward college. Grieve admitted some of the players looked at Johnson as "a pain in the neck."

"He's the type of guy who wanted to be a leader," first-base coach Rich Donnelly said of Johnson. "But with Buddy and L.P. (Larry Parrish) here it was hard to project him into that role. Then, when they left (Parrish had knee surgery), in his mind he was the one to take over. But you can't force leadership on players. Leadership is gained by the respect players have for you."

Grieve knew he wanted to get rid of Johnson, but had few ideas. Already, he had an idea he might have to eat $1 million in contracts by releasing the over-the-hill Hooton the next spring. He did not look forward to telling owner Eddie Chiles that he had poured $2 million down a free-agent rathole. He felt that he had reached a crisis.

Then the phone rang.

Toronto General Manager Pat Gillick was on the line. The Blue Jays were trying to hold off a late-season challenge from the Yankees for first place in the East. Johnson had played for the Blue Jays in 1983 and 1984, and Gillick thought they could use him again.

Not only was he willing to assume Johnson's contract through 1986 with a club option for '87, but he would part with three minor-league pitchers–Matt Williams, Greg Ferlenda, and Jeff Mays. (None would make an impact with the Rangers.)

Grieve called it "a phone call from heaven."

In seventy days and three trades, the Rangers had parted with thirty-eight years' experience. Their players' average age had dropped from 31.0 to 29.7, and the transformation was only beginning. Like Bell, Tanana, and Johnson, veterans Bill Stein (38), Hooton (35), Alan Bannister (34), Glenn Brummer (31), and Chris Welsh (30) were in their last year with the Rangers.

While systematically banishing experienced players, the organization was pursuing young talent to replace them. This job fell largely to Sandy Johnson and his group of scouts, with Grieve overseeing the operation. Their first project was to identify the top pick in the June draft. By virtue of their 69-92 record in 1984, the Rangers held the third pick overall in the draft.

It was essential that they find a quality player. In Grieve's mind, it was also essential that player be a pitcher.

As the draft shook down, there was little question of what was going to happen with the first two picks. Milwaukee, picking first, would take catcher B. J. Surhoff from the University of North Carolina. San Francisco, picking second, would take first baseman Will Clark from Mississippi State. That would leave the Rangers free to pick the best pitcher in the country.

Texas identified that player as Oklahoma University wild man Bobby Witt. He was a raw talent, having won only seventeen games in two college seasons despite striking out 231 in 196 innings. He had once struck out seventeen in a game against Cliff Gustafson's powerhouse at the University of Texas. With the Olympic team, he had gone 3-0 with an 0.69 earned run average, striking out thirty-six in 26 innings. But he was basically a one-pitch pitcher—his fastball was in the 90-95 MPH range—and his wild streaks were legendary.

That did not slow Grieve's enthusiasm after drafting Witt. "We picked third," he said, "and got the #1 player on our list."

In that same draft, the Montreal Expos used their first-round pick, the seventh of the draft, to select Oklahoma State strongman Pete Incaviglia, otherwise known as "The Big Guy." Incaviglia's home-run stroke was the hitting equivalent of Witt's high, hard fastball. Both packed the rough-around-the-edges power of a Charles Bronson movie.

Scouts were not as high on Incaviglia as Witt. He had set an NCAA record with a hundred home runs, and was coming off the kind of a junior season Ring Lardner would have crafted. In seventy-five games, Incaviglia had batted .464, a Big Eight record, with an NCAA-record 48 home runs and 143 RBIs. His slugging percentage was a phenomenal 1.140. Yet some scouts derided Incaviglia for his defensive shortcomings—a catcher and third baseman in high school, he was used as a designated hitter as a freshman at Oklahoma State, in right field as a sophomore, and in left field as a junior—and a supposed lack of hustle. It was his arrogance that really bothered scouts.

Montreal General Manager Murray Cook found it a problem, too, as Incaviglia refused to sign a contract with the Expos. He told reporters he wanted to play for a team in the United States, not Canada, but in truth this was all about money.

Agent Bucky Woy and Cook battled back and forth throughout the summer, with Incaviglia holding the leverage of a possible return to Oklahoma State over Cook's head. Once, according to Incaviglia, he was told a deal had been reached. He packed his bags and headed to the airport. There, he was paged by Woy, who told him that the Expos were reneging. Incaviglia returned home, once again putting his career in Woy's hands. His father questioned whether Pete was getting good advice.

"He had my father calling him at home," Incaviglia said. "I told him, 'My parents just want to know what's going on.' He explained things to my father ten and eleven times."

Woy told the Expos he would keep Incaviglia out of baseball until the January draft, at which time the Expos would lose the rights to their top choice. "I took a lot of heat," Woy said. "People didn't like to see the top prospect sitting out. A lot of people told Pete I was making a hell of a mistake. June, July, and August weren't easy. People were playing baseball, and Pete was shining his car. People told Pete, 'Your agent is an idiot.' Pete never flinched."

Woy, a Dallas-based agent who made his name marketing Lee Trevino, was not particularly experienced in dealing with baseball teams and baseball players. Bob Horner was the only significant player he had represented before Incaviglia. But he made several trips to Stillwater, Oklahoma, and came away convinced that Incaviglia was a special player. Among his demands of the Expos was that Incaviglia be given a major-league contract and a chance to go straight from Oklahoma State to the majors.

"I just didn't think people gave him enough credit," Woy said. "His statistics were so good, I think it worked against him. It actually hurt him, in my opinion. All the scouts said the same thing—it was the aluminum bat, college pitching was bad that year. When you think you have a great athlete, with the capabilities of doing great things, that's what this business is all about. You do your homework, get up a lot of nerve and you hope you're right."

When the Expos rejected Woy's demands, Incaviglia hung in limbo until after the Royals beat the Cardinals in a seven-game World Series (and the Rangers had completed their woeful season with a 62-99 record and second consecutive last-place finish). It took that long for Woy to successfully lobby Commissioner Peter Ueberroth's office to allow another club to arrange contract terms and then trade for Incaviglia's rights. Without Ueberroth's approval, a team would be tampering if it talked to Woy or Incaviglia.

Woy began calling other clubs after getting Ueberroth's approval. He found receptive ears in Arlington, although Grieve balked when the Expos' Cook said it would take a #1 draft pick like Witt or Jeff Kunkel to obtain his rights. Sandy Johnson was in Incaviglia's corner, and eventually persuaded Grieve to get back in touch with Cook.

Grieve quickly pounded out a contract deal that met Woy's approval. Incaviglia would get what amounted to a two-year deal. In the first year he would receive a $150,000 signing bonus and the major-league minimum salary, $60,000. If the club exercised its option for the second year—as it surely would, whether Incaviglia was playing in Arlington or Tulsa—Incaviglia would receive a guaranteed $172,000.

"There was big money involved for a guy who'd never played professional baseball, let alone in the big leagues," Grieve said. "We decided giving him that contract would not be the risk it would be for any other player. Spending that money to get a twenty-one-year-old power hitter made sense."

Cook eventually realized something was better than nothing, which was what he would wind up with if Incaviglia remained unsigned. He told Grieve he would give up the draft rights for right-handed curveballer Bob Sebra, who had gone 0-2 with a 7.52 ERA in a 1985 trial, and utility man Jim Anderson, who had already been released by the Rangers once.

Texas had done what no other team in baseball would—signed Incaviglia to a big contract and agreed it would give him the chance to go straight to the majors. It was not the kind of decisive move the club was known for.

"You can't always play it safe," Grieve said. "You have to go for it now and then. If we think he has a realistic chance, shoot, go for it. One thing is for sure: He thinks he can (do it). He has no doubt about it."

Grieve credits Johnson with persuading him to take a chance. "Sandy Johnson pushed and pushed and pushed," he said. "We got a first-round draft choice and all it cost us was a major-league contract. It's something that you're only going to do once in your lifetime."

Grieve was not through dealing. Among other things, he still needed to find more pitching, and he wanted to find a new shortstop. Curtis Wilkerson wasn't the shortstop he wanted to build his infield around.

Wilkerson, whose .312 average at Oklahoma City had prompted the Rangers to release veteran Bucky Dent in the spring of 1984, had been the Opening Day shortstop for two years. A switch-hitter, he sometimes shared the position with veteran Wayne Tolleson. Through two full seasons, Wilkerson carried an offensive history that raised eyebrows. His batting average was .248 with the bases empty, .235 with runners on base, .213 with runners in scoring position and .170 with runners in scoring position with two outs. Mix in his knack for untimely errors, and it looked like a position that could be improved.

Kunkel was no sure bet. After his confidence was zapped by Rader in 1984, his father, American League umpire Bill Kunkel, died of cancer in May of 1985. He went into a funk. He hit .164 in his final eighty games at Oklahoma City, finishing the year with a .195 batting average. He was promoted in September, but all that got him was torn cartilage and a partially torn ligament in his left knee when he collided with George Wright chasing a pop fly in Oakland.

Grieve let it be known that he was interested in improving his pitching and middle-infield situation. Among those with the biggest ears was new Chicago White Sox GM Ken "Hawk" Harrelson, a flamboyant player while with the Boston Red Sox. Harrelson still liked to be on the front page. He wore ostrich boots, a ten-gallon hat and a look that said, "Let's make something happen." Harrelson had been hired to restore the White Sox to the division-champion status they had held as recently as 1983, and he felt it would take some trades if they were going to do that after finishing 85-77 in 1985.

Grieve and Harrelson started talking about deals at the World Series. Among Harrelson's propositions as they continued talks was a deal involving more than ten players from the two teams, including Rangers Gary Ward, Larry Parrish, and Don Slaught. "It was too many players involved for me to come up with something to even talk about," said Grieve.

Harrelson narrowed his wish list to reliever Dave Schmidt, who had closed out 1985 by eliminating California from the pennant race with a 6-0 complete-game performance in a spot start, and Tolleson. Grieve had concocted his own plan of attack in consultation with Johnson, and Harrelson played right into his hands in the late November talks.

Grieve told Harrelson, "We have to have (Edwin) Correa."

"No problem," answered Harrelson.

"If we lose Tolleson we have to have a middle infielder," countered Grieve. "How about Scott Fletcher?"

Harrelson hedged for a moment.

"I don't want to . . . but I guess I can."

Grieve's pulse raced, but he kept driving up the price, eventually also extracting a minor-league second baseman, Jose Mota, from Harrelson. Grieve began smiling as soon as he hung up the phone.

"I knew we had made a good deal . . . and so did he (Harrelson)," he said later. "We didn't have to wait and see."

Correa, a nineteen-year-old right-hander from Puerto Rico, came heavily recommended by Luis Rosa, Johnson's man in Latin America. He had been a pro since he was sixteen, and was coming off a 13-3 season at Class A Appleton. Not only that, but he had already won a major-league start, beating Seattle 3-2 on the last day of the 1985 season.

"He's one of the top minor-league pitching prospects in all of baseball," Harrelson said on the day the trade was made. "He's a thoroughbred, no doubt about it. I would be surprised if he's not on (the Rangers') staff on Opening Day."

Fletcher, twenty-seven at the time of the trade, had been the White Sox's regular shortstop when they won the American League West in 1983, but his stock in the organization had dropped after Ozzie Guillen was acquired from San Diego in 1984. He'd batted only 301 times in 1985.

Grieve considered Fletcher-for-Tolleson at least an even trade, meaning he had gotten Correa and Mota for Schmidt, a former twenty-sixth-round draft choice who had never saved more than twelve games in a season.

Harrelson knew he was mortgaging at least some of the White Sox's future for, hopefully, some immediate improvement. "He (Grieve) made a hell of a deal," Harrelson admitted. "As far as talent, he got a ton."

Grieve agreed. "There's no doubt," he said, "that just talent for talent, we got more in this trade than they did."

Bobby Valentine could hardly control himself when reached on one of his frequent off-season ski trips. In his six months with the organization, it had added Bobby Witt and Correa to a group of young pitchers that already included Jose Guzman and, waiting in the wings, Mitch Williams.

"I'm real excited," Valentine said. "I think we gave up two guys who were outstanding young men and had credible years for us last year," he said. "I appreciate what they did. But in getting Ed Correa, I think we may have the finest stable of young arms of any major-league team."

* * *

While willing to trade, Grieve was quiet when it came to negotiating for free agents. Having signed Cliff Johnson, Burt Hooton, and Dave Rozema the year before, Grieve showed no real interest in any of the free agents available in the winter of 1985—a group headed by Kirk Gibson and including consistent stopper Donnie Moore and catchers Carlton Fisk and Butch Wynegar.

If Johnson and Hooton were worth a $3.5-million gamble the year before, why not Gibson, Rozema's best buddy, and Moore?

Good question. But since Grieve's 1984 folly, Commissioner Peter Ueberroth had forced the owners to open their books. It was a step in the stalled Basic Agreement negotiations, ostensibly, but it also awakened an industry that within the last year had seen the Chicago Cubs pledge $16.2 million to retain free-agent pitchers Rick Sutcliffe, Dennis Eckersley, and Steve Trout; Bruce Sutter sign a six-year, $11-million contract with Atlanta; and Orioles owner Edward Bennett Williams spend almost $10 million for Fred Lynn, Lee Lacy, and Don Aase.

Agents and players whispered of collusion (eventually affirmed by federal arbitrator Tom Roberts) while baseball executives spoke only of an improved business sense.

"There's been a great deal of talk in owners' meetings about cost containment," said Rangers president Mike Stone. "How can we contain costs in a sport that is in bad economic shape? What you see more and more is ownership coming together and saying, 'How come you did this? How come you paid that guy so much money?' It has implications for everybody. There is more peer pressure. I wouldn't say there is an agreement, but there is peer pressure. You don't operate in a vacumn anymore."

No one in baseball was offering more than a three-year contract—a result of a study Cubs General Manager Dallas Green conducted for the owners' Player Relations Committee. It showed:

• The year prior to signing a contract of three years or longer, 104 targeted players averaged 133 games, 13 homers, 63 RBIs and a .280 batting average.

• The year after signing a contract of three years or longer, they averaged 124 games, 11 homers, 56 RBIs, and a .273 batting average.

• The second year after signing, they averaged 117 games, 12 homers, 54 RBIs, and a .267 batting average.

"The economic realities," said Stone, "are coming home to roost."

7

"Amazing, Isn't It?"

Joey Valentine was like almost every other boy growing up in America in the late 1960s. He did not really understand what was going on outside his little community of Stamford, Connecticut, but he understood one thing better than any man alive: his car.

Joey did not yet know himself, but he knew the Chevy's limits backwards and forwards. Two hundred miles on a tankful of gas was as much as you could coax out of that 1963 Impala convertible. It was a fact established by that unforgiving teacher, experience. Anything more than two hundred miles and, hey, stick out your thumb and hit the highway. You're a walking man.

When his younger brother Bobby wanted to borrow the convertible to visit friends at a distant college, Joey gave him specific instructions. "You can't get more than two hundred miles on a tankful," he said. "Make sure you put some gas in it. You're always leaving it without any gas."

Bobby smiled, took the keys, and left.

The next morning, Joey Valentine went down to the driveway, slipped behind the wheel of the Impala and turned the ignition key. The engine cranked and cranked, but wouldn't turn over. Joey was getting hotter and hotter; he reached the boiling point when he checked an odometer that showed 242 new miles and a gas gauge that was beyond empty.

Joey went inside to consult his younger brother, who, as usual, was sitting at the kitchen table, eating his cereal and reading box scores.

"You went 242 miles," he screamed. "I never went that far."

Bobby flashed him a can-you-believe-it smile.

"Amazing," he said, "isn't it?"

Years later, that story stayed fresh for Joe Valentine. "I can't think of Bobby without thinking of that car," Joe said. "He went door to door, driveway to driveway, and stretched it to the end. That's just the way he is."

There appears to be some truth to that analogy. Bobby Valentine has a way to stretch every situation to its absolute, unquestionable, unthinkable max—especially when there is somebody telling him he will fall short.

At least half the people Valentine called for advice about his opportunity to manage the Rangers told him to forget it. Stay as a coach with the New York Mets and wait for a job without built-in land mines. You've got a great future, they told him. Don't squander it on Eddie Chiles and his group of underachievers.

That lit the fire.

"People around here wondered what he was doing," says brother Joe, who still lives in Connecticut. "He came home and said the Rangers were going to be the #1 team. He really feels it. He's always had these kinds of feelings, and when he has them, you tend to believe him and have those feelings, too."

It didn't take long for the Rangers' loyal fans to realize Valentine was different from any of the twelve managers who had preceded him. It was his energy level that separated him from the pack. This was a hands-on guy who never seemed to need rest.

While his predecessor, Doug Rader, hid in the clubhouse before games and alienated fans with an uncaring outlook, Valentine immediately became a good-will ambassador for his team. Despite loss after numbing loss in 1985, Valentine could usually be found before games sitting atop the first-base dugout—smiling, signing programs, and shaking hands with a long line of fans.

When Valentine was unable to get the Rangers out of last place in the American League West that year, he took the blame. "He will always think that," said General Manager Tom Grieve. "He is a hard judge of himself, and he never thinks he does enough."

Valentine embarked on an ambitious program in his first off-season with the Rangers, spreading himself like butter on too many crackers. As usual, he put in time overseeing his three restaurants in Connecticut. And much of that time was spent in the kitchen, not just out front shaking hands, although he did that, too, getting so wound up at a New Year's Eve dance contest that he dislocated his shoulder. He also took ten days off to go skiing (his #1 recreational passion since the end of his playing days). But he spent most of his time promoting the Rangers. He was more active on the Rotary Club circuit than any manager in the franchise's sorry history.

The crowning touch came the day before he left for spring training in Florida. He flew down from Connecticut to take part in a six-hour Ranger telethon, a ticket-pushing extravaganza staged by the club's flagship station, KTVT. He dominated the show, looking as if he had been born in a black tux and red bow tie—kind of a cross between Frank Sinatra and Wink Martindale. Valentine served as emcee for the six-hour show. When the lights finally went off, he hustled across town to do a live spot on one of the Dallas-Fort Worth market's Sunday-night sports shows.

That first spring, he bounced around the Rangers' rundown complex in Pompano Beach like a Florida love bug. Now you see him; now you don't. Before the players arrived, Valentine led preparations for the team, going to the extreme of hanging upside down in a batting cage to string netting that was stolen later the same night. When the players arrived, he started his workdays around 7 A.M. and often didn't quit until 11 P.M.

He not only scheduled an unprecedented number of workouts, he also ran them. It wasn't unusual to see him hit forty-five minutes of ground balls to infielders on one of the complex's two diamonds, then sprint to the other field to throw forty-five minutes of batting practice. He actually had the audacity to instruct major-league players in the art of playing baseball, constantly speaking to them in groups or one-on-one.

"He doesn't say do as I say," Grieve said. "It's do as I do."

Valentine even fought Florida's rainy weather. He regularly helped Pompano Beach's overmatched grounds crew, doing what needed to be done to keep the two diamonds usable. He ran pumps, and went so far as to borrow a vacuum cleaner from clubhouse man Joe Macko to try to clear puddles.

Valentine earned respect from his players with every hour he spent on the field. "We've worked harder than we ever have before," said pitcher Mitch Williams. "But you know Bobby got here at seven. How are you going to complain . . . ?"

The late Paul Richards, then a consultant and unofficial baseball guru to the Rangers, said at the time that he had never seen a manager work as hard as Valentine. Richards added that he certainly didn't remember himself working as hard when he was a manager with the Chicago White Sox and Baltimore Orioles: "I hired people to do that stuff."

Valentine's unusual work habits and high visibility don't always endear him to other baseball men. Some see this as self-promotion, perhaps missing the point that there was nothing phony about the hours Valentine put in. Three years into his tenure in Texas, *Inside Sports* magazine ran a list of the "five most popular reasons for Bobby Valentine's unpopularity." Among them were "his New York arrogance," "his mouth," and "he smiles too much."

"People think I'm a blowhard," Valentine says. "There are always those doubting Thomases who want me to walk my talk. But I didn't take on this personality when I became a manager. I've had this personality all my life."

His energy level definitely comes naturally. As a child, Bobby never saw his father asleep when others were awake at his house. Joe Sr. was always up by the time his sons started their day. "Sleep never was a big thing in my family," Bobby once said.

Valentine says his father slept when the urge hit him. "My father would be sitting down in his chair and he'd doze off for a ten-minute nap before breakfast. Then he'd get up and be good for another ten hours."

That trait was passed down to Bobby. "I can sleep anywhere when the time is right. I could sleep on that table if the time was right and I needed it," he said that spring, pointing to a small table in his cramped office in Pompano Beach. "I've done it at my restaurants. I've been going all night, and it was a half hour before we were opening, and I'd hop up on the desk in my office and sleep for half an hour. I sleep on planes and buses. It's a good time for it. And I never lie awake."

Valentine proved his boast about sleeping when the Rangers found themselves unexpectedly on the fringes of a pennant race in 1986. It came at a time when he had just negotiated to open two restaurants in Arlington, including one a few blocks from Arlington Stadium. Good businessman that he is, he did not want to miss out on the boom that a down-to-the-wire race in September could create, so he and his father spent many long hours plying their carpentry skills at the Collins Street restaurant after August games. Some nights Valentine never slept, catching naps as best he could the next day. There were nights when his office door was closed a couple hours before a game for reasons other than private meetings: Valentine was sleeping.

Joe Sr. has always been most comfortable when he was working. Joe Jr. calls him a "workaholic," and Bobby remembers that one year his father built a redwood deck and added kitchen counters while visiting his son's Seattle home for a week. His father remembers that trip, too.

"He always called me to visit when there was something that needed to be done," Joe Sr. says. "He would say, 'I'm going to have somebody out to do this or that,' knowing that I'll do it."

It has always been that way.

Bobby tells a story about the Christmas Eve night that a sprinkler pipe burst at one of his restaurants, causing the dining-room ceiling to collapse. "The ceiling caved in. This is a catastrophe, a catastrophe!" Valentine remembers, his voice rising. "My dad came out that day and evening, and while I was working with a broom to clean up the mess, he got all the sheetrock, tape, everything we needed, and before dinnertime he had put up a whole new ceiling. Remember, this is Christmas Eve. We couldn't even get a work crew. That's impressive, huh?"

Valentine could never imagine telling his father there was something his son couldn't do. Bobby never did that while growing up on the sports fields of Rippowam High in Stamford, and he wasn't about to start.

"I would almost be afraid to do that," he says. "I can't imagine that. It would insult him."

Valentine became a capable workman on his own. During the 1988 season, he embarked on an ambitious project worthy of radio handyman Al Carrell. Working in the mornings before home games, he built a redwood deck off the second floor of his ranch house in east Fort Worth. This was no puny project. The deck was to stand almost ten feet off the ground, and it had to be strong enough to support 3,000 pounds in a corner where he was putting a hot tub.

Why would a man with a $300,000 income from the Rangers, which he claimed did not even cover taxes from his restaurants, tackle such a project? "I had this guy out to look at it," Valentine said, "and he said there was no way I could do it. Besides, I needed something to do. I was getting up at six, drinking a pot of coffee listening to (Norm) Hitzges' morning sports talk show, and it was only eight by the time I finished the coffee. [My son] Bobby doesn't even get up until eight-thirty."

Valentine stated his motto years ago—sleep is overrated.

You could never say Bobby Valentine was a normal kid. He did all the normal things, but he did them with abandon. He also did some things none of the other boys in Stamford would dare try, let alone master.

Ballroom dancing, for instance.

Valentine, a born ham, was studying dance steps when most Little Leaguers were afraid to be seen with a girl, much less do the rhumba with one. At fourteen, he and his partner finished second in a national contest, the result of his mother, Grace, playing both shower-room attendant and taxi driver for years.

Often, there wasn't enough time for Valentine to even shower between baseball practice and dance class, so Grace put a bucket of water in the car before heading to the field.

Valentine spread himself many ways while at Rippowam High School in Stamford—playing the lead role in the senior play, *Teahouse of the August Moon;* slipping into costume to play the school's Indian mascot at basketball games; and scoring well enough on his college boards to be accepted at Yale. But athletics were the hottest of his passions.

In fact, he was such a natural football player that his development was not retarded by his decision to drop out of Pop Warner ball at age eleven, rather than get a crew cut. He was fond of his pompadour look. Besides, he had already decided that he didn't like being told what to do, and he had no idea why a haircut would make him a better football player.

Valentine didn't return to organized football until he was a freshman at Rippowam High. In his first game for the varsity, he took a kickoff and ran eighty-five yards for a touchdown. It was a hint of things to come. By the time Valentine was a senior, he had made his #32 into a local legend. He was an All-State player as a sophomore, when he scored a state-record twenty-one touchdowns, and again as a junior.

But it was the Rippowam-Stamford High game in 1967 that really separated Valentine from the area's other skilled players. He set another record with six touchdowns, including one of ninety-eight yards, to lead the Rippowam Warriors to a 40-6 victory. He finished his career with fifty-three touchdowns, becoming the only three-year All-Stater in Connecticut history.

Valentine didn't know it, but he had become a role model for another pretty good athlete, National Football League quarterback Steve Young. Growing up in Greenwich, Connecticut, a decade behind Valentine, Young and his friends paid their own form of respect to Valentine when they were in Stamford.

"We used to drive by his house in Stamford," Young told the *Star-Telegram's* Jim Reeves, "and say, 'That's where Bobby Valentine lives.'"

More than eighty schools offered Valentine football scholarships, including

USC, which had a pretty good #32 of its own: O.J. Simpson. John McKay convinced Valentine to sign a letter of intent, but it turned out to be worth only the paper it was printed upon.

Valentine enjoyed football, but he *lived* for baseball. Maybe it was because no baseball coach ever told him to get a haircut.

Valentine's baseball ability showed itself early, as it always does with the good ones. At age nine, he got bumped up from the minors to the majors in Little League. Bobby had always played with older kids anyway, tailing brother Joey, who was three years older. "Bobby always said, 'I can't play with kids younger than me, or my age, because I can't learn anything from them,'" said his father, Joe. "That was his motto. And he always seemed three or four years ahead of his time."

Valentine used the speed that had made him such a breakaway threat as a scatback to unnerve others on the bases, as well as to run down balls considered uncatchable in the outfield. He could hit, too. There was no questioning his tools. When it came time for the baseball draft in June of 1968, the fact that Valentine had already signed his intent to accept a football scholarship at USC didn't keep the Los Angeles Dodgers from using their #1 draft choice on him.

Valentine was the fifth player chosen in the draft, following Tim Foli, Pete Broberg, Marty Cott, and Thurman Munson. But Valentine had hoped to be picked before anyone else. "That made me furious," he later said.

Al Campanis, then the Dodgers' general manager, made a trip to Stamford to court Valentine. "He told me I could go to USC and play against the best the Pac-8 had to offer, or I could sign with the Dodgers and compete against the best players in the world," Valentine said. "I left the next day for the Dodgers rookie team in Ogden, Utah."

A rotund former left-handed pitcher named Tommy Lasorda was in his third year managing that team in the Pioneer League. It didn't take the two long to form an alliance. Valentine was one of the team's top players, as he was expected to be. He hit .281 and led the league with sixty-two runs and twenty stolen bases in sixty-two games. It was a good team, too, finishing first with a 39-25 record. Among Valentine's teammates on that Ogden team were Tom Paciorek and Steve Garvey.

The following spring at the Dodgers' camp in Vero Beach, Florida, Valentine pulled off one of the all-time upsets in the organization's history. Lasorda's choice for side wagering beat Maury Wills and Willie Davis in a sixty-yard dash known as the "O'Malley Relays." (Perhaps his victory explains why Valentine would borrow the idea of the race to break the tedium of his own spring trainings almost two decades later.)

That same spring, Lasorda and the Dodgers undertook a conversion of Valentine, trying to turn the center fielder into a shortstop, reversing the usual direction of switches between those two positions. The process cemented the bonds between manager and player.

By then Lasorda had been promoted from the rookie-league club in Ogden all the way to the Class AAA Pacific Coast League farm club in Spokane,

Washington, replacing Roy Hartsfield. During the winter Lasorda had lobbied unsuccessfully to stock his team with many of the same players who had been in Ogden only one season before. Bill Schweppe, the Dodgers' farm club supervisor, felt that would be too big a gamble with so many good prospects. So Valentine and the others were penciled in for a year with double-A Albuquerque.

But, for Valentine, that changed when an injury caused Spokane shortstop Bill Grabarkewitz to be promoted to the big-league team eighteen games into the 1970 season.

Campanis asked Lasorda if he wanted to promote shortstop Jimmy Johnson from Albuquerque. Lasorda said no, Johnson wasn't who they wanted. They wanted Bobby Valentine.

"To play shortstop?" asked Campanis.

"That's right," Lasorda confirmed.

Campanis told Lasorda they would run him and Valentine out of town, but that did not daunt Lasorda's enthusiasm for the move. "Let 'em try," he said, "but he's the guy *I* want. Let me tell you, that kid is a winner. He loves to play and he can play."

Converting Valentine to shortstop had been discussed all winter, as Wills was starting to wear down and there was no real heir apparent at the position. Still, with the exception of three weeks that spring, Valentine had never played shortstop, and this was the highest level of the minor leagues. It was asking a lot of an eighteen-year-old, less than one year removed from the Rippowam Warriors, but Lasorda heard no reservations from Valentine.

Lasorda stuck Valentine right into the lineup. Valentine's defense was shaky, to put it mildly, but Lasorda was sure it would get better. Every day, he and Valentine would be the first ones at the field, with Lasorda hitting Valentine hundreds of ground balls. It was not helping the team to win, but Lasorda had committed himself to helping Valentine develop, because he was sure the kid could play in the major leagues in a hurry.

Valentine's league-leading error total (thirty-eight in 111 games by season's end) became the source of grumbling in the clubhouse. Some older players simply resented the close relationship between Lasorda and Valentine.

In late June, a group of players sent coach Dick McLaughlin to speak to Lasorda about Valentine. They wanted him taken out of the lineup. Lasorda later remembered it as his first real challenge as a manager.

He assembled the team, determined to make it clear the inmates were not going to run his little asylum.

"Apparently," Lasorda said, "there are some people here who think they can run this team better than I can. They think we should have someone other than Bobby Valentine playing shortstop."

All eyes were on the floor, especially Valentine's.

Lasorda continued. "Before addressing that issue, I think everyone in here should get a baseball, take it to that young man and get his autograph. Because one day, when most of you are punching a time clock somewhere, Bobby Valentine will be playing in the major leagues. That baseball will mean something to you. As long as I'm the manager of this team, he is the shortstop, because he is going to play in the major leagues someday."

Valentine would always remember that show of loyalty. It didn't take him long to prove Lasorda correct, either. The next year, Valentine was selected the Coast League's MVP, hitting a league-leading .340 with fourteen homers and eighty RBIs. He also earned a reputation for toughness, overcoming a fractured cheekbone after being hit in the face with a pitch from Greg Washburn during the PCL playoffs and playing throughout the year on a bad right knee that required surgery during the winter.

Lasorda was horrified when Washburn hit Valentine in the head during the playoff series against the Hawaii Islanders. He thought Valentine might be dead: as it was, Lasorda found that the left side of Valentine's face had been caved in. Lasorda remembers Valentine asking him for a favor while on the ground: "Don't let them put me on a stretcher." With help from his teammates, he walked to the clubhouse in center field.

The next year, 1971, Valentine reached the majors, playing for the Los Angeles Dodgers with the promise of staying a long time. But in truth, the knee surgery had cost him much of his speed, as he hit .249 with only ten doubles and five stolen bases as a rookie. He also had lost some of his range at shortstop and was used largely as a utility man.

After the next season, he was included in a seven-play deal with the nearby California Angels. Valentine, Grabarkewitz, Frank Robinson, and pitchers Bill Singer and Mike Strahler went to the Angels in exchange for pitcher Andy Messersmith and third baseman Ken McMullen. Valentine had to prove himself again.

He was in the process of doing exactly that until the night of May 17, 1973. He was hitting .302 and had stolen six bases. But his promising start became a bitter recollection after a ball hit by Oakland's Dick Green sent him crashing into the fence in left-center field at Anaheim Stadium. Valentine made a leaping attempt at a catch, then tried to brace himself with his left leg. His spikes hung in the fence, shattering his tibia. Bad as the break was, Valentine got more bad news when the cast was removed from his leg about a month later. The shin bone had not set right and was jutting out at the front of his leg. It was not a sight for the squeamish. Doctors recommended rebreaking the leg and setting it again, but that would have wasted the initial recovery time. Valentine declined, taking his chances.

His career was over. His speed was almost completely gone, and without that he was an ordinary player. Valentine returned to the Angels in 1974, but no matter how hard he tried, he could not turn the injured leg into a good one again.

After the 1975 season, which Valentine spent with four different teams, he went to the Dominican Republic to play winter ball for Lasorda. He and Lasorda had a deal: Valentine would play every game, and when the season was over Lasorda would evaluate his progress and his chances of becoming an everyday player in the major leagues.

Late that winter Lasorda took Valentine out to a dinner they would both remember. Lasorda, who had made a deal, told Valentine he didn't have it anymore. Afterward, they both cried.

"He told me that I'd never be the player he (had) thought I'd be," Valentine said. "That hurt. We were both crying. But he told me something else. He told me that if I wanted to stay in baseball, I should start thinking about managing."

Valentine, at age twenty-five, did exactly that. He played four more seasons, drifting from San Diego to the New York Mets before finishing his playing career with the 1979 Seattle Mariners, a collection of inexperienced and over-the-hill players who labored through a 67-95 season. While spending much of his time on the bench, compiling only 408 at bats in his final three seasons, Valentine began studying baseball's inner game.

When his playing career ended, he became a minor-league instructor. Although stories of his love affair with the Dodgers yielded years of speculation about his replacing Lasorda as the Dodgers' manager, it was the Padres, not the Dodgers, who offered him his first coaching job.

Valentine jumped from the Padres' organization to the Mets in 1982, again as a minor-league instructor. But after the 1982 season, he was promoted to the Mets' third-base coach, working for manager George Bamberger. When Davey Johnson took over in 1984, Valentine stayed on as third-base coach, consistently declining chances to manage in the minor leagues. He felt that the major leagues were the best place to learn how to manage in the major leagues.

His lack of experience didn't keep the Rangers from considering him for their vacancy in 1983, nor offering him the chance to manage two months into a woeful 1985 season. Valentine, as always, was full of himself—and full of enthusiasm for the challenge ahead.

"There's a lot more talent there than the record shows," Valentine told reporters with the Mets in Houston, hours before formally accepting his first manager's job. "But everything is a risk. If the risk is small, then so is the reward. If the risk is large, the reward can be that much greater."

An Early
Return On
V-Ball

Teams of Senators and Rangers had been coming to Pompano Beach, Florida, for twenty-five years before Bobby Valentine's one and only spring there. There had been few changes in the team's facilities over the years, but the town had grown from a sleepy bedroom community and had blended into thriving Fort Lauderdale, its neighbor to the south.

Former Rangers publicist Burt Hawkins swore there had been thatched huts when the expansion Senators located there in 1961; now there were high-rise retirement complexes like the Sea Ranch along the beach. Property prices had soared as developers moved northward from Miami Beach.

Strange things happened in South Florida in the springtime. Normally tranquil grocery stores became chaotic as senior citizens battled with the college kids who sped down I-95 from the Northeast and the Midwest for spring break in Fort Lauderdale, where traffic could be bumper to bumper for miles. Good restaurants, like Bobby Rubino's or the Raindancer, had hour-long waits every night. In some bars, wet T-shirt contests remained the rage long after most of the country had moved on to body-building and other forms of self-worship.

Most of the ballplayers congregated at one time or another at the Laughing Fish, the bar at the Holiday Inn that served as the team's headquarters. Bartenders Lenny and Larry made good conversation, and the big-screen television stayed tuned to the college basketball games on cable. With the New York Yankees training ten minutes away in Fort Lauderdale, the Rangers could more easily blend in with the tourists. They could move around without directing much attention to themselves. Only hard-core fans cared enough about such an indistinguished franchise to show up at Pompano Beach's Municipal Field.

So few people witnessed Pete Incaviglia's crash onto the scene here in the spring of 1986. Incaviglia, eager to impress, had reported early, along with the Rangers' pitchers and catchers. It took him only one round of batting practice the first day to come across like some kind of Paul Bunyan, who carried a bat instead of an axe. After putting the pitchers through their first workout, Valentine stuck around to throw batting practice to his prize pupil. Reporters gathered to watch the show.

Pitch . . . home run to left.

Pitch . . . home run to right.

Pitch . . . home run to center.

Valentine could barely stop laughing long enough to throw the ball. He became so engrossed in the display that after one pitch he forgot to get behind the pitcher's screen. Incaviglia lined it back at him. Valentine twisted to avoid it, but the ball caught him square in the back, dropping him as surely as if he had been shot. Incaviglia started toward the pitcher's mound, but Valentine didn't lie there long. He jumped back up and began to berate Incaviglia. "Get back in there!" he yelled. "I'm not through with you yet."

So Incaviglia stepped back into the right side of the batter's box, and a few pitches later launched a line drive that made everyone very quiet. It screamed out toward left field, headed for a collision with the wooden fence. But instead of hitting the fence and bouncing back, it sent a baseball-sized section of the fence flying. He had literally knocked a hole in the fence.

"That's one-inch plywood," Valentine said. "Awesome."

No one had ever seen this before—certainly not at Municipal Field, a park whose size helped to explain how the Rangers had hit only four homers two springs earlier—but lots of people would see the hole at the top of the fence. It became legend in the Grapefruit League. Rangers publicist John Blake was happy to take visiting reporters to the left-field fence, enjoying the role of tour guide at a national monument.

Valentine remembered that first-day session with awe. "From the second swing on, I had the fear of God," he said. "I couldn't see the ball after he hit it. I lost some of his home runs right off the bat. I throw batting practice to a lot of guys—and it was only batting practice, I know that—but I've never seen anything like it. He's going to make the president of the ball company very happy, because he's going to put a lot of dollars in his pocket."

Hitting instructor Art Howe joined Valentine in singing the praises of Incaviglia. "An incredible display," Howe said. "The wind was blowing in and he was hitting like it was blowing straight out. He's got a great swing, not like a (Dave) Kingman-type big swing. It's going to be fun working with him . . . but it won't be much fun throwing to him. He's got the best bat speed I've seen getting through the strike zone. I've played with some pretty good players in my lifetime, too."

Said Grieve, "That is about as hard as a human can hit a ball. Nobody can hit a ball harder. I don't care who he is."

It was a satisfying first day for Incaviglia. "People always said the aluminum bat was why I hit so many home runs," he said. "It was only batting practice, but I think I showed aluminum wasn't the reason . . . I want to make the ball club, be on the roster when we leave here. I want to have a good season and help the team win. I think it's about time to bring a winner to Arlington."

Incaviglia had been bred to destroy baseballs. His father, Tom, a former minor-league infielder, established a daily regimen during the 1970s in Monterey, California. He would work at the post office in the morning and the family business, Incaviglia Liquors, in the evenings. In between he would take his three sons, Pete, Tony, and Frank, to a field for batting practice. "He would throw pitches to those kids all day," said first baseman Pete O'Brien, who grew up in nearby Pebble Beach. "He worked his tail off for his boys."

Even as a boy, Incaviglia's preference was for balls that traveled a long way. "I've always been able to hit the ball farther than other people," said Incaviglia. "I enjoy it more than anything I do, anything I could do. It's always been what I do. I love it. I can't describe the feeling, but when I hit the ball out of the park I feel like I've accomplished something."

He caught the eye of crusty old Paul Richards. "He probably hits the ball farther than anybody with the exception of Frank Howard and Jimmie Foxx," said Richards. Added White Sox scout Ellis Clary, "All I know about him is he can hit it out of the Grand Canyon."

Incaviglia came to his first spring training with a forty-eight-inch chest and forearms and thighs that were the product of a summer and fall spent in the weight room. "My overall strength is designed for baseball," Incaviglia said. "It is designed for what I do—hit the ball out of the park, into the gaps. You have to have strength to do that. You are given God-given talent, too. I've been blessed with having good bat speed, making good contact. That's why I'm successful. I never think about home runs. I go to the plate thinking about making good solid contact. If I made good solid contact, the ball is going to go out of the park, so I don't have to think about it."

Valentine had begun calling Incaviglia the "Fat Kid," but the nickname did not really fit. Wrote *Dallas Times Herald* columnist Frank Luksa, "Some piece of blubber. Weight lifting since high school has Pete muscled like an NFL linebacker. A Randy White-sized chest sets off his 6-2, 225-pound frame. Incaviglia carries as much fat as a tire iron."

Said Valentine, "He has a wait problem all right. He probably can't wait for his next at bat."

Searching for comparisons to Incaviglia, the names of Kansas City slugger Steve Balboni and former Rangers meteor Dave Hostetler were mentioned to Tom Grieve. "Anyone who compares Incaviglia to Balboni ought to be scouting a girls soccer team," Grieve said. "There is no comparison between Balboni and Incaviglia. Balboni has never taken a swing as good as Incaviglia's in his life."

Despite never having played in the minor leagues, Incaviglia would break camp with the Rangers that spring. Valentine made the decision on March 24, saying that Incaviglia would open the year as the regular right fielder, where erstwhile center fielder George Wright was the incumbent. "He without a doubt won the position," Valentine said. "I based it on the risk-reward ratio. I think the rewards could be so great it's worth the risk. He's an impressive guy. I've been impressed with him from the beginning. I think I'm going to continue to be impressed with him. I will give him fifteen years before I'm tired of writing his name in the lineup."

At the time Valentine made the announcement, Incaviglia was hitting a spring-training .306 while leading the Rangers with three home runs and 10 RBIs. "There was no doubt in my mind, but I didn't want to come in and step on anybody's toes," said Incaviglia, who set his rookie goals at 30-40 home runs and 100 RBIs. "If I can fit in with Larry Parrish, Gary Ward, Pete O'Brien, and Oddibe McDowell, and help them win, that's all I want. We have a quality lineup, and I just want to be a part of it."

It was Valentine, however, who would add a telling postscript to Incaviglia's amazing spring. "He has to prove that he can take a pitch out of the strike zone," Valentine said. "When he starts seeing seasonal fastballs and the breaking balls get sharp, can he take the fastball up and out of the strike zone and the breaking pitch away? If it turns out pitchers don't have to put the ball in the strike zone, then we're talking a horse of a different color."

Incaviglia was one of twenty-five players in that crowded camp who had never played in the majors or had played less than a full season there. It was a rare place of equal opportunity, and nothing seemed impossible. Perhaps only ten players had truly secure spots on the roster, leaving fourteen other spots open for the other forty-two players in camp.

It was a real blend of faces, with end-of-the-road types like pitcher Mickey Mahler and catchers John Stearns and Luis Pujols trying to prolong their careers while future major leaguers Chad Kreuter (#63) and Paul Kilgus (#59) got their first look at the big time.

From that group emerged a corps of six rookies who would return to Arlington to open the season against defending AL East champion Toronto. Half of the pitching staff would be rookies, including one who had never won a professional game and two others who had spent most of 1985 pitching Class A ball. Bobby Witt, Mitch Williams, and Edwin Correa were the heart of a pitching staff that *Dallas Morning News* columnist Randy Galloway would tag as "Witt 'N Wild," adapting the name from a water park near Arlington Stadium.

Witt, the Rangers' #1 pick in the 1985 draft, was the pitching star of camp. That came as a great surprise to anyone who had seen him pitch the previous summer at Class AA Tulsa. Witt, a twenty-one-year-old with Nolan Ryan tools, had gone 0-6 with a 6.43 ERA in his professional baptism. He had walked 44 and struck out 39 in 35 innings. "Raw" was still the adjective most often used with Witt when he reported for work under first-year pitching coach Tom House.

But hitters seemed overmatched against Witt's fastball, which he threw about 90 percent of the time. He struck out 15 while giving up one hit in his first 10 innings of work in exhibition games. He had won Valentine over by the time he worked three hitless innings against the New York Yankees March 21. Valentine made that clear when he was asked what more Witt had to do to make the team. "Stay healthy," he answered.

Witt did that, finishing his first spring 4-0 with an 0.75 ERA in seven consistent game appearances. Williams was not quite as impressive, but he seemed much more under control than he had the previous spring, when O'Brien had refused to face him in batting practice and bullpen bystanders scrambled whenever Mitch headed to the mound.

Williams was thriving under House's guidance. The wild left-hander and the bespectacled pitching coach–a.k.a. Professor Gadget–were renewing a relationship that had begun when House was a minor-league instructor for the San Diego Padres. "When I first got out of high school, I was a pitching coach's dream," said Williams, twenty-one. "I did a lot of things wrong, I had a good arm and I had a lot of motivation to play the game. I wanted to learn. If you want to learn, you're the perfect guy for Tom House. He's the only guy I've ever worked with who I could walk on the mound and within five pitches he knows what I'm doing–right or wrong. He can pinpoint what's the matter. Around Tom House, I've never had a problem throwing strikes."

Now *there* was a news bulletin.

After a sour experience in a camp run by Doug Rader in 1985, Williams had walked 117 batters in 99 innings at Class A Salem, then walked 48 more in 33 innings after being promoted to Tulsa. We're talking some kind of wild. "Last year there were times I just wanted to say, 'The hell with this,' " Williams said. "It was that bad."

But House tinkered with Williams's mechanics in the Instructional League, sending an improved model to Pompano Beach. He compiled a 2.25 ERA in his outings, walking only five in 12 innings. "Super," said House. "He's around the dish with everything."

House successfully lobbied Valentine to go with Williams–a risk Valentine called the biggest of all that spring, bigger even than giving Incaviglia and Witt their chances. "I hired my pitching coach because I respect him and consider his opinion a valid one," Valentine said. "Mitch has done a good job this spring. He's done what Tom House said he would during spring training: throw strikes. He's made a lot of progress. With his competitiveness and confidence level, he might continue to do what Tom says he's going to do: . . . be a credible major-leaguer this year."

Edwin Correa came to camp ahead of both Witt and Williams. Although he wouldn't turn twenty until after Opening Day, he had the experience the others lacked. He had been signed by the Chicago White Sox when he was only sixteen, and had already spent three full seasons in the minor leagues, twice helping Appleton to the Class A Midwest League championship. He had finished 1985 with the White Sox, beating Seattle in his only start, and had pitched regularly in the Puerto Rican League during the winter. He came to camp ready and earned a job by going 2-0 with a 3.46 ERA in his 'A' game appearances, striking out 25 in 26 innings.

Correa was the most outwardly confident of the young pitchers. "We look young. We are young," Correa said. "But we think like old men. We are young in age but not experience. We are not just ready to pitch in the big leagues, we are ready to win."

Starter Jose Guzman and reliever Dwayne Henry also left Pompano Beach with the Rangers. Valentine, in his first full season as a manager, would open the year with a staff that was labelled "The 36-36 Club," because its five starters (Mike Mason, Guzman, Correa, Witt, and Mahler) had combined for 36 career victories while its five relievers (Dave Rozema, Greg Harris, Ricky Wright, Williams, and Henry) had combined for 36 career saves.

This was normally not considered a safe way to do business.

You couldn't tell that on the afternoon of April 6, however. Incaviglia used the final exhibition game to hit his seventh homer of the spring, a club record, and help the Rangers beat the Chicago Cubs in Oklahoma City. They finished the Grapefruit League with a record of 15-13.

"I think we've got great talent here," said Incaviglia, already comfortable as a team spokesman. "I don't think anybody in the division has better talent than we do."

Valentine shrugged off the team's lack of experience. "When I call down to the bullpen and tell (coach) Tom Robson to get Mitch up, I don't ask how old he is. I keep looking at this thing," Valentine said, pulling a lineup card out of his pocket, "and I can't find where it says age. Just name and position. There's nothing on it about age."

Valentine's goal leaving Florida was understated: "To be the most improved team in baseball."

A freak accident had put Charlie Hough on the disabled list to start the season. He'd broken his little finger exchanging hand slaps with a friend of his who had just been appointed to a judgeship in Miami, leaving Guzman as the Rangers' Opening Day starter. Guzman had been considered a sure thing to make the starting rotation when spring training began. He had secured his spot on the team the previous September, when he went 3-2 in five starts after being promoted from Class AAA Oklahoma City. He had beaten Seattle 7-2, Minnesota 2-0, and Oakland 4-2 in his last three starts of the season.

Guzman was an exception to the fast-lane approach of player development that had begun under Grieve and Valentine. He was only twenty-two at the time of his Texas debut, but he had already played five seasons. Scout Orlando Gomez had spotted Guzman pitching for John F. Kennedy High School in Santa Isabel, Puerto Rico, and had signed him when he was seventeen. Guzman had come up the hard way, developing a selection of pitches in the process of hurling for farm clubs in Sarasota, Burlington, Tulsa, and Oklahoma City.

That Guzman was the real thing was demonstrated on Opening Night. He was to face Dave Stieb and the Toronto Blue Jays, defending champions of the powerful AL East, before 40,602 at Arlington Stadium. His nerves would be given a stress test.

No problem.

In the top of the first, Guzman retired Lloyd Moseby, Tony Fernandez, and Rance Mulliniks in order. In the second, he retired Willie Upshaw on a grounder to second baseman Toby Harrah, struck out George Bell, and retired Jesse Barfield on a tapper back to the mound. In the third, Ernie Whitt and Cecil Fielder grounded out before Damaso Garcia dropped a single into left field for the first hit of the game. A double play grounder from Upshaw helped Guzman protect the scoreless tie into the fourth inning, when the Ranger offense started making noise.

Don Slaught drove an 0-2 curveball from the fiery Stieb into the left-field bleachers to give Texas a 2-0 lead. Curtis Wilkerson, starting at shortstop in place of Scott Fletcher, raised the lead to 3-0 by walking, stealing second, and scoring on a two-out single by leadoff man Oddibe McDowell. A three-run homer by Larry Parrish off rookie reliever Mark Eichhorn increased the Texas lead to 6-0 in the fifth inning.

Guzman gave up three runs on four hits during the Blue Jays' sixth inning, but collected himself nicely. He retired the last seven men he faced before Valentine called in Greg Harris to pitch the ninth. Harris preserved a 6-3 victory for Guzman, who had given up eight hits and walked none in eight innings. He was the first rookie to win on Opening Day since the Dodgers' Fernando Valenzuela in 1981.

Not a bad way to start the season.

Rookies Correa and Witt started the second and third games of the Toronto series, which the Blue Jays won 3-1 and 11-10. Baltimore followed Toronto into Arlington for a weekend series that would match Mason, Mahler, and Guzman against the Orioles' Storm Davis, Mike Flanagan, and Scott McGregor. The Friday night game revealed a lot about the season that would follow. Texas trailed 4-3 entering the ninth, having closed from 4-1 on Incaviglia's first career homer —a two-out drive to right-center field in the eighth inning.

With one out in the ninth, pinch hitter Tom Paciorek doubled into left field. Harrah hit a fly for the second out, and reliever Don Aase issued what looked like a harmless walk to McDowell. Wrong. When Aase followed the walk with a wild pickoff throw to first base, Paciorek chugged around third base and charged toward home plate. First baseman Eddie Murray's relay throw to catcher Rick Dempsey had Paciorek dead at the plate, but Paciorek slammed into Dempsey, knocking the ball loose. As Dempsey hit the ground and the ball rolled slowly toward the seats, McDowell never stopped. He slid across home plate before the dazed Orioles could recover, completing a ninety-yard dash from first base. The Rangers had won 5-4 by playing what Paciorek called "Magoo" baseball.

Mahler, a likable left-hander whose fastball could be timed by a sundial, teamed with Harris for a 2-1 victory over the Orioles on Saturday night. The

Rangers overcame a 1-0 lead thanks largely to Fletcher's bat control and McDowell's speed. These Rangers were, indeed, making things happen. Good feelings continued the next day despite a 3-2 loss. Guzman failed to protect the 2-0 lead he took into the seventh inning but was impressive enough that Earl Weaver said it looked like "he learned to pitch in heaven." Standings said the Rangers were 3-3, but they felt a lot better than that about themselves.

They felt even better after they opened the season's first road trip with three consecutive victories in Milwaukee and Baltimore. Correa lost a shutout in the eighth inning of a 10-1 victory, then a three-run ninth rallied Texas for a 7-5 victory over the Brewers. Witt put together the weirdest pitching line of the season in that game: 5 innings pitched, no hits, 2 runs, 2 earned runs, 8 walks, 10 strikeouts and 4 wild pitches. Brewer hitters kept chasing his sliders, which more often than not crashed to earth in front of the plate. Witt faced 23 batters, but only three put the ball in play. "Once he collects himself," Valentine said of Witt, "I think we will see nine innings of that stuff."

The next day, in Baltimore, a seven-hit, six-run fifth inning set the tone for a 12-3 drubbing of Scott McGregor and the Orioles. It was only April 18, but at 6-3 the Rangers had moved from the bottom to the top of the American League West. That was too good to last, of course. Texas finished April with a 9-10 record. But it rebounded to win its first three series in May, taking four of six games from the Yankees and two of three from the Detroit Tigers. The Rangers' first-ever doubleheader sweep of the Yankees was included in that stretch, as Mason and Guzman pitched the Rangers to 6-3 and 9-1 victories.

Valentine's brash team demanded more attention when it arrived in Cleveland. Hough, back from the disabled list, and Indians' left-hander Neal Heaton kept hitters under control through five innings. But Larry Parrish's fourth home run in four games started an unprecedented bombardment by the Rangers in the sixth inning. Texas scored eight runs in the sixth inning, four more in both the seventh and eighth innings and another pair of runs in the ninth. When the Cleveland Stadium scoreboard stopped spinning, it showed 19 runs and 22 hits for the Rangers—both club records. Paciorek went five-for-six, both Incaviglia and McDowell had three hits, and veteran second baseman Toby Harrah drove in four runs with two doubles.

"It was just one of those things," said Parrish. "We weren't doing a whole lot before the sixth, but after that everything we did worked out. We couldn't do anything wrong. Everything was in the hole."

It was the fifth victory in a six-game stretch for the Rangers, keeping them in a tie for first place with Gene Mauch's California Angels. "Another outstanding team win," Valentine said, beaming before reporters in his shabby office in the visiting clubhouse. "Everyone contributed, some guys a little more than others. I can't say enough about the way the guys are playing."

Paciorek, whose ties with Valentine dated to Ogden, Utah in 1968, had been signed as a $200,000 free agent before the season. In addition to serving as a bench player, his role was to keep the young team loose. He accomplished that with his impersonations of other Rangers, including Valentine, and a willingness to tell any joke, no matter how vulgar or absurd. "There's a lot of good offensive players on this team," said Paciorek. "Guys who can hit and who can run. Bobby is very aggressive. We're always moving on the bases. That puts a lot of pressure on the defense. And when you find holes, it makes it a lot easier." The Rangers were finding all the holes.

While Texas and California jockeyed between first and second place, everyone else in the West, including defending world champ Kansas City, took their lumps in early-season trips through the East. Despite their 20-20 record, the Rangers were only one-half game out of first through May 23. They had recently suffered two critical injuries, losing catcher Don Slaught for almost two months when he was beaned by Boston's Dennis "Oil Can" Boyd and Parrish for one month when he pulled a ribcage muscle, but moved into first May 24. Witt and Williams survived a rain delay and teamed for a 3-2 victory over Boston, and a two-out single in the ninth by Vietnam vet Bobby "Ace" Jones salvaged the win. This was euphoria on Interstate 30.

Although Roger Clemens cooled Texas by coming within four outs of a no-hitter the next afternoon, the Rangers kept their hold on first place for thirty-two consecutive days—the longest stretch at the top in the franchise's history. They went 17-9 after the loss to Clemens, proving they were no longer the dregs of the "AL Worst." Chicago, the team that had given Texas Correa and Fletcher, failed to win once in six games during that stretch. Seattle left Arlington without a single victory after a four-game series in which the Rangers rescued themselves from deficits of 5-3 in the ninth, 5-4 in the seventh, and 4-3 in the ninth. An average crowd of almost thirty thousand turned out at Arlington Stadium for the weekend series against the Mariners, including 34,735 for the Saturday-night doubleheader sweep.

Local newspapers responded by sending extra reporters on a six-game trip to the West Coast. The Rangers' offense went into hiding, dropping two of three games in Oakland before the first series of the year against the second-place Angels, who had fallen 3½ games off the pace. Fans at Anaheim Stadium assumed a hushed reverence as Hough and young right-hander Kirk McCaskill began to battle in the Monday opener.

An error by Angels center fielder Gary Pettis and a single by Steve Buechele produced an early run for the Rangers, and it appeared it could be the only run of the day. Hough was at the top of his game, changing speeds on his knuckleball and getting away with his occasional fastballs. With defensive help from Harrah and McDowell, he took a no-hitter into the ninth inning. In a move to help Hough at the start the ninth inning, Valentine inserted the speedier Wright into left field for Gary Ward.

Tension built when Hough got a called third strike past pinch hitter Ruppert Jones to start the ninth. Jack Howell, another pinch hitter, lifted a fly ball down the left-field line. It was a long run for Wright, who had been playing the left-handed-hitting Howell to pull Hough. But Wright caught up with the ball. In fact, he overran it. The ball deflected off his glove when he reached behind his body for it. Howell arrived at second base with what was ruled an error on Wright.

But Hough had lost his concentration. Rookie Wally Joyner, the next California hitter, pulled a single through the right side of the infield to end Hough's no-hit bid. It also scored Howell, tying the game 1-1 with one out. Doug DeCinces struck out for the second out, but Hough then walked Reggie Jackson, moving Joyner to second. Hough struck out the next hitter, George Hendrick, but the one-and-two knuckleball bounced to the screen after Hendrick's swing and miss. Catcher Orlando Mercado chased the ball as Joyner went from second to third, but Joyner surprised everyone by continuing around third toward home plate. He scored easily.

Hough, as alert a fielder as has ever played for the Rangers, had forgotten to cover home plate. Not only did Hough lose his no-hitter in the ninth, but the Rangers lost the game, 2-1. It was a loss that would follow Valentine's team for the rest of the season, setting a horrible tone in the series against California.

Texas scored a total of one run against Mike Witt and Don Sutton the next two nights, and left Anaheim with its lead down to one-half game.

Mauch brought the Angels to Arlington the next weekend. By sweeping a four-game series against Oakland, the Rangers had pushed their lead over California back to two games. It didn't last through Saturday. The Angels destroyed rookie starters Guzman, Correa, and Witt, outscoring Texas 25-8 for their second three-game sweep of the Rangers. The teams had matching 38-32 records entering Wednesday night's meeting of McCaskill and Witt. Three walks and a wild pitch helped the Angels take a 4-0 lead in the third inning en route to a 7-1 victory—the lone hit off McCaskill a homer by Buechele—and sole possession of first place.

Texas briefly regained the West lead by winning four games in a row, but by the All-Star break had slipped back to second place, 1½ games behind the Angels. But it was still a very good first half for Valentine and his Rangers. They were 47-41, needing only fifteen more victories to equal their total from 1985.

"[Our] winning attitude since the first day of spring training . . . has really put us where we are," said Mason, who was 6-2 at the break despite missing three weeks with a pulled hamstring. "We have played through some things that could have killed us. It's the influence of the coaching staff, the whole management. It is something we have never had. We've had managers come here to win, but couldn't instill a winning attitude, which is really making everybody believe in themselves. Before, people believed we could win, but the emphasis just wasn't the same. If we won, got hot, great. Now, if we win, or get hot, we're supposed to win because we're that good."

With the scrappy Scott Fletcher setting the tone, the surprising team had proven that it was willing to play hard—very hard.

"That's just an attitude," Valentine said. "It's wanting it more than the other guy. In a hundred-yard sprint, usually the fastest guy wins. In a weight-lifting contest, it's usually the strongest guy that wins. In baseball, it's not always the best team that wins. It's usually the one that plays the best. You play best when you have that desire to do better. You don't always need to have the best talent."

While his baseball team was on a roll, owner Eddie Chiles' business was nearing a financial collapse. His fortune was still tied to the price of oil, and the news on West Texas Crude got worse all the time. Things were so bad that Chiles decided he should sell his share in the Rangers to minority partner Gaylord Broadcasting, the television subsidiary owned by Oklahoma City publisher Edward L. Gaylord.

Gaylord had come aboard in October of 1984. To ease the pressure on Chiles, he'd bought one-third of the team as well as a right of first refusal to match any further purchase from Chiles. Only intervention by Commissioner Peter Ueberroth had gotten the deal approved, as American League owners had disapproved of increased ownership by broadcasting entities.

Ueberroth used his "best interest of baseball" powers to override the owners' rejection. "I thought it would work out," Gaylord said of the minority purchase. "I didn't see any reason why it wouldn't. I'm glad it's over so we can get on our way."

Now Gaylord had reached an agreement to buy Chiles out for an estimated $50 million. It seemed a simple enough transaction, but with this franchise things were never as simple as they seemed.

After the break it took just one game for the bloom to come off Valentine's rose. Beginning a seven-game trip to Detroit and New York, the Rangers went down 2-1 to Walt Terrell, the right-hander Eddie Robinson had sent packing in the ill-fated trade for Lee Mazzilli. Williams and Harris, as effective as any team's late-inning tandem during the first half of the season, combined to blow a 1-0 lead in the ninth. Harris, who had fifteen saves at the break, forced in the winning run by walking Alan Trammell and Kirk Gibson.

"I couldn't have thrown a strike if I'd aimed it," Harris said after the game. "It's a horrible day to come up with a day like this. We needed to come out in the first game and get a victory right out of the chute, get a quick start."

But pitching wasn't the reason Valentine was livid afterward. Terrell is not a strikeout pitcher, yet he fanned leadoff man Oddibe McDowell four times. McDowell had been one of the few players who had failed to attend an optional workout at Arlington Stadium on the last day of the All-Star break.

Valentine benched McDowell the next day. "Oddibe needs a couple of days to get himself back in shape where he's ready to play every day," Valentine said. "He wasn't ready. He didn't participate in the workout. We had an early workout, and he didn't participate. That disappoints me."

McDowell said he had his reasons for missing the workout, but did not give them. "I didn't go to the workout because I had reasons not to go," he said. "I called in and said I was not coming."

After leaving Washington with the rest of the Senators, Ted Williams made a game attempt to get the Rangers off to a good start in the team's new Southwest surroundings. Like this sombrero, Texas baseball was never a good fit for the Splendid Splinter. (Photo by Paul Iverson)

Williams broke the monotony of the Rangers' initial season in Arlington during a visit by Dizzy Dean.
(Photo by Paul Iverson)

With home-grown talent Jim Sundberg blossoming as the top defensive catcher in the American League, Billy Hunter got the most out of the Rangers for one summer. His hard-driving style didn't work so well the next year, and like Ted Williams, Whitey Herzog and others before him, he fell victim to ownership's lack of patience. (Photo by Paul Iverson)

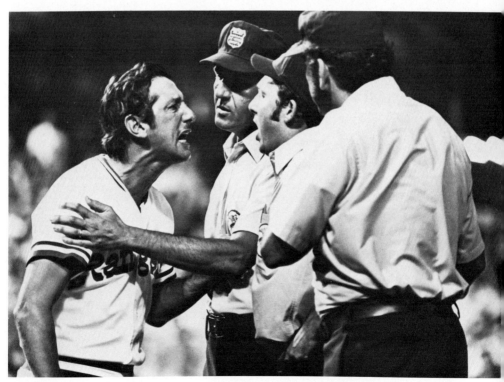

Billy Martin's formula for instant, short-term success worked well with a young team in 1974, but an amazing September rally still left them short of Reggie Jackson and the Amazin' A's. (Photo by Paul Iverson)

A 1973 sellout crowd at Arlington Stadium watches as 18-year-old high school ace David Clyde winds up to deliver his first pitch in the big leagues. Clyde was big business at the box office that year but had only 17 other career wins after beating Minnesota in his debut. (Photo by Linda Kaye)

With no commitment to developing their own players, the Rangers ran through a cast of veterans at or past their prime under the direction of owner Brad Corbett. Jim Fregosi was one of many who did a nice job for a short time in the late '70s, but none were good enough to bring a title to Texas. (Photo by Paul Iverson)

Wayne Tolleson's hustle typified the obscure team that Doug Rader managed into first place at the All-Star break in 1983. But after the break, and for the next two seasons, reality returned for Tolleson and the Rangers. They kicked away enough games to finish last in 1984 and 1985. (Photo by Louis DeLuca)

The presence of third baseman supreme Buddy Bell brought promise to the Rangers for seven springs. Bell was the highest paid, best-liked, and most frustrated Texas player. In the spring of '82, he said the Rangers were the best team he ever played on; they lost 98 games that year. (Photo by Louis DeLuca)

Mickey Rivers was a pleasure to watch and a treasure to listen to while finishing up his career. Asked for his goal one year, he said, "To stay injury-prone." After hitting .300 in 1984, Rivers was released in the spring of '85 so Doug Rader could keep rookie Tommy Dunbar on the roster. Rader said the Rangers wouldn't need Rivers' "comic relief"; they finished last that year, and needed all the laughs they could get. (Photo by Louis DeLuca)

During their first year in Arlington, the Rangers said goodbye to one bespectacled slugger, Frank Howard, and hello to his successor, Jeff Burroughs. The south winds would eventually cause Burroughs to seek a trade that sent him to Atlanta for five players, including legend-to-be Roger Moret. (Photo by Paul Iverson)

George Wright, a top prospect, and Gary Ward, acquired in a trade, were expected to provide pop at the plate while playing solid outfield. But moments like this one, being witnessed by Cliff Johnson, were few and far between during 1985. (Photo by Louis DeLuca)

Oddibe McDowell, an All-American at Arizona State who batted .400 in triple-A, signaled the dawn of a new era when he was promoted to the major leagues in May 1985, two days after Bobby Valentine replaced Doug Rader as manager. But for McDowell and Olympic teammate Bobby Witt, the jump to the big leagues included an attempt to escape the Rangers' legacy of losing. This night, they were the last two out of the dugout after a tough loss. (Photo by Louis DeLuca)

Toby Harrah came from Washington with the Rangers in '72, then returned in a 1985 trade for Billy Sample to end his career in Texas. Harrah played shortstop, third base, and second base as a regular, then joined Bobby Valentine's coaching staff. (Photo by Louis DeLuca)

Despite a horrible beginning in 1982, Larry Parrish became the Rangers' all-time home run leader. It was a shock to many when he was released in 1988, less than one season removed from a trip to the All-Star Game. (Photo by Louis DeLuca)

With losses climbing and attendance dropping, the Rangers were open to any and almost all promotions during the early '80s. Danny Darwin had to wait behind the Bud Man to take his turn on the Arlington Stadium mound in 1984. (Photo by Louis DeLuca)

Short of pitchers during the surprising 1986 season, Bobby Valentine gave Florida State All-American Mike Loynd a chance to go from the College World Series to the major leagues in two months. Loynd's animated style, a la Mark Fidrych, worked in his rookie year but vanished after he was chased off the mound by Toronto's Lloyd Moseby in April '87–a sidelight to the Rangers' 1-10 start. (Photo by Louis DeLuca)

Adapting to life after a 95-mph fastball, Frank Tanana was the team's pitcher of the year in 1984 before an '85 trade for flop Duane James. (Photo by Louis DeLuca)

Journeyman Greg Harris came from obscurity to give Bobby Valentine 20 saves during the honeymoon season in 1986. (Photo by Louis DeLuca)

Rangers president Mike Stone checked out Steve Howe's recovery from cocaine addiction before signing him in 1987, but the move smacked of desperation after Howe disappeared during a mini-camp the following January. He was soon out of baseball for good. (Photo by Louis DeLuca)

Mitch Williams looked at peace with Larry Parrish's dog, Spec, but "The Wild Thing" kept things interesting during four seasons in the Texas organization. The key to a nine-player trade with the Chicago Cubs before 1989, it coast Texas only $25,000 to draft him from San Diego. (Photo by Louis DeLuca)

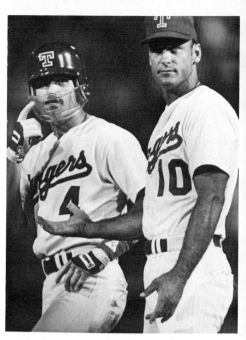

Pete O'Brien slowed to give coach Tim Foli a forearm after one of the drives that made him a steady 20-homer, 85-RBI player during seven full seasons with the Rangers. (Photo by Louis DeLuca)

Hitting instructor Art Howe helped catcher Don Slaught get used to a protective shield on his helmet after getting beaned by Oil Can Boyd in May, 1986. Slaught eventually fell out of favor with manager Bobby Valentine and was traded to the Yankees, while Howe was hired to manage the Houston Astros in 1989. (Photo by Louis DeLuca)

Speed was never the best of Larry Parrish's attributes; here Oakland's Mickey Tettleton applies the tag as Parrish can't even stand to look. (Photo by Louis DeLuca)

A friendship begun when both were languishing on the bench with the New York Mets resulted in a chance to manage for Bobby Valentine when Tom Grieve replaced Joe Klein as the Rangers' general manager. Both were committed to building from within, and for the first time in franchise history, both of the team's top executives were willing to admit how far the Rangers had to go. (Photo by Louis DeLuca)

When Eddie Chiles' efforts to sell the team to Oklahoma City publisher Edward Gaylord were rebuffed by American League owners, George W. Bush put together a successful deal for his ownership group in 1989. It didn't hurt his efforts any that his father had just taken office as President. (Photo by Louis DeLuca)

Carney Lansford knocks the ball out of Scott Fletcher's glove on a slide into second. The Scooter had two excellent years at the plate but a huge salary increase, a severe drop in his batting average, and his limited range in the field – not to mention Tom Grieve's coveting of designated hitter Harold Baines – led to his trade to the Chicago White Sox midway through the 1989 season. (Photo by Louis DeLuca)

While Bobby Valentine's personal portfolio included a chain of restaurants, his focus was squarely on the game once in uniform. This night, the best efforts of the Chicken couldn't even get a peek his way. (Photo by Louis DeLuca)

The efforts of agent Bucky Woy and backing of Bobby Valentine helped Pete Incaviglia jump straight from Oklahoma State to the major leagues in 1986. Incaviglia whetted appetites with 30 homers as a rookie, but developed a love-hate relationship with fans who jeered him for strikeouts, shaky outfield play, and salary disputes. (Photo by Louis DeLuca)

Bobby Witt displayed tons of potential during his first four seasons but never mastered the art of just winning. Given their heritage of trading away raw talent—Dave Righetti, Ron Darling, Walt Terrell, et al—Witt had a surprisingly long shelf life in Texas. (Photo by Louis DeLuca)

The Arlington Stadium scoreboard told the story as Nolan Ryan flirted with first perfection, then no-hitter No. 6, against Detroit in 1989. Dave Bergman broke it up with a one-out single to left field. The Rangers spent $3 million to get him away from the Houston Astros, and he rewarded them with an amazing season for a 42-year-old: 16 wins, 301 strikeouts, and five no-hitters into the eighth inning in 32 starts. (Photo by Louis DeLuca)

Charlie Hough was on his way out of baseball when Eddie Robinson signed him at a bargain-basement price in 1980, but turned out to be the decade's most consistent starter in the American League. Hough's knuckleball took him within two outs of a no-hitter against California in 1986. (Photo by Louis DeLuca)

Steve Buechele did not want to be compared to Buddy Bell when the Rangers brought him to the big leagues, but his sparkling defensive play made it a natural comparison. (Photo by Louis DeLuca)

This is a youth movement? Entering the '90s, the Rangers' two most consistent pitchers were their oldest – 41-year-old Charlie Hough (left) and 42-year-old Nolan Ryan. (Photo by Louis DeLuca)

Before Rafael Palmeiro (front) slumped after the All-Star break, he, Ruben Sierra (right), and Julio Franco gave the Rangers the best three-hitter combination in the American League for much of 1989. The Three Amigos are expected to provide the nucleus of the lineup that will take Texas into the '90s. (Photo by Louis DeLuca)

He also wasn't playing.

It was an unsettling situation for a suddenly nervous team, even though Valentine reinstated McDowell to the lineup after one game. He should have also kept Harris on the bench. Detroit swept the four-game series, with Gibson incredibly getting the game-winning RBI in each game. Harris negated an eleventh-inning homer by Slaught in the third loss, serving up a three-run homer on an oh-and-two curveball to Gibson. Rookie Eric King threw a six-hit shutout to complete the sweep.

Texas continued the post-break slide at Yankee Stadium. New York slugged eight homers in sweeping the three-game series, including two apiece by Rickey Henderson and Don Mattingly. After averaging 4.7 runs per game in the first half of the season, the Rangers scored 11 during this seven-game losing streak. But California won only twice during that stretch, pushing its lead to 3½ games.

Neophyte Mike Loynd, who had pitched for Florida State in the College World Series only two months earlier, snapped the losing streak when the Rangers got back to Arlington. The junkballer beat Cleveland 5-3 in his major-league debut, keeping the Indians off balance with his histrionics on the mound. Joe Carter swore revenge. "I'll get him next year," Carter said, "if he's still in the big leagues."

Loynd's unlikely victory began a stretch of good baseball. Texas won thirteen of seventeen games, closing to within 1½ games of California on August 14.

None of those victories was as remarkable as a 13-11 win over Baltimore August 6 at Memorial Stadium. Rick Dempsey performed his Jerry Lee Lewis act on the tarp during a pre-game rain delay. What followed was the first major-league game to include three grand slams. Harrah, Larry Sheets, and Jim Dwyer each hit one. Sheets and Dwyer's slams came during a nine-run fourth inning that put the Orioles ahead 9-6. Texas trailed 11-6 after seven, but homers by Buechele and Pete O'Brien and a two-run double by Parrish put the Rangers ahead for good 12-11 in the eighth.

Mauch apparently found that kind of Texas victory amusing. He had seen the Rangers first-hand and was not impressed. "I like the idea of having to beat a club that has to score nine runs to win," said the California manager. "I also like my pitching."

Mauch didn't stop there. "If we can't handle the Texas Rangers, I have to give up. I shouldn't say that, because the Texas Rangers are having one great season, but I figure that if we win ninety, that should be good enough in our division."

Some Rangers took Mauch's comments as a sign of panic. "If he was content with what was going on, he wouldn't say anything," opined Mason. "He's panicking because they can't get away from us."

By rebounding from the seven-game slide after the All-Star break, the Rangers earned respect in other baseball circles.

"I think they're for real," said Toronto outfielder Jesse Barfield. "They're a real scrappy club right now. They have as good of a shot as anybody in the

West. They remind me of us last year. They never give in and you need that to win a division. I'm happy for them because they're playing their hearts out."

Texas followed the Baltimore series by winning two of three games against Toronto, coming from behind for 9-7 and 7-6 victories. "What they showed us and Baltimore is that they won't lie down and die," commented Blue Jays pitcher Dave Stieb. "They've been winning without their starting pitching, and that's a pretty good sign. The best thing they've got going for them is their confidence level."

And, it appeared, the schedule.

Texas was finishing a stretch of nineteen games against powerful East opponents Baltimore, Milwaukee, and Toronto at the same time the Angels played only West cabooses Minnesota, Seattle, and Oakland. Ahead was a stretch during which the Rangers played six series against Kansas City, Chicago, and Boston while the Angels faced Detroit, Baltimore, and New York.

"That's going to be tough on them," observed Gary Ward. "They have to go to the East, and by the time they get through with the East it will be time for them to play us again."

Texas also appeared to have the best of the schedule in September, playing fifteen in a row against Seattle, Minnesota, and Oakland before the first of the seven remaining games against California. "That's when we can legitimately say we can begin our killing run," said Mason. "That's when we've got to hold back from complacency, when we have to buckle down."

No sooner had Ward and Mason spoken than the Rangers hit the skids. Texas had traveled to Toronto after a 4-2 homestand, and on a rainy night at Exhibition Stadium–the place Doug Rader had called the "Voodoo Palace"–young right-hander Joe Johnson shut down the Rangers in a 6-1 victory for the Blue Jays. Correa gave up home runs to George Bell and Cliff Johnson. It was the start of the finish for a team which had been surprising even to themselves.

Toronto swept the weekend series, scoring 12 runs off Hough in a 13-1 victory on Saturday and overcoming a 5-0 Rangers lead on Sunday. Mason failed to protect the lead and Ernie Whitt applied the finishing touch in the eleventh, lining a pitch from Jeff Russell just inside the right-field foul pole for a home run. California, meanwhile, had swept a series against Oakland, increasing its lead over Texas from 1½ games to 4½ games. That lead jumped to five games when, after a gloomy off day in Kansas City, Frank White's eleventh-inning homer off thirty-year-old rookie reliever Dale Mohorcic gave the Royals a 9-8 victory. It briefly took the Royals' minds off manager Dick Howser, who recently had left with a brain tumor less than a year after helping bring Kansas City its first world championship.

Texas never got closer to the Angels than three games, remaining in second place the rest of the season. It came out of the crippling four-game losing streak to win eight of eleven games, finishing August 17-12. But the Angels, behind Joyner and DeCinces, kept winning. Mauch's team went 19-10 in August, then kept winning in September.

The losing battle took its toll on Valentine. In Chicago, umpire Dan Morrison ejected him from a 3-1 loss on August 31 when Valentine attempted to intervene in a dispute between Morrison and Williams. Two days later, Valentine and umpire Steve Palermo continued a personal feud that had peaked earlier in the year when Palermo had ejected both Incaviglia and Valentine from a game in Boston. There were no ejections from this altercation, which started when Palermo said something to Steve Buechele, but it was ugly. Valentine ripped Palermo to Texas reporters after the 8-6 loss September 2, saying Palermo was letting his feelings about Valentine affect his judgment. Valentine cooled down the next day, sending word to Palermo that he would like the chance to discuss the difficulties. Palermo declined, but Valentine had breakfast with crew chief Joe Brinkman. Brinkman tried to explain to Valentine how he could alter his on-field approach and perhaps avoid his frequent ejections—at the time, nine in 262 games. But the summit didn't seem to accomplish much.

A week later, the tag team of Big Pete Incaviglia and Little Bobby Valentine got thrown out of another game. This one was in the Metrodome, on September 11, and as usual Incaviglia did not agree when plate umpire Larry Barnett called him out on strikes for taking a curveball from Frank Viola. Valentine sided with Inky, but Barnett ran him out in a hurry.

The next day, Valentine learned that he had been suspended for four games by American League President Bobby Brown. In his report to the league office, Barnett wrote that Valentine had accused him of betting on the game—a charge Valentine strongly denied. Valentine was unable to do more than watch Friday and Saturday's games from the Metrodome's upper deck and Saturday's from inside a television truck.

Valentine wasn't the only casualty that September. Chiles's sale of the team to Gaylord Broadcasting was shot down by American League owners at a joint owners meeting September 23 in Newport Beach, California. President Bobby Brown said the vote against Gaylord was originally unanimous, but sources indicated that nine owners had voted for passage on the first ballot, only one short of approval.

The sale was blocked by owners from smaller markets, led by Milwaukee Brewers owner Bud Selig. Having read that Gaylord Broadcasting president Bill Banowsky said he planned to make the Rangers' TV network, KTVT-Channel 11, a "superstation second to none," the group feared further television saturation; a perceived threat to their home-game attendance.

"At this particular time, [the owners] felt that for a TV company to own a baseball team was not something they could approve," said Brown. "There were no objections to their staying in a minority position, no objection to them personally . . . If they made jeans or automobiles, it would be no problem."

Kansas City owner Avron Fogelman was in the bloc of owners opposing Gaylord's bid for majority control. "Proliferation of TV is a problem," he said. "It could be baseball's biggest problem. Baseball owners today are not assuming anything. It's not a matter of questioning anyone's integrity."

Gaylord seemed undaunted by the defeat, which Chiles also took graciously. "It's a great situation," Gaylord said of his minority interest. "When we got in, the team was in the cellar. Now it's making money. We're very happy. We have got an investment, but we don't have the day-to-day responsibility for the team. I'm disappointed for Mr. Chiles, but frankly I'm relieved I don't have to take on more responsibility."

Chiles estimated he had lost $20 million since taking over the team from Brad Corbett, but he did not display his combative side after the defeat. Perhaps he still enjoyed owning a team that had been the most pleasant surprise of the year in the majors.

About ten days after the rejection, Chiles announced that he was taking the team off the market. "I'm not looking for options. I could look for a buyer, sure, if I wanted to. Right now I don't want to. We have a hell of a baseball team and the finest management group in baseball. My feeling is just keep it, enjoy it. I've sweated out a lot of bad years with these teams. Now I can sit and enjoy the good times . . . "

After looking forward to playing California seven times in the final ten days, the Rangers came to Anaheim with the need to pull off one of the greatest runs in baseball history. They trailed the Angels by nine games with ten remaining, beginning with a three-game series on the West Coast. A Friday night crowd of 45,677 watched the Angels recover from a 2-0 deficit against Mason and the Rangers to clinch the division title with an 8-3 victory.

Texas finished the season 87-75, with Valentine causing a splash on the season's final day. After a promotion in which the Rangers' players literally gave fans the jerseys off their backs, Valentine grabbed hold of a microphone and delivered an inpassioned thank-you speech to the crowd. Fans cheered throughout the speech, but went crazy at his final line: "You ain't seen nothing yet."

It had been an amazing season in many ways. Incaviglia failed to reach his lofty Florida goals but still hit 30 homers and drove in 88 runs. Parrish and O'Brien had solid seasons, combining for 51 homers and 184 RBIs. Fletcher had hit .300. Correa had won 12 games, including a three-hit shutout at Yankee Stadium, and struck out more batters (189) than any American League rookie in sixteen years. Witt had set a league record with 22 wild pitches, but went 7-0 in his last 12 starts to finish 12-14. There was a reason for Valentine's strut.

Grieve and he had escaped, if not erased, the stigma that had followed the franchise from Washington in 1972. They were the Arlington Hillbillies no more.

"The test of things like that is a test of years, not one year. But we've made great strides," Valentine observed. "I'm really proud of this situation right now. I think there's pride in this organization now."

With sixteen crowds of more than thirty thousand, the Rangers increased their attendance by more than half a million, setting a personal record with 1,692,021.

"The best thing that happened to our team this year was we regained the confidence of the fans," Grieve said. "They liked to come to the ballpark. They preceived our organization as heading in the right direction, one that has a plan and will stick to it. They've seen the performance of a team loaded with young players, who in their minds should get better, and a team that's fun to follow, to root for in years ahead.

"The image of the team in the eyes of the fan has been improved . . . The performance by the whole organization made that possible. The players are visible to the fans. Bobby signs autographs sitting on top of the dugout. The organization as a whole has made an effort to be visible to the fans, to show we care, we appreciate their support."

Said Charlie Hough, "It's been an important year, probably more important for the guys who have been here a stretch, even the guys who have been here just the last year or two. They have seen enough confusion, which is what it has been. I think it was an important year for the franchise itself to handle things as well as it did this year . . . There was no panic, that's important for the players."

What next?

Grieve was not about to pop off after only one successful year. "I use the analogy of playing golf," he offered. "Somebody who is learning to play golf and shooting 110, 108, if he plays a lot and has any ability to begin with, probably can shoot 88 or 87. But it's harder to make the next jump. It's hard to shoot 78 or 79 unless you're pretty good at it. That's where we are. We've been shooting 100, 110 the last few years. Now we're getting down in the 80s. To get down into the 70s may take a lot of fine-tuning, and can be even more difficult."

Valentine, of course, had the Rangers winning the Masters next year. He was too full of himself and his team to have time for reality. He couldn't wait for 1987.

A Silver Lining In Right Field

The winter of 1986-87 was a euphoric time for the franchise. Skeptics had become believers. Believers had become fanatics. Even the accountants were happy. The Rangers had turned an operating profit for the first time, and expected a bigger one in 1987. Despite the slide of oil prices and the area's collapsing economy, ninety-eight percent of the Rangers' season-ticket holders kept their seats at Arlington Stadium.

"I guess what I felt the most happy about last year was that people started to identify with the Rangers," said club president Mike Stone. "They started to feel like, 'This is our ballclub, it's in our area and it's part of us. It's exciting baseball, it has an exciting manager and exciting young players. It's something I want to be a part of.' That really means a lot to me."

Stone remembered the scene at Arlington Stadium in 1984, his first year on the job. "It was like being chronically on the road," he said. "It was sad. It was frustrating. I felt sorriest for the twenty-five guys sitting in the dugout, saying, 'Geez, are we in Cleveland? Are we in Detroit?' That hurts."

Bobby Valentine, named the American League's Manager of the Year by United Press International, put himself through a Tommy Lasorda-style off-season. He was everywhere, speaking to everyone. Rangers Public Relations man John Blake, who was handling Valentine's schedule, estimated that he made sixty public appearances in eight states. For *Sports Illustrated* he filmed a national commercial with Terry Forster—in one of his restaurants, of course—

and a local Ford commercial with first baseman Pete O'Brien. He taped several radio spots for Epson computers. For a man supposedly at rest, and with a wife and young son at home, his schedule seemed out of control.

In late January and early February, he fulfilled obligations for fifteen consecutive days. Included were motivational speeches in Fort Lauderdale and Fort Worth, banquets in Los Angeles, Cleveland, Dallas, Fort Worth, and Arlington, and a baseball clinic in Connecticut. He also spoke at a breakfast of exhibitors at the Fort Worth Fat Stock Show, hyped the Rangers in Tulsa, Oklahoma, and, with Tom Grieve, accepted the Big D Award, the highest compliment that can be paid by the Dallas All-Sports Association.

"We've got probably the best salesman there is in Bobby Valentine," said Rangers ticket manager Mary Ann Bosher. "He sells the club everywhere he goes. All you have to do is listen to him to get enthusiastic."

A record crowd of over one thousand attended the annual Mid-Winter Baseball Banquet. "I've been in sports since I was ten years old," said eighty-five-year-old George Schepps, the banquet's coordinator, "and the hottest product to market I've known is Bobby Valentine."

KTVT, the Fort Worth television station owned by minority partner Edward Gaylord, found that the Rangers were easier to sell to advertisers. "You can go in with a smile on your face," said Charley Edwards, KTVT's general manager. "You don't have to back in the door."

For years, the Richland Mall in Waco had been a regular part of the club's annual public relations caravan through Texas and surrounding states. "In years past we would grab people walking by and force an autograph on them," said Jim Small, an assistant in Blake's PR office. "Holtzie (radio announcer Mark Holtz) would stand out in the middle of the mall and hawk stuff. This year it was incredible. There were probably six hundred people there. We signed autographs for two and a half hours."

Public reaction to the Rangers had changed. "Before, we'd go out and try to drum up interest . . . " Small said. "When we would go out, there would be a lot of questions like, 'Why did you trade Sundberg?' Afterward, everybody would bolt for the door. Now we finish talking at one o'clock, and they keep you there until 1:30 asking questions about the team. It's great. Everybody is pumped up about it."

While there had been little past interest in Rangers players as marketing tools, that also had changed. Businesses wanted players at their grand openings. Don Slaught and 1986 rookies Pete Incaviglia, Bobby Witt, and Mitch Williams picked up a quick $500 an hour signing autographs at a baseball card show.

Expecting a big season, KTVT reorganized its programming. It had originally decided to carry no Ranger games after September 3 in 1986, but signed up for thirteen of the final sixteen road games in 1987. "It's our belief that this team is going to be more successful," Edwards said. "When you don't feel strong about a team you tend to gear down in September and October. You won't have the viewer support . . . We feel very positive, as everybody else does, [about] where (the Rangers) can go this year and in the future."

Year sixteen of the longest running comedy in the American League was beginning to open, and finally ticket lines had replaced punch lines.

Blue skies.

Nothing but blue skies.

It was a quiet winter for General Manager Tom Grieve. He rarely heard from other clubs, as they knew he was satisfied with the team he would be bringing into the 1987 season. He had no depth with which to make a deal, but that wasn't really the point. He was satisfied.

Grieve's decisions were easy ones. Darrell Porter and Tom Paciorek, productive bench players on one-year contracts, had to be re-signed. Gary Ward was a solid outfielder, but the emergence of Ruben Sierra and Incaviglia left him with nowhere to play. His $865,000 salary, highest on the team, had been a sore point last year and he would not take a big pay cut. So Ward would not be re-signed.

Grieve was barely noticed at the winter meetings in Hollywood, Florida. He stuck around the minimum number of days at the Diplomat Hotel, and he picked up only twenty-three-year-old Cecil Espy, a candidate for the fourth outfielder's job, which had been held by Ward.

Ward's place atop Grieve's mental list of overpaid players was quickly filled by reliever Greg Harris. The right-handed junkballer had been a great find when the Rangers purchased him from San Diego before the 1985 season, and a bargain when he saved twenty games while earning a $310,000 salary in 1986. But Harris demanded to be paid for his success, eventually winning a 100 percent raise to $620,000 in arbitration. It was to be one of Harris' few victories in 1987.

History now shows that the Rangers arrived at their new six-diamond complex in Port Charlotte, Florida, headed in the wrong direction. Their amazing leap from a seventh-place 62-99 record in 1985 to a second-place 87-75 record in 1986 had given them new status. Since 1901, only twenty-eight major-league teams had jumped over five or more teams in a single year. Twenty of those twenty-eight teams finished with worse records the year after their dramatic about-faces.

No wonder the attitude of the Rangers' management was best described as guarded optimism. Some magazines, including *Sports Illustrated*, picked Texas as the pre-season favorite in the American League West. But not Grieve and Valentine.

"I expect to be a strong, competitive team from day one until the end of the season," Grieve said in February. "I expect us to be in a pennant race the whole year. We have the ability to do that. You don't know what your opponents are going to do. I think we should play solid baseball all year, but I wouldn't pick us as pre-season favorites. California and Kansas City should be the pre-season favorites."

Valentine echoed that cautious theme. "I don't think we ever had the respect last year that we are going to have at the beginning of . . . this year, " he said. "One of our jobs this year is going to be to maintain it. My expectations are that we [will] continue to grow as a team, continue to improve individually. When this season is over, our team will be even more prominent on a national level and our individuals will be even more recognizable."

After using thirteen rookies in 1986, Valentine said that "the sophomore jinx is not a jinx at all. It's the inability of people to recognize the reality of the situation, an unwillingness to put forth the effort it takes to improve."

There was little real competition for jobs in the spring. Rookie Jerry Browne, after a successful September trial in 1986, moved into the second-base job held by Toby Harrah the previous two seasons, despite being outplayed in the spring by handyman Curtis Wilkerson. Rookie Bob Brower, a former Duke University fullback, outplayed Espy to move into the fourth outfielder's position. Sidewinder Scott Anderson provided the real surprise, dominating hitters to earn a spot in the bullpen.

Working out before the season opener in Baltimore, Larry Parrish said the team's biggest enemy would be the new level of expectation surrounding it. "Last year, not much was expected from the young guys," Parrish said. "It was one of those situations where anything we got from them while they were learning was going to be fine. We had such a good year, everybody expects us to have what it takes to win the division. The fans. The media. They're not going to have the same attitude this year when we're losing."

Valentine declared the Rangers ready for Opening Day despite their having lost the final five exhibition games. "We can handle it," he said a day before the opener.

Three pitches into the 1987 season, Oddibe McDowell was circling the bases at Memorial Stadium, having led off the game with a home run off Mike Boddicker. But Baltimore got that run back in the second inning when a knuckleball from Charlie Hough got past Don Slaught and allowed an Oriole to score from third. Hough and Boddicker battled through seven innings, keeping the score tied 1-1.

Texas had a chance to take the lead when Parrish led off the eighth with a long double to center field. Brower, the rookie who had scored 130 runs at Oklahoma City the year before, was sent in to pinch run. Slaught flied out, bringing third baseman Steve Buechele to the plate. Buechele sent a line drive screaming into left field. For a moment, he thought he had given the Rangers a 3-1 lead, but the ball caromed sharply off the top of the fence to left fielder Ken Gerhart. When third-base coach Tim Foli saw Gerhart trying to throw out Buechele at second base, he began wildly signaling Brower to keep running. But Brower couldn't immediately see Foli, and hesitated as he headed into third. Brower headed for home when the throw skipped past second baseman Rick Burleson, but was beat there by Eddie Murray's throw and catcher Terry Kennedy's swipe tag.

"I barely nicked him with the tag," Kennedy said. "If he'd been there a half-step sooner, he'd have jumped over me."

Brower pointed a finger at Foli. "I couldn't see him," he said. "He was way down the line. I had to hesitate."

Hough was replaced by Greg Harris after a leadoff single by Alan Wiggins in the eighth inning. Wiggins advanced to third base two outs later, but Buechele got Harris out of the inning by making an incredible catch on a foul pop by Murray. Buechele back-handed the ball a half-step before he collided with the rolled-up tarp, which flipped him into a box seat. It was a heart-pumping play.

It was also a meaningless play.

With one out in the ninth and pinch runner Rene Gonzales on first base, Harris made a lazy throw to first baseman Pete O'Brien. The throw bounced in the dirt five feet to the right of O'Brien, who was screened off by Gonzales, and went to the fence. Gonzales moved all the way to third base on the error by Harris, then scored the winning run on Larry Sheets' sacrifice fly.

This was not a good way to start a season—although it would prove prophetic. "If they're all like that," Valentine said, "we'll have an exciting season."

Texas used Sheets' misplay of a fly ball by Scott Fletcher to take a 6-4 victory in the second game of the season, but returned to Arlington 1-2 after the Orioles pounded Mike Mason 8-6 in the final game of the series.

Back home the next night, Jose Guzman failed to make it through the first inning of the home opener. He was replaced by Mike Loynd before many in the crowd of 42,415 had fought through the traffic jams along Interstate 30. Guzman retired only two of the first nine Milwaukee hitters, falling behind 3-0 before he got the first out. By the time the inning was over, the Brewers led 8-0 and Guzman had a 94.60 earned run average. Milwaukee went on to an 11-8 victory.

Hough got bombed the next night, with some help from Guzman. Valentine put Guzman into the game in relief when Hough was knocked out in the fourth inning, and by the time that inning ended the Brewers had scored eight runs. Texas battled back but couldn't overcome the damage, losing 8-6 when Oddibe McDowell popped up with two on in the ninth. The Rangers lost an agonizing 7-5 contest on Sunday afternoon. Paul Molitor greeted Harris with a game-tying homer in the eighth inning and the Brewers went on to win in the twelfth, sending Texas back on the road with a 1-5 record.

Valentine used a rainout in Boston to try to quiet rumors about his possible return to Los Angeles as Tommy Lasorda's hand-picked replacement. The rumors had heated up since the spring, when Eddie Chiles had put the team back on the market. They had come to a head when Dodgers General Manager Al Campanis lost his job after telling Ted Koppel's "Nightline" audience that blacks lack the "necessities" to manage baseball teams. Los Angeles writers speculated that Lasorda would soon move into the front office, leaving the manager's job open for Valentine.

Valentine thought such talk had become a distraction for his struggling team. "I would not under any circumstances take that job with the Dodgers," Valentine said, "just as I wouldn't accept the nomination of the Republican Party in the next presidential election, and just as I wouldn't take the job as the next head football coach at SMU. None of them will be offered. . . . I hope this is my team for a long time. I love these guys. I live and die with them, and I expect to live a lot more with them. When I came here, I took this to be a relatively permanent thing. I didn't think it would be a quick fix. I thought it would be a long, hard battle. But it will be won. The battle will be won."

He said a phone call from a player's wife to his wife, Mary, had convinced him it was time to make his commitment known. "She said something like if Mary wasn't around when she came back in May, goodbye, good luck," Valentine said. "That disturbed me a little."

Nothing disturbed him as much as the team's direction. Things didn't get any better in Boston. Al Nipper, never one to inspire fear, beat the Rangers 4-1. He gave up nine hits in eight innings but benefitted from an absence of timely hitting by Texas batters, who went 0-for-10. Don Baylor's three-run homer off Edwin Correa was all the support Nipper needed. Texas took a 4-1 lead against Bruce Hurst the next day but Hough could not protect it. He was gone after going 2-1 on Dwight Evans with the bases loaded in the sixth inning—a decision Valentine would quickly second-guess. Evans drove the second pitch from Dale Mohorcic over the Green Monster for a grand slam, giving the Red Sox all the offense they needed for a 5-4 victory.

The Rangers stumbled on, getting no help from the American League schedule. In Milwaukee, the Brewers were the Rangers' mirror image. Rookie manager Tom Trebelhorn had gotten the Brewers off to a 9-0 start, including a no-hitter by second-year left-hander Juan Nieves, that was the talk of baseball. A crowd of over 41,000 came to County Stadium to see a Friday-night mismatch of left-handers—Ted Higuera vs. Mike Mason.

Parrish homered off Higuera in the second inning, giving the Rangers a brief lead. Mason caved in after five shutout innings, giving up three runs in the sixth inning. Milwaukee, which had scored twenty-six runs in the weekend series in Arlington, went on to a 10-2 victory, scoring seven runs off the Texas bullpen in the eighth inning. Dan Plesac nailed down a 4-3 victory for Bill Wegman the next day.

The Rangers hit bottom Sunday, when Harris blew a 4-1 lead late in the game. Pete Incaviglia's two-run homer had put Texas in control, but the lead crumbled in the ninth.

Mitch Williams started the inning by walking Glenn Braggs. Greg Brock, a left-handed batter, followed with a single grounded past Browne. Williams jerked with anger when Valentine brought Harris in to face the right-handed-hitting Rob Deer, who drove a hanging curveball from Harris to the top of the left-field bleachers, tying the score 4-4. "That one just hung," Harris said. "I threw the first one outside, and I tried to throw that one inside to him, and it didn't break. I throw something that breaks, I get him out."

Harris got within one out of getting out of the inning, but then walked Jim Gantner on five pitches. Shortstop Dale Sveum, the Brewers' #9 hitter, then lined a chest-high fastball into the right-field seats for his sixth career home run. Milwaukee had won, 6-4, raising its record to 12-0 while dropping the Rangers to 1-11.

It was the ninth straight loss for Texas.

Afterward, while the stadium rocked, Harris sat by himself in the dugout, trying to figure out why he had thrown Sveum a 3-2 fastball instead of the curveball that earned him $620,000 a year. "That's how I got him out in our park," Harris said. "I just jammed him all day and got him out. I just didn't get it done. I just didn't have enough to get him out."

Inside the cramped visitor's clubhouse, players and coaches walked around with blank faces. Hardly a word was spoken as they showered and headed to the waiting bus.

"Now the streak has got to be over," Buechele said twenty minutes after Sveum's home run, his eyes still glassy. "It has to be. You get all the writers in the whole wide world and have them put together a story and they couldn't put together a worse ending than that. It happened, and now it's over with. That's the end. It's got to be."

O'Brien echoed that theme.

"The streak is going to be over. We're not going to lose 161 ball games," he said. "We know the streak is going to end. But it's frustrating when you can feel a ball club start playing pretty good baseball through eight innings. We felt we would win it. But we'll be back. That's not going to keep us away from the ballpark."

Basically, with a slight comic twist two days later, that was the 1987 season for the Rangers. Following an off day at home, all coaches and players were required to attend the annual "Welcome Home" banquet April 21 in Arlington. It turned out to be not only a gloomy event, but also a costly one. McDowell opened an eight-stitch gash in one of his fingers buttering a dinner roll at the banquet, and was out of the lineup for nine consecutive games. Talk about bad starts.

Hough ended the losing streak at nine games when the Rangers opened a homestand with a victory over Baltimore. Texas began playing well, winning seven of eight games after the losing streak, but by the All-Star break had only been able to raise its record to 41-45, trailing first-place Minnesota by the deceptive margin of 6½ games. It shed some excess baggage along the way, returning Scott Anderson to the minor leagues after he compiled a 9.53 ERA in his first eight appearances and trading Mason (0-2, 5.59) to the Chicago Cubs after he balked at an assignment to Oklahoma City.

Valentine searched for the positives in a season that had gotten away. "If we didn't have the type of guys we have, there were a few times in the first half that we could have said, 'Wait till next year,' " Valentine said. "The guys have stayed confident. I really believe they have been prepared for the long run. The long run is only about half done. The fan support has been a major contributor to our continued optimism. The fans haven't given up on us, so we haven't given up on ourselves."

Despite the 1-11 start, attendance had never been better at Arlington Stadium. The Rangers averaged 24,285 for their first forty-one dates – a pace that would have given them a season attendance of 1.9 million had they maintained it.

Steve Howe and the Rangers had something in common: desperation. Howe, a one-time National League Rookie of the Year, was out of baseball because of his addiction to cocaine, and the Rangers needed left-handed pitching. It was a marriage born as much of convenience as of conviction.

Howe, last seen blowing a chance in Minnesota, had been either suspended or released four times since 1983 because of his drug problem. But scout Doug Gassaway had raved about Howe's fastball and slider in Mexico, and the Rangers were curious enough to take a look. Howe's agent, John Lence, arranged a tryout in Los Angeles, and the Rangers sent out quite an entourage: club president Mike Stone, General Manager Tom Grieve, and alcohol-drug abuse counselor Sam McDowell.

Grieve said he was convinced to pursue Howe after watching him throw for about fifteen minutes. "It didn't take a genius to see he was throwing the ball really well," he said. "What convinced us he was a good person and ready to continue his commitment off the field (came from McDowell and Stone). They talked to doctors and talked to Steve. Sam staked his reputation on Steve. That was enough for me."

Before the Rangers could sign Howe, the twenty-nine-year-old left-hander had to convince John Johnson, president of the National Association of Professional Baseball Leagues, to lift a suspension placed on Howe after he'd failed a drug test while pitching for the San Jose Bees. That done, Howe still needed Commissioner Peter Ueberroth's permission to return to the major leagues. The Rangers did not see that as a problem, since they wanted Howe to pitch first at Class AAA Oklahoma City anyway. Grieve understood that Ueberroth would rule on Howe's eligiblity in "one week to one month . . . hopefully."

Texas called a news conference to announce Howe's signing on July 13, the final Sunday before the All-Star break. Howe, his wife, Cyndy, and his two children, including a one-month son, arrived looking as if they had just been to Sunday school. Howe wore a solemn blue blazer over a charcoal shirt, smiled frequently, and had all the answers. This time, he swore, things were going to be different.

"The programs don't change. You as a person have to change. People I know have told me that I've changed. It's a maturing process," Howe said. "This is my last step for a success story. I got back. I never quit. I am proud of the effort. Nobody can ever take that away from me."

Howe knew he would face skeptics. "People are going to have questions about me no matter what I do or when I come back," he said. "I can't let what people think of me or my situation affect me. If I do, then I am taking away from myself and . . . it might be better to stay away from the game. Yes, I did fail, but on the positive side, yes I did come back, and yes there is life after chemical dependency. So we as a people, myself even, tend to look at the negative side of everything and hammer it. I wouldn't be here if I wasn't sure I can succeed. If I didn't have the feeling inside of myself, I wouldn't be here. All I can say is watch and see."

Grieve, too, put up a confident front after Howe signed a minor-league contract that gave the Rangers options for both 1988 and '89.

"The only thing we're liable for is a minor league contract," Grieve said. "None of the money is guaranteed, although we hope that we'll pay it for him to help in the major leagues. It's a chance to get an extra draft choice, a #1 draft choice. You don't get an opportunity like that very often. He's got a lot of pitching left."

Three years earlier, Howe had told a reporter about a man who was reading a newspaper while his son pestered him to play. The father kept reading, until he finally realized he had to occupy his son. He cut out a page with a picture of the world on it, cut the picture into a dozen pieces, and gave it to his son. "Put this together and then we'll play," he told the boy.

It was only a few minutes before the child returned with the picture intact. "How did you do that so quickly?" the father asked. "Easy," said the boy. "On the other side of the world was a picture of a man. Put the man together and the whole world falls into place."

Howe was still trying to put the man together.

Early on, there wasn't much doubt about the pitcher. The night after the news conference, while Larry Parrish represented the Rangers in the All-Star Game at Oakland, Howe demonstrated to Grieve and a crowd of 7,427 at All Sports Stadium in Oklahoma City that he could handle the public part of his bargain. In his first work in the United States since July 1986, Howe pitched three hitless innings and was the winning pitcher in Oklahoma City's 5-4 victory over Iowa. He struck out two and walked none, throwing 24 strikes and 14 balls. He seldom went to his changeup or his curveball, sticking with low fastballs and sliders. "I think," he said, "the question has been answered about whether I can still pitch."

It was a good night for Grieve, who watched from the box seats behind home plate. "This may sound bad after he does good, but I knew he could do it," Grieve said. "It's not a big surprise after seeing him throw. He threw low strikes both times I saw him throw."

Before long, Valentine and Grieve grew anxious to see Howe in a Rangers' uniform. But every time Stone called Ueberroth, he was told to be patient.

With Valentine publicly hinting that he had to have Howe, the Rangers demanded a meeting with Ueberroth. Chiles and Stone flew to New York on August 5, where an animated session in Ueberroth's office left them back where they had begun. Stone was steaming. He was also in a vise, with Valentine and

Ueberroth taking turns at the handle. Valentine didn't say much on the record, but he clearly felt his authority to pick his own players would be undermined if he could not activate Howe.

Stone eventually sided with Valentine. On August 6, the Rangers called a news conference to announce that they were promoting Howe from Oklahoma City. Howe, who had been squirreled away in an Arlington apartment for two days, again attended the news conference. "I'm grateful for their faith in me," he said. " . . . If you are loyal to me, you will get your money's worth from me."

Chiles said of the decision, which would later cost him a $250,000 fine, "We think we're doing the right thing. We think it's legally, ethically and morally sound. We reached our judgment and this is it. I can't tell you what the commissioner will do. I have no idea. In this case, I felt the ball was in our court. It was our turn at bat, and we took it."

Grieve said the Rangers were not concerned about the reaction within baseball. "I think all of us feel what we're doing is in the best interest of our franchise, our fans," he said. "As Eddie says, we don't wake up every day worrying about what twenty-five other ball clubs think. If they don't agree with it, that's their problem, not our's."

Locally, the decision to fight Ueberroth was popular. A *Dallas Times Herald* phone survey found 73.2 percent of callers in favor of the stance taken by the Rangers. "This is ridiculous," said one of the callers, a sixty-one-year-old woman. "I think something like this could send him back to drugs."

It was all good fodder for the autobiography Howe had in the works. But nothing happened during the last two months of the season that was quite as dramatic as what it took for the Rangers to get Howe. He was just another mediocre pitcher on a mediocre pitching staff. In twenty-four appearances, Howe compiled a 3-3 record with one save and a 4.31 ERA. It wasn't a triumphant return, but it was good enough for the Rangers to exercise their option on a two-year contract, guaranteeing Howe $900,000 if he would only stay clean.

Howe went home to Montana after the season. Much of his time was spent working on snowmobiles in a friend's shop. All seemed to be well until the middle of January, when the Rangers flew him in to Arlington to attend a mini-camp with some other pitchers.

Howe attended the first session on a Monday, impressing team officials with his conditioning—he had lost eight pounds in the off-season—and his attitude. "He was healthy, optimistic, looked great," Grieve said. "We felt very confident we were well on the way to having a successful end to the Steve Howe story." But Howe failed to show up at the stadium the next two days, including a scheduled workout on Wednesday. He called equipment man Joe Macko to say he would be running late, that he was looking for houses. Valentine and Tom House waited in the clubhouse for him until 6 P.M., but he neither arrived nor answered the phone in his hotel room. That night Grieve called Howe's agent, John Lence, and was told that Howe had run late because of a trip to a storage facility.

But the Rangers found out that Howe had gone Tuesday night with some of

his teammates to Lace, a topless bar near the ballpark. There, he had apparently gotten quite drunk, which was a clear violation of his aftercare program. He
then disappeared for almost forty-eight hours, and never accounted for his
activities during that time span.

Howe refused to discuss the details of his absence with reporters but provided his own version of the truth in his 1989 book, *In Between the Lines: One
Athlete's Struggle to Escape the Nightmare of Addiction.* He wrote that he and his
roommate for the mini-camp, pitcher Brad Arnsberg, began drinking whiskey
that night, then went to Lace. Howe said he then began using "crank," and went
into "hiding."

Wrote Howe, "When confronted by Tom Grieve, Bobby Valentino, and Sam
McDowell, I tried out a story, which at the time I was pretty proud of. It went
like this: I had a couple of drinks in the room, and then we went to Lace. I met
some people, and we all went to a party. At the party, a wild dancer from the
club must have slipped something into my drink because I was suddenly so
whacked out that I decided I couldn't return to the camp and take the urine
test."

When Howe did take the urine test, it was positive for amphetamines and
alcohol. It was time for another news conference—by the third team in three
years to release Howe because of his addiction. Valentine was in Switzerland
skiing, and Stone did not choose to attend. Grieve had to go this one alone. "It
was not a situation where we had a lot of room for leeway," he said. "It was not
three strikes and you're out. It was one strike."

The incident seemed to shock everyone around the Rangers. "I will swear
on the Bible he was doing great," said McDowell, the former major-league
pitcher-turned-therapist. "For the first time in Steve's life, he was in a state of
recovery."

To Grieve, Howe had appeared less jumpy, more relaxed on Monday. "I can-
not believe it," he said. "The guy looked perfect on Monday. I would have bet a
lot of money, and made a lot of stupid statements, based on what I saw. It was
a shock."

And a sad sidelight to a sad season.

The one consistent bright spot in the entire 1987 season was second-year
outfielder Ruben Sierra. He had flashed his potential by hitting 16 homers and
driving in 55 runs after joining the Rangers for the last four months of the
1986 season, and now he was backing it up. From July 7 to September 10, he
hit .306 with 17 homers and 56 RBIs in sixty games.

It was proof that scouts had been justified in raving about the young outfielder from Rio Piedras, Puerto Rico. Many people compared him to Roberto
Clemente, whose #21 had been adopted by Sierra. He played the same position,
right field, had the same strong build, an arm almost as strong, and a stroke
that made the bat sing.

Actually, it's incorrect to say that Sierra adopted Clemente's #21. In truth,

Valentine forced it on him after a slow start to the 1987 season. Edwin Correa, a neighbor of Clemente's in San Juan, had worn the number but agreed to give it up for his countryman.

"I knew Ruben wanted it last year," Valentine said. "They both wanted it because Roberto is such a big part of the culture in Puerto Rico. I just felt it would be glorifying his name a little more if that number was on the field every day rather than every fifth day."

Valentine fell in love with Sierra on first sight in Pompano Beach that spring of 1986. The relationship was cemented in a conversation at the end of Sierra's rookie season. Valentine told Sierra he was impressed with the player's skills, but that Sierra needed to refine them. Sierra said he was willing to do whatever it took.

"A lot of people are going to look at me," he said. "I want people to look at me and say, 'This guy is good. He's going to be the greatest player.' That's what I want to be."

Along with Charlie Hough, Sierra was among the few real blessings the Valentine-Grieve regime had been left by their predecessors. Scout Orlando Gomez had signed him in 1983, two years after bringing Jose Guzman from Puerto Rico to the Texas organization. He had been a raw talent in those days, noticed for his tools, not his statistics. He never hit more than thirteen homers in a minor-league season and averaged .261 below the majors. But he was special, and that was noticeable.

Joe Klein may have put it best. "Ruben Sierra," he said, "is a piece of marble that is capable of being molded into a statue."

Chicago White Sox manager Jim Fregosi raved about Sierra. "I thought he was the best player I saw in the American Association, on a par with Eric Davis," Fregosi said. "Numbers. You don't write up reports on guys who had successful years . . . You write up reports on the talents and physical abilities. Once things fall in place, those guys don't spend enough time in the minor leagues to have big numbers."

Sierra's development began with simple survival after his father died in an automobile accident when he was four. He was raised by his mother, in government-subsidized apartments where the rent was as little as $10-$20 per month. "There is poverty," Gomez, the scout who signed Sierra, told *Dallas Morning News'* writer Tracy Ringolsby. "Even if you are a native, if you go into that area, you have to be careful."

"You can see any kind of [stuff] there," said Sierra. "Anything you can think of. If a guy gives me trouble, I move right away. I never turn my back. I say, 'Hello. See you later. I have to do something.' "

Sierra spent many days playing baseball at the Roberto Clemente Sports Academy in San Juan, refining skills he knew even then were special. "Nobody teach me baseball, I was born like that," he said. "It is something God give to me. I think all the time that I want to take advantage of what God give me. Not everybody else has that."

Toronto scouts had established a rapport with Sierra when he was fifteen, and thought they had the inside track to sign him when he turned seventeen. But Gomez topped the Blue Jays' $15,000 offer and signed him for $22,500.

A natural right-handed hitter, Sierra learned to switch-hit in his first season with the Rangers' organization. While others struggle for years to make the conversion, Sierra was such a natural that he began hitting for a higher average from the left side of the plate. His first hits from both sides of the plate in the majors were home runs.

"He can see somebody do something and do it himself, right then," Hough said of his teammate. "Ever see him dance? He could be a professional dancer. I'm not so sure the best way to coach Ruben isn't to show him movies of great players. Show him films of Clemente and Mantle."

Broadcaster Mark Holtz had christened Sierra "The Golden Child," which referred to both a popular movie at the time and Sierra's love for gold jewelry. He wore several heavy chains around his neck and rings on every finger. He was as hard to miss off the field as on it.

Sierra spoke English but often acted as if he didn't, trying not to embarrass himself by saying the wrong thing. This created a certain skepticism among his new teammates.

"Last year, there were definitely some questions about him off the field," Larry Parrish said. "There were a lot of questions. But this year he has shown up at the park ready to play."

Veteran Darrell Porter agreed. "He works hard. That's the reason he's having the good year. That's what will determine if he has a great career," Porter said. "The guys who work hard are the ones who have great careers. I think Ruben will be that kind of guy.

"He wants to be like his man. A lot of people talk about idols. I think the one he's trying to follow, he's very, very serious about. He wants to play like Clemente did."

Sierra had played in 219 consecutive games before returning to Puerto Rico in September for an uncle's funeral. He struggled to get back into his groove after returning to finish the year, and on the last Friday of the season reached one goal with his thirtieth homer, a shot off Seattle rookie Clay Parker. It made him one of only five players in history to drive in at least 100 runs and hit 30 homers in a season before age twenty-two. The others: Hall of Famers Jimmie Foxx, Mel Ott, Eddie Mathews, and Hal Trosky.

"I'm glad he got that homer," Valentine said. "It was big for him."

The same was true for the year, which he finished with 109 RBIs despite hitting only .263. How much better would he be when he did something about that average?

Despite big offensive years from Sierra, Parrish (who set a club record with 32 homers), O'Brien (23 homers, 88 RBIs) and Incaviglia (27 homers, 80 RBIs), the Rangers never got over the hump in 1987. They got back to .500 with a dramatic victory over Milwaukee on July 26, but it seemed to take all the team's energy to reach 49-49. Once there, they nose-dived, losing six of seven games, and never recovered. They went 12-17 in August and 14-18 in October and September, finishing the season on an especially sorry note. Seattle won seven straight against Texas during the final two weekends of the season, dropping the Rangers from fourth place into a tie for last with California, the team it had chased down the stretch only a season before.

"As a group, we have not played well," said Hough, who finished the year with eighteen victories. "For some strange reason, we haven't combined the good hitting with the good pitching to win close games—the 3-2, 2-1 games. We haven't won the 9-8 games either. We've been at times erratic defensively, and yet I look out there and think we have a good defensive team. We have given up the extra run that inevitably comes back to haunt us. But I see no reason we can't, with the personnel we have, the guy handling the ball club, correct these problems. I certainly feel good about being part of the future."

No one beat Hough for finding fresh air in a sewer.

No one expected a 75-87 season when the Rangers went to spring training—except *Times Herald* columnist Skip Bayless, who predicted it exactly—but there was some consolation. The franchise set an attendance record of 1.76 million, which allowed Valentine to spend the winter asking why Chiles shouldn't have patience. After all, Valentine would say, we have made money for him the last two seasons. Valentine was right, of course, but that was irrelevant.

No matter how many times Valentine had preached to his team about not having reached its destination, the Rangers had lost their edge.

10

Shock Treatment

If 1988 were to be any better, improvements in the Rangers would have to come from within. Tom Grieve spent the winter like a modern-day Nero, fiddling while his franchise grew older, if not better. His only trade sent Don Slaught to the New York Yankees for right-hander Brad Arnsberg.

Slaught had fallen from favor because of rookie Mike Stanley's bigger bat, but he would go on to become the Yankees' regular catcher. Arnsberg arrived in Texas nursing an elbow injury he sustained while relieving for the Yankees the previous August. That didn't make Grieve regret the trade. He just wanted to find a new home for Slaught and his $531,500 salary. Grieve's only other significant decision that winter was not to offer Greg Harris a contract, freeing the late innings for Mitch Williams.

At the winter meetings at the Loews Anatole in Dallas, Grieve's activity was limited to a lukewarm pursuit of free agents Dave Righetti, Atlee Hammaker, and Bob Horner. Righetti and Hammaker re-signed with the Yankees and Giants, respectively, and Horner passed on a guaranteed $600,000 to accept a bigger salary with the St. Louis Cardinals after Jack Clark jumped to the Yankees.

During spring training, *Dallas Times Herald* columnist Frank Luksa facetiously demanded that Grieve face a firing squad for his off-season malingering. "Suspect failed to answer telephone or mail," wrote Luksa. "Family alarmed. Friends worried. Search warrant obtained. Approached door to Rangers general manager office. 'Do Not Disturb' sign in evidence. Forced entry made. Phone covered with cobwebs. Filing cabinets rusted shut. Lights out. Cuddly family of bats in residence. Suspect found unconscious between dead potted plant and dusty fishbowl. Disoriented when awakened. Shown picture he had clutched to bosom, suspect screamed. Figure in autographed photo later identified as Greg Harris."

Pitching was the top priority in the winter and spring, with minor-league instructor Dick Egan added as bullpen coach and an assistant pitching coach. After all, the 1987 Rangers had outscored every American League West team and had still tied with California for last place. "It was one of those years," pitching coach Tom House said. "Everything that could go wrong did go wrong. If it repeats itself, I don't deserve to be where I am, and some of these pitchers don't deserve to be where they are."

House continued to talk up his team, but counted only Charlie Hough and Jose Guzman as proven starters. "I think we have enough talent," House said. "I don't know about that phrase 'proven talent.' But I've seen what other organizations have, the raw tools, and we're as good as or better than anybody around. What we've seen is how valuable experience is."

Valentine hoped the Rangers' interest in veterans like Righetti and Hammaker would shake up a pitching staff that included youngsters Bobby Witt, Paul Kilgus, Edwin Correa, Guzman, and Williams. "There might have been a message sent out—that we're looking to improve," Valentine said. "We want pitching to be one of our stronger suits this year."

House carried the point further. "It's time for the youngsters to start having some results to show for their talents. I've always been a supportive pitching coach, but I'm going to . . . tell them it's not just having potential or how they look in a big-league uniform that counts. It's winning ballgames."

Valentine, too, said he planned to stop coddling his young players, pitchers in particular. "If I don't see improvement in the normal progression, they might need a shock treatment, or whatever you call it when you get a door slammed in your face," he said. "But I don't think we will have to do that. Two years ago, the ideal progression would be for the group of young pitchers to be where Guzman and Mitch Williams are. If Correa and Witt had progressed as much as Guzman and Williams, we wouldn't be having this conversation."

Spring training was not encouraging. Designated hitter Larry Parrish had supplied much of the offense over the last two years, hitting sixty homers and driving in 194 runs in 1986-87. He underwent arthroscopic surgery on his right knee the week before camp opened. At thirty-four years of age and 225 pounds, he was straining on his swing.

Then there was Correa, who had missed the last half of the 1987 season with a stress fracture in his shoulder. He had rested during the winter, then gotten permission to throw the month before camp opened. When he got to Florida, he convinced Valentine that he would be back in the starting rotation when the season opened. "I think his arm is very sound," Valentine said after Correa took his regular turn four times in eleven days. "That he's sound is very good news. I was not sure Eddie could keep on this pace."

But pitching against his old team, the Chicago White Sox, on a sunny March 23 at Sarasota's Payne Park, Correa gave up six runs in three innings. In the semi-privacy of the clubhouse, he broke down and cried. His shoulder hurt and he could not deny it. "Between innings it's like a nightmare," Correa said.

Correa knew he would not accompany the Rangers to Arlington for the season opener against the Chicago White Sox. "I wanted to go with the club, I wanted to perform, I just wanted to do it," Correa said. "I want to be the Eddie who two years ago was unbelievable."

One week later, Correa received bad news from Dr. Frank Jobe. Jobe recommended exploratory surgery, which he said could be career-threatening if he found what he suspected: a tear in the shoulder lining. "I don't know what to say about this," Correa said. "I am just going to pray that I will be all right."

Valentine was shocked by the long-range implications. "The last thing I expected was for him to walk in here and tell me there might be a new problem."

Still, Valentine left Florida feeling good about his team. It was a strange optimism, considering that the final roster included retread Steve Kemp and such minor-league journeymen as first baseman Larry See and pitchers Mike Jeffcoat, DeWayne Vaughn, and Guy Hoffman.

"The easiest thing to say is we aren't as good as people thought we were in 1986, that we'll need a few years to get really good," Valentine said. "I think that's bull. We have a very good ballclub, and we have been good for the last two years, minus forty-five days . . . I don't see any team in the division I like better, or in the league, for that matter."

Valentine rejected an idea that his third full season as manager would be crucial for his personal survival and credibility. "To me, this is the same as any year I'll ever manage," he said. "This . . . is not a do-or-die year for [me or for] Bobby Witt, Oddibe McDowell, Pete Incaviglia, Pete O'Brien, or any of our players. I do think I'll manage every game as if it's do-or-die. That's the way I've managed every one of them."

Club president Mike Stone agreed with Valentine's assessment, saying there was no pressure from Chiles to produce immediate results.

"Bobby and Tag [Grieve] put a great deal of pressure on themselves," Stone said. "They're both winners. But a crucial year? No . . . "

Everything clicked on Opening Night. O'Brien homered twice, Cleveland contributed two unearned runs, and Hough and Williams combined for three pickoffs in a 4-3 victory over the Indians at Arlington Stadium. It seemed the kind of victory that separated 1987's 75-87 finish from the 87-75 season that had preceded it.

But Cleveland bounced back to win the next two games 5-1 and 4-1 behind young pitchers Greg Swindell and John Farrell, and the Rangers finished that first homestand 2-4 and April 8-13.

Less than a week into May, Valentine had to use the "shock treatment" he had talked about in the winter. Witt had shown nothing in his first six starts, struggling with his control as badly as ever. Valentine decided something had to be done after a terrible outing against Milwaukee May 5 ran his record to 0-5 and his ERA to 7.68. Witt had walked 35 batters in 36⅓ innings, and Valentine could no longer watch it. He optioned his "Hope diamond" to Class AAA Oklahoma City, but said he hoped Witt would be back by the first of June.

Witt was dumbfounded. "There's nothing I can do about it," Witt said. "It's just throwing strikes. That's the whole thing."

House felt that he had tried everything. His latest attempt had included subliminal tapes tailored to improving Witt's concentration. "When all the other pieces look like they should fit, and there seems to be a block, it's got to be that somewhere in his conscious or subconscious mind he's not allowing his body to do what it was born to do," House said. "With a guy like Bobby, why wait five to eight years for [success] to happen? This will speed up the process."

Valentine was himself dumbfounded when he was greeted with a contract extension after returning from a 2-5 road trip to New York, Baltimore, and Milwaukee. The Rangers were 10-16. At Stone's urging, Chiles had decided to head off any rumors by extending Valentine's contract through the 1991 season.

Chiles said he held himself more responsible than Valentine for the team's poor start. As much as anything, he said, the problems were financial. The Rangers' payroll of about $6.5 million, like the team's record, was the lowest in the major leagues.

"I don't blame Bobby because he doesn't have all the talent in the world," Chiles said. "We compete on limited resources in this franchise . . . he does extremely well with what he has to deal with."

Valentine was one week from becoming the first of thirteen Rangers managers to spend a full three years with the organization.

"I'd say this organization is starting to put [its past] behind [it]," Grieve said, "just like we're starting to put behind us the practice of trading our best young players for veteran players. We're still trying to put behind us [our past instability] . . . You can't do that after a year or two."

Chiles had changed since the early days when he called team meetings and put armed guards at Arlington Stadium.

"In the last two years, Eddie Chiles has been very supportive of the Rangers' management," said Grieve. "Eddie Chiles has let Rangers management make all the decisions . . . He hasn't tried to make the decisions himself. I think people realize that."

The Valentine extension puzzled players but was well received in the clubhouse. "He's a good manager, but he's a jockey," offered O'Brien. "It's like Sparky (Anderson) said, put a Clydesdale in the Kentucky Derby with a great jockey and he's still a Clydesdale. It goes back to the fact that we have to start playing better."

Valentine was delighted. "This is my team," he said. "I want to win with this team. As far as my commitment, my life is committed. I don't know how long I'm going to live. But one thing I want to do is win (the World Series). I've never quit at anything."

In 1988, he might as well have quit. His team ran off a string of eight consecutive victories over New York, Baltimore, and Kansas City after the Valentine extension, raising their record to 18-16. The eighth victory in that streak, a 6-3 win by new starter Jeff Russell over the Royals, matched the club record for consecutive victories. "Once you get a tie, you might as well break it," Valentine said. "This is probably as good a team as this franchise has had since it's been here, so it should have the longest streak."

Oh, sure. Kansas City beat Hough 5-4 the next night, and the Rangers proceeded to lose 19 of 32 games. They fell to 31-35, eleven games behind the Oakland Athletics. Included in the stretch was some hideous short relief, illustrated by a 10-8 loss to the White Sox on June 4 at Comiskey Park.

The Rangers took an 8-4 lead into the ninth that night, but Williams allowed a leadoff homer to Ivan Calderon, then gave up two singles and fell behind Donnie Hill two balls, no strikes. Valentine called for Dale Mohorcic, who finished the walk of Hill to load the bases. Rookie Mike Woodard singled to cut the lead to 8-6 and load the bases for Gary Redus. Redus drove a flat, 3-1 sinker into the left-field bleachers for a game-winning grand slam. "I don't know if I choked, or what," Mohorcic said. "Whatever it was, I'm sick of it."

Valentine continued to run an Oklahoma City shuttle. Jerry Browne, the Opening Day second baseman, was sent down June 9. Oddibe McDowell, one-time poster boy of the Rangers' youth movement, followed him one week later. By mid-June, seven of twenty-four players on the Opening Day roster had spent time in Oklahoma City.

"It's a sign that we're out to win," reasoned Hough. "Right now it's a thought that we're trying to develop players, but not at the expense of not winning today's game. They are looking at it like the most important game of the year is the one in the next couple of hours. I can't blame them."

Grieve concurred with the assessment. "Over the course of time the emphasis subtly shifts from development to winning. We're somewhere in the middle."

No matter how much they emphasized winning, it was difficult to do. With the All-Star break approaching, Valentine found his team 39-44. Its offense wasn't clicking, and he was tired of waiting for Larry Parrish to start producing. After sixty-eight games and 248 at bats, Parrish was hitting .197 with only seven homers and 26 RBIs. Fastballs he once crushed were now sailing past a slow bat, and Parrish rejected pleas from hitting instructor Art Howe and Valentine to try a lighter model.

A top-brass meeting was called for July 6 at Arlington Stadium to discuss Parrish. Valentine wanted to release him, and neither Grieve nor Stone objected. It would cost the club some money, but the three agreed that Valentine could do as he wanted. The move was to be made during the All-Star break, but after Baltimore's Oswaldo Peraza shut out Texas on July 8, Valentine decided he could not wait.

Parrish was gone the next day.

It was not the cleanest of breaks. The story of his impending release appeared in the *Times Herald* before Parrish got the word from Valentine, who leaned against a tarp down the right-field line to tell Parrish goodbye. Parrish had been an All-Star one year before, but in the end all the Rangers seemed to want was to hustle him out of town. There were few efforts by Grieve to trade him. "That didn't seem to be a very viable possibility in my mind," he said. "We did not shop him around to twenty-five major league teams . . . Because of his contract, he couldn't be traded [without his permission]. There really wasn't much of a market for his services. I knew what we were going to get in return at this point in time – nothing."

Parrish received the remainder of his $534,627 salary and a $250,000 buy-out on his $925,000 contract for 1989. Many of his teammates felt Valentine gave up on him too early. "He's got some good years in him," O'Brien said. "I'm confident he will come out of it."

Parrish left the Rangers feeling he had been short-changed during his seven seasons in Texas. He walked out of the clubhouse in Baltimore carrying a chip on his shoulder – the result of the club's having declined to renegotiate a bad contract he signed in 1985. Among other things, that contract called for $100,000 to be subtracted annually from his base salary as deferred income; Parrish thought the deferred money was in addition to the base.

"When I got here (in 1982)," Parrish mused, "it was a funny organization. You couldn't make more than Buddy Bell because he had an agreement with Eddie Chiles. It was just a funny situation. (Finances) probably bothered me more than anything. This was supposed to be the year when I could have gotten some payback, or revenge. I could have finally made what a guy who hits a lot of home runs and drives in runs should be making."

While in Texas, Parrish played on one team with a winning record and three that finished in last place. "I'm going to walk away from this franchise saying I didn't win as much as I should have won there," he said just before leaving. "We never got a shot to win."

Chiles had yo-yoed on the issue of selling the team since the American League owners had rejected Gaylord Broadcasting's buyout attempt in 1986. He had entertained potential buyers the following spring in Port Charlotte, and appeared close to selling the team to a New York group headed by Warren Crane that April. But by May he had taken the franchise off the market again, saying, "I intend to keep them and win the American League pennant. It's a closed chapter."

It wasn't, of course. Chiles kept his pursuit of a buyer out of the papers in early 1988, but his age and shrinking fortune left him no real choice. His Western Company of North America filed for Chapter 11 bankruptcy February 2, two weeks before the Rangers headed to Florida to get ready for the 1988 season. Chiles insisted that the bankruptcy had no bearing on his baseball team, but he knew he couldn't hang onto it forever.

Chiles was waiting for a local buyer, but the oil collapse had taken most potential buyers down the same road as Chiles. In July, Chiles confirmed that he had been holding negotiations with members of the Tampa Bay Baseball Group, investors who had pledged to bring the major leagues to Tampa. He admitted that he had not included a clause restricting movement of the franchise in the negotiations. "Sometimes when you've got your neck in a noose," he said, "you can't call the shots."

Chiles and Tampa auto dealer Frank Morsani met in a Tampa hotel room August 24. Before they left, they shook hands on a $46.4-million deal for Chiles's controlling interest in the Rangers plus Arlington Stadium and its adjoining 119 acres. The deal was announced two days later in a simple press release. There was no news conference and no sign of the principal buyers, Morsani and New Jersey developer Bill Mack. It was obvious that the Mack-Morsani group might move the franchise to Tampa. Chiles dismissed it all as preliminary, saying that he expected Edward L. Gaylord to use the right of first refusal he had negotiated as part of his 1984 minority purchase of the team. "I think [he's] highly interested in the team, and it's going to be a very likely situation that [he] will end up with the team."

Gaylord did not exactly come rushing in to prove Chiles right. He said he expected to carefully weigh the matter, using most of the thirty days given him to make the decision. In the meantime, Morsani revealed his intentions in a round of calls to Dallas-Fort Worth reporters two days after the sale.

He said promising to keep the team in the area would be giving away a useful bargaining chip for his MXM Corporation. "You could [devalue the franchise] by making such a statement," he said.

Two days later, Morsani turned off even more fans with his plastic smile and cool, noncommittal stance at an Arlington Stadium news conference. Interest was so great it was carried live on both radio and television, and Morsani received a George Allen-like reception from fans. Wrote the *Fort Worth Star-Telegram*'s Jim Reeves, "He hit the ground slithering."

But give Morsani a certain amount of credit. It wasn't what he said that got him in trouble. It was what he didn't say—that he wouldn't move the team. It would have been easy to say one thing while planning to do another, but Morsani left it open.

It was the second time a Mack-Morsani group had attempted to purchase a major-league team, and the man involved in the other attempted purchase, former Minnesota Twins owner Calvin Griffith, sounded a warning for Ranger fans. "I think everyone who cares about baseball in that area should be worried about his intentions," he said. "All he wants is to get a team for Tampa."

The Dallas Morning News editorialized about the situation on the Monday after the sale. "The Rangers may be 20-something games out of first place," it wrote, "but dadgummit, they're our losers and we want them to stay here until they figure out how to get around the bases often enough to win the World Series."

Not everyone felt that way. "It's not like we're losing a winning team," said Arlington disc jockey Michael Hernandez. "It's not like we're losing the Mets or the Yankees. I love the game, but I can watch it on cable. I live and die with this team, but if they leave, it's no big loss. They almost cause me more aggravation than pleasure."

Gaylord indicated that he had heard a new bid to buy the Rangers would be more successful than his failed attempt two years earlier, but he kept Chiles and Morsani waiting for his answer. He had still not given it when Chiles and club president Mike Stone headed for a September owners' meeting in Montreal. There, Chiles did an incredible thing. He invited the assembled reporters up to his suite, and told them he'd made a mistake in selling the team to the MXM group without a clause in the contract stipulating that the team stay in Dallas-Fort Worth. "I'd feel a lot better and sleep a lot better if I had that clause in the deal," he said. "But a deal is a deal. I confess I made a bad one. I was a little careless in the negotiations, and it turned around and bit me. I should have foreseen that eventuality (of a move) and done something about it."

On September 14, Gaylord announced that his company was exercising its option to block the Mack-Morsani sale. While any attempt at relocation would have been fought by the commissioner and others who wanted baseball in the Dallas-Fort Worth area, the nation's television market, Gaylord's act was almost as significant to the fans as Tom Vandergriff's original wooing and winning of the Washington Senators. Gaylord explained later that he had felt obligated to keep the team out of the hands of "New Yorkers and other foreigners."

Morsani expressed no regret about his candor. "We've always gone into everything with the cards face up."

Chiles was the happiest of all about Gaylord's decision, although he knew that Gaylord still faced a rough road to approval by the American League ownership. He still might not have found a way to unload the team, but at least his "mistake" had been erased.

Texas did not find a replacement for Larry Parrish at designated hitter that season. It tried seventeen different players over the course of the season, including journeymen Barbaro Garbey, James Steels, Kemp, and See. They combined to bat an all-time league-low .196 — one point higher than the New York Mets' pitchers. That said a lot about their dismal mood during the season's second half.

The ultimate defeat came on August 23, when the Rangers took a 7-3 lead into the ninth against Kansas City. Williams, Mohorcic, Hoffman, and Craig McMurtry combined to walk six batters in an eight-run ninth inning for the Royals. In one incredible stretch, Mohorcic, Hoffman, and McMurtry threw thirteen consecutive balls as Kevin Seitzer walked to force in the tying run and George Brett walked to force in the winning run. Both Valentine and catcher Jim Sundberg, who had re-signed with the Rangers after being released by the Chicago Cubs, were ejected by umpire Tim Tschida during the inning. After his ejection, Sundberg threw his catcher's gear out of the dugout, one piece at a time.

"It was probably 1977 when I got that angry, when I physically showed my anger," Sundberg said. "It was just the frustration of the situation."

Valentine knew the feeling. "That," he said, shaking his head, "was terrible. That ninth inning was terrible."

During the second half of 1988, about the only bright spot on the team was

Witt. He returned from Oklahoma City July 10 with his career resurrected. After completing only two of his first sixty-two major-league starts, he reeled off nine consecutive complete games, and overall, finished twelve of his sixteen starts.

Witt drew rave reviews from around the league.

From Baltimore's Mickey Tettleton, July 10: "He's come up with a forkball that's outstanding. I thought he was great, the best I've ever seen him. You've got to sit on the fastball but the other pitch keeps you off balance. He's going to be tough."

From Detroit manager Sparky Anderson, August 9: "Witt really pitched well, just outstanding. He deserved to win the way he pitched."

From Minnesota manager Tom Kelly, August 19: "He's been pitching real well since he got recalled. He must have learned his lesson. I give him a lot of credit. He pitched a hell of a game."

Witt developed confidence he had never had before. "It seemed like before it was a struggle to get through five," he said. "Now I'm going out there feeling a lot better. I'm confident."

Despite Witt's revival, the Rangers continued to sink as the season dragged on toward its conclusion. A 14-14 August was followed by a 9-19 September which meant the team had to at least split a four-game series in Seattle to avoid finishing in last place.

Mark Langston dominated the Rangers in Game 1, leaving the teams tied for last place. But Mariners starter Mike Moore failed to get out of the second inning the next night, giving the advantage back to Texas. Dwayne Henry, on his annual visit from the minors, served up an eleventh-inning homer to Scott Bradley Saturday night, so the teams were again even. But Sierra hit a two-run homer in the first and Paul Kilgus and McMurtry combined on a five-hitter on the last day of the season to keep the Rangers out of the basement.

They finished the season 70-91. "It was a tough last couple weeks looking at salvaging something," Valentine said. "This was a good way to end it. Next year, we'll try to get things the same as they were in this game and different from most of the season."

Valentine knew there had to be changes in his team—big changes.

During that last weekend in Seattle, when he was just trying to keep his team out of last place, Valentine spoke candidly with two reporters. They talked of the future, and names like John Kruk, Jesse Barfield, Von Hayes, and Dale Murphy were bandied about. They talked of the past, and there Valentine found the best reason for hope.

"You know," he said, "this year might have gone exactly right."

No longer could Grieve and others kid themselves that the Rangers were close to the top. They finished 33½ games behind the Oakland A's, a team that had been rebuilt while the Rangers spun their wheels, and no amount of Band-Aids could put Texas in Oakland's league. It would take a renewed commitment to get better. It would be expensive.

And, one way or the other, it would be interesting.

11

Marching Through Atlanta

Tom Grieve never had made much of a blip on baseball's wintertime radar. But it didn't take long to see that the off-season of 1988-89 might be very different from any that had preceded it.

Don Mattingly was the first clue.

Not surprisingly, Yankees owner George Steinbrenner and Mattingly, baseball's best hitter, spent much of the 1988 season fighting with each other. Mattingly even said he'd welcome a trade out of pinstripes. Grieve's ears perked up. Mattingly was the kind of hitter the Rangers needed to add to their offense. He could not only hit a fastball, but he could hit a good fastball. He could hit for power (35 homers, 145 RBIs in 1985) but also for average (.352 in 1986), and he did not strike out very often. That was a key: In 1988, the Rangers topped a thousand in strikeouts for the third straight year, the first American League team to do that in twenty years.

But no matter how much Bobby Valentine might covet Mattingly, he had seldom considered actually getting him. This time was different. When Grieve went to the annual general managers' meeting in Palm Springs, he asked Yankee General Manager Bob Quinn about Mattingly. They talked about smaller deals—the Yankees wanted third baseman, Steve Buechele for Mike Pagliarulo—but Grieve kept twisting the conversation back to Mattingly.

Other teams were interested, of course, but by the end of the long weekend Quinn returned to New York thinking the Rangers' offer was the best of the bunch. Grieve was offering Pete O'Brien, Mitch Williams, and Jose Guzman in a three-for-one package. Quinn was hoping to turn it into a ten-player deal that would include Mattingly, Pagliarulo, and infielder Bobby Meacham for seven Rangers—O'Brien, Guzman, Williams, Buechele, outfielder Bob Brower, and two prospects.

Grieve did not publicly confirm the talks. But he did not deny them, and he did not seem to mind when the *Times Herald* ran a story on the front page of its November 7 sports section headlined: "Rangers exploring deal for Mattingly."

"We've had talks with lots of teams," Grieve admitted. "We are looking at any ways we can find to improve. That is what we have been doing, and what we will continue to do." He did not even rule out a proposal as outlandish as Quinn's seven-for-three deal. "I wouldn't necessarily rule out a trade like that," he said. "But they are few and far between."

It was only one month after the end of the season, but Grieve was clearly itching to begin remodeling his team. He didn't even want to wait until the upcoming winter meetings in Atlanta. "That is almost a magical date for making things happen, but we would like to do something before that," he said. "I'd love to go to the winter meetings with something already done."

This was going to be a different winter.

Before looking elsewhere, the Rangers had to put out a little fire at home. They had neglected to sign shortstop Scott Fletcher to a contract extension during the 1988 season, when he was hitting .276 and committing only eleven errors, and now it was going to cost them. A shortage of shortstops throughout baseball made even a singles hitter with limited range and a below-average arm—that is, Fletcher—a prized commodity.

Philadelphia, Cleveland, Montreal, and Toronto entered into a bidding war for Fletcher. Phillies General Manager Lee Thomas established the ground rules, saying that the only way to get Fletcher to leave Arlington, where he had recently purchased a home, was to offer significantly more than the Rangers. Fletcher had never made more than $575,000 during a seven-year career in which he spent much of two seasons on the bench, and he had never been selected to an All-Star team. But the market called for him to be paid like an All-Star.

Thomas made the first offer of more than $1 million a year to Fletcher. Sources close to the negotiations later revealed that the Phillies offered three years at $3.3 million when the highest offer on the table was the Rangers' two-year package worth $1.6 million. "I'm not trying to force Texas to go into their vaults," Thomas said. "but I don't really care what they think."

Thomas eventually raised his offer to $4.05 million for three years. Cleveland came close to that package and both Montreal and Toronto (which envisioned Fletcher as its second baseman) were in the same ballpark. Grieve had to compete with them. On the last day of November, Fletcher signed a contract that made him the highest-paid player in Texas Rangers history and the highest-paid athlete in Dallas history—Herschel Walker and Mark Aguirre included.

The agreement struck by Grieve and Fletcher's agent, Richie Bry, called for

Fletcher to receive $1.2 million in 1989 and a guaranteed $3.9 million over three years with a club option for a fourth year in 1992. Fletcher also demanded contract language that would allow him to be paid in the event of a baseball strike in 1990, as well as a clause that would allow him to veto trades to eight teams of his choosing. For its baseball issue the next spring, *Sports Illustrated* would get Fletcher to pose in a bank vault in his Rangers' uniform.

"He was a shortstop at a time several teams needed shortstops," Grieve said. "He was at the right place at the right time."

Fletcher offered no apologies for becoming baseball's latest millionaire. "A lot of clubs made very good offers to me," he said. "It wasn't like I was taking them that high. The value was there."

Bry saw the signing as a sign that teams were willing to bid against each other for premium players, as they had until the free-agent market dried up in 1985. "I think the free-agent process has obviously changed," he said. "It started changing before Scott. It started changing last year when the Dodgers signed a contract with [Kirk] Gibson. I can't say I was astonished. Scott was the only shortstop on the market, and he was a consistent one. I'm pleased for him."

To Grieve, retaining Fletcher had been essential to the building process that lay ahead. "Scott is a player who always gives you 100 percent effort," he emphasized. "He has performed admirably and has been a solid team player who is being rewarded for that effort. Hopefully this delivers a message to the players and also to the fans that we will hang onto our players."

* * *

Although they made $3 million offers to pitcher Mike Moore and second baseman Steve Sax, who were free agents, there was no mistaking the Rangers' priority. They wanted a solid hitter to put in the middle of their lineup–most likely behind free-swinging Ruben Sierra and in front of Pete Incaviglia–to correct their 22.6 percent decrease in run production from 1987 (823) to 1988 (637). With Incaviglia hitting behind him, Sierra batted only .213–a 73-point drop. Pitchers had figured out that Sierra wouldn't take a walk; if he did, they could recover by getting Incaviglia to chase an inside fastball or an outside curveball.

It didn't seem to matter what position the new Mr. X played. "The ideal guy is the best hitter available, period," said Grieve. "I don't have a preference whether he's a position player or a designated hitter." Valentine talked about a cross between Ted Williams and Lou Gehrig with a little Ron Cey mixed in for good measure. "It could be a .275 hitter who drives in runs and can hit a few dingers," theorized Valentine. "We're going to get good production out of Inky, if he's with us, but obviously there are certain pitches he doesn't handle well. Ruben has certain pitches he doesn't hit real well. O.B. has certain pitches he doesn't hit well. A solid hitter handles all pitches. That's what we want. But who the heck *doesn't* want those guys?"

Talks with the Yankees had gone nowhere, with Quinn hedging so long that Grieve took the three-for-one proposal off the table. Grieve next turned his attention to five-time batting champion Wade Boggs, who was being shopped by the Boston Red Sox after his embarrassing extramarital affair with girlfriend Margo Adams. Grieve was having productive talks with Indians General Manager Hank Peters regarding second baseman Julio Franco, a lifetime .295 hitter, and also had the names of Philadelphia's Von Hayes, California's Johnny Ray, San Diego's John Kruk, Toronto's Jesse Barfield, Atlanta's Dale Murphy, and Chicago's Harold Baines on his shopping list.

Because he figured it would take an experienced starting pitcher—most likely Guzman, although Bobby Witt's name came up, too—to get one of those hitters, Grieve also wanted to add a starting pitcher. That's where free agents like Moore and Houston's Nolan Ryan came in. Owner Eddie Chiles had authorized an increase in the paltry team payroll, and Grieve had earmarked much of it to buy an arm. He made a serious pitch for Moore before Moore signed with Oakland. Then, after telling at least one reporter that he didn't plan to bid for Ryan because he would only be giving the future Hall of Famer leverage with the Astros, Grieve turned his attention to Ryan.

In concrete terms, he spent the month between the general managers' meetings and the winter meetings spinning wheels. Nothing was settled when he headed for Atlanta on December 3. "I'm disappointed . . . " he said. "We've tried hard, worked hard, but so far we haven't been able to accomplish anything."

That changed. His first twenty-four hours at the Peachtree Marriott were a whirlwind of meetings in which it quickly occurred to Grieve, Valentine, scouting director Sandy Johnson, and the other Rangers executives and scouts that anything might be possible.

There was serious talk about a three-way trade between the Rangers, Padres, and Cubs in which the Rangers would send Guzman and infielder Curtis Wilkerson to the Cubs for shortstop Shawon Dunston, then send Dunston to the Padres. But that deal bogged down when Padres' boss Jack McKeon refused to put Kruk in it, instead offering the Rangers talented young catcher Sandy Alomar, Jr. The Rangers already had a catching prospect they liked in Chad Kreuter, so Alomar did not hold much appeal.

But after a few conversations with Cubs General Manager Jim Frey and super-scout Hughie Alexander, the Rangers realized something they had not even hoped: that the Cubs were willing to trade Rafael Palmeiro, who at age twenty-three had batted .307 in his first full major-league season. That wasn't all. The Cubs also loved Mitch Williams, absolutely loved him, *had* to have him. Their scouts had also fallen in love with Kilgus, the curly-haired lefty whose guts compensated for a lack of velocity.

This was interesting.

It didn't take long for talks to heat up. "Palmeiro's available," one of the Rangers' inside men said Sunday night, "and we're going to get him. We won't even have to give up Guzie, either."

Grieve was less succinct but was clearly excited about something when he met with reporters. "We're closer to doing something this year than the last couple of years," he said. "But sometimes you get your hopes up, think you're going to be able to do something, and it doesn't come through. I think there's some real possibilities, but you can never be sure you're going to do something until a team calls you and says you have a deal."

Grieve laid out the parameters of his negotiations. "If we trade a young guy who is a key player for us, what we have to get in return is a young player who is going to become a key part of the team. We're not going to trade a young player for a veteran player who will only be here for a year or two."

Around eleven o'clock the next morning, a news conference was scheduled to announce a trade between the Rangers and Yankees. No one knew what to expect. With Grieve in a mood to do business, nothing was ruled out before announcement of the deal: Brower for Meacham. Grieve appeared embarrassed to have gathered reporters for such a bombshell.

Meanwhile, there was word in the hotel lobby that another deal had been done, but a hitch had apparently developed. An hour passed, then two, and still there was no news conference. Panic began to take hold in the Rangers' suite. Was Frey trying to back out of the deal? Valentine thought so.

It was a question about whether minor-leaguers Pablo Delgado and Luis Benitez could be traded. They had been signed less than a year before. A rule that had been put into effect after Incaviglia refused to sign with Montreal, then was traded to Texas–called "the Incaviglia rule"–stated that a player had to spend one year in the organization that drafted him before he could be dealt. But Delgado and Benitez, natives of Puerto Rico, were signed as free agents, not drafted. The Rangers contended the rule should not apply to them, and Valentine went screaming down to the hotel lobby to get a ruling from Commissioner Peter Ueberroth. Assured that Ueberroth's office would not intervene to block the deal, Valentine went back upstairs smiling. About thirty minutes later, the trade was announced.

It was a dilly involving nine players, including five left-handed pitchers–a definite attention-getter. Texas sent Williams, Kilgus, Wilkerson, Class AA lefty Steve Wilson, Delgado and Benitez to Chicago in exchange for Palmeiro and left-handed pitchers Jamie Moyer and Drew Hall. It was the largest number of players traded in one deal at the winter meetings since the Rangers and Seattle had completed an eleven-player deal in 1980.

The prospect of having Palmeiro in his lineup delighted Valentine. "If at the end of the [last] season I had to draw a sketch of the kind of player we really needed, I would have said one of the top five hitters in either league, who hits from the left side and doesn't strike out," Valentine said happily. "He is that hitter."

In addition to his .307 average, Palmeiro had 41 doubles, five triples, and eight homers for the Cubs in 1988. But manager Don Zimmer also saw a hitter who had driven in only fifty-three runs, including none that had brought in the game-winning run. Grieve didn't worry about the knock on Palmeiro as being unproductive. "We were looking for an offensive player," he said. "If he continues to mature he could become a good hitter who also supplies power. We think we acquired a hitter who can challenge for the American League batting championship for many years."

While it was Williams the Cubs wanted, Valentine was pleased that they had taken the young left-hander instead of the more reliable Guzman. The Rangers had nurtured Williams for four seasons, but still saw him as too wild to close out games consistently. Valentine also considered him selfish because of Williams' obvious displeasure when another reliever got a late-inning assignment he wanted.

Zimmer vowed patience with Williams. "As a manager, I know he's going to throw balls, and I can live with that," Zimmer said. "But he can throw three balls and then strike a guy out with the next three pitches. I've seen him do that."

The principal players involved took the trade hard. Palmeiro declined to return phone calls from reporters for the first forty-eight hours after the deal, and Williams' wife, Dee, spent much of the time in tears. "I'm pretty surprised," Williams said. "I'm sad about leaving Texas because I really enjoyed the people and the fans. I don't have anything bad to say about the Rangers' organization. I have to look at it as a case of where another team really wanted me."

After the announcement, Grieve spoke briefly with reporters, then hurried to his suite for a meeting with Peters and another ten Cleveland Indian executives. Grieve and Peters had discussed a Julio Franco trade after the general managers' meetings in Palm Springs; now Grieve wanted to talk further. Peters had inquired about Pete O'Brien in every preliminary discussion, but no other Ranger could replace the popular first baseman, whose contract was a potential problem after the 1989 season. Palmeiro had played mostly left field with the Cubs, but Rangers scouts assured Grieve he could be O'Brien's replacement at first base.

Grieve wanted to make sure he got to the Indians before they sent Franco elsewhere. Franco had been a productive player for five years with the Indians, batting over .300 in each of the last three years. He had been a leadoff hitter as well as an RBI man, scoring 86 runs while stealing 32 bases in 1987 and driving in 90 runs in 1985. Grieve had already acquired one good bat for his lineup, but he wanted another.

Talks with the Indians went well. Names were discussed, with Peters telling Grieve he would have to have twenty-two-year-old second baseman Jerry Browne as a replacement for Franco. Peters also expressed an interest in Oddibe McDowell, which was welcomed by the Rangers. McDowell had finished the 1988 season in a three-way platoon with Cecil Espy and Brower, tying newcomer Espy for the team lead in stolen bases despite almost 100 more at bats than the rookie. His home run production had dropped from 18 in 406 at bats in 1985 to six in 437 at bats. It was an understatement to say he was available.

Grieve also took the time Monday night to give Nolan Ryan's agent, Dick Moss, an offer better than the Rangers' initial 1-year, $1.2-million package. It had been his most productive day ever as a general manager.

Early Tuesday morning, the frenetic activity resumed with word that

Peters and the Indians had said yes to the three-for-one package for Franco. The Rangers sent O'Brien, Browne, and McDowell to Cleveland and received a player many people saw as a problem for Valentine. But concerns about Franco's history of erratic behavior didn't keep the Texas organization from celebrating.

"I was surprised we could get him," scout Doug Gassaway said of Franco. "Talk to big league scouts and they will tell you he is the best second baseman in the game, including [Ryne] Sandberg and everybody. I believe we're in business."

Grieve knew the cost was high. "We went into the deal with Cleveland prepared to overpay for Julio Franco," he said. "In return we got a player who will be a good player for us. The worst people can say is we overpaid to get a good player." Indians manager Doc Edwards praised Franco. "He is one of the best hitters in either league," he said. "We just needed help at a lot of positions, and this was a way we could get it."

It had taken him six years to do it, but Franco had worn out his welcome in Cleveland. Twice he had failed to show up for games, once vanishing altogether in New York and once bolting the clubhouse after a pre-game dispute. He had spent time in a Dominican jail for carrying a gun in his car. "Early in my career I wasn't grown up," he admitted. "I made mistakes. People who go to college make mistakes. People in business make mistakes. You've got to learn to live with it and react a different way."

Grieve dismissed questions about the reputation that followed Franco to Texas. "Omar Minaya, our scout in the Dominican Republic, recommended him wholeheartedly as the right kind of player to acquire," Grieve said. "We see him in our weight room working hard when Cleveland is in town. You hear a lot of things, but usually those kinds of things are blown up or just not true. If there is something to his reputation, it's the job of the manager to handle them. That was not a concern for us."

Valentine seemed excited about having a player who, one way or the other, figured to liven up a clubhouse that had seemed quiet since Mickey Rivers' release in 1985. "Part of the reason for the changes was to establish a new chemistry," Valentine said. "We thought we'd gotten a little stale. We had a mind-set on our team that Oakland was better [than we were]. To stay the same wouldn't have changed the mind-set. Our reaction was to put it into gear. I think we're better offensively after these moves, and we kept our (starting) pitching intact."

Grieve could hardly believe that he had found a way to add two .300 hitters without disrupting his starting pitchers. He felt sure he would have to part with a young pitcher, most likely Guzman. "The biggest thing that has happened with all the trades is we haven't given up any starting pitching," Grieve said. "We have kept our starting staff intact with the inclusion of Jamie Moyer in the place of Paul Kilgus."

Grieve had gotten the attention of his peers in the American League West and his veteran players. Neither had ever seen the Rangers rock and roll like this. "I think it's obvious nobody is going to concede the division to the Oakland

A's," said Oakland manager Tony La Russa, whose team had finished 33½ games ahead of Texas in '88. "Texas has improved themselves tremendously. They're two-for-two."

Grieve caught his breath for a moment after his third trade in two days, then went back to work to sign Ryan. The future Hall of Famer had spent the last nine years pitching in Houston but was insulted when owner John McMullen tried to cut his salary from $1.3 million to $1 million after his 12-11 season at age forty-one in 1988. He was exploring the open market and had even traveled to Atlanta for face-to-face meetings with representatives of other teams.

Ryan and Moss holed up in a hotel across Peachtree Street from the Marriott. On Tuesday night, executives and owners from as many as four interested teams (Texas, California, San Francisco, and Houston) trekked back and forth to Ryan's room. A brush fire of a bidding war developed, with Angels owner Gene Autry fanning the flames. He had developed an emotional attachment to Ryan when he was pitching four no-hitters for California in the 1970s, and was desperate to get him back. He offered a guaranteed $2.5 million for one year or a two-year package that could have topped out at almost $4 million.

Grieve reacted by raising the Rangers' offer. His greatest lure was geography. Ryan had lived in his hometown of Alvin, Texas, while playing for Houston, and only about 230 miles separated Alvin from Arlington. If Houston was not attractive to Ryan anymore, Grieve hoped to convince him that the Rangers were the next best thing to staying home.

Valentine could hardly sleep that night while thinking of the chance to land Ryan. The next morning, after hearing that the Rangers had won the war for Ryan, he danced across the hotel lobby and hugged scout John Young. The signing became official that afternoon.

While Grieve had pitched the idea of home and family, he backed up his pitch with money that staggered those who had watched the Rangers pinch pennies throughout the Chiles era. Ryan would be paid a guaranteed $2 million to pitch for Texas, replacing Franco ($1.225 million) as the highest-paid player in club history. He would receive a $200,000 signing bonus, a base salary of $1.6 million and a guaranteed buyout of $200,000 if Texas chose not to pay him $1.4 million to pitch in 1990.

While that was impressive, what would stick with most of the fans back home was the terrific little sound bite Ryan laid out for TV cameras. "I am," Ryan said, "a die-hard Texan." He said he was sorry he hadn't been able to end his career in Houston but happy he could continue it in his home state.

"I really wanted to remain in Texas," he said. "I'm certainly disappointed the Houston situation didn't work out. Houston is my home. I went home with the idea of finishing my career, pitching in a World Series in an Astros uniform. I am not going to get the opportunity to do either . . . The overriding factor was what I felt was best for myself and my family. This was a decision not just made by me. I have teenage kids. We will be able to maintain our home in Alvin, and our kids can keep going to the schools they are in."

Valentine behaved as if he had just added the Mona Lisa to his art collection. "To date, this is the one most important transaction the Texas Rangers have ever made," Valentine gushed. "Very simply, that is because Nolan Ryan is not only as fine a performer but as fine a human being as any organization could have associated with it. We're extremely fortunate to do it."

Grieve echoed that message. "For the Rangers, this is probably one of the greatest days in the history of the franchise. Nolan Ryan is arguably one of the best pitchers who has ever pitched. We are thrilled having him in our organization."

In addition to the money and the Texas location, Ryan cited the Rangers' make-it-happen posture as one of the things that made him say yes. "I think the Rangers showed at these meetings they are doing everything they can to put the best ballclub on the field," he said. "I think the aggressive attitude will show on the field next year."

McMullen, the Astros' owner, clearly misgauged the market for Ryan. He reacted angrily over the whole affair. "It goes back to the lunacy of the whole sport," he said. "I have to say I'm pretty surprised. It was all started by Autry out in California, who has a love affair for Nolan Ryan. The interesting part about it is that he didn't get him. That just shows what a folly it is. A team is more important than one player."

McMullen would have gotten an argument at the Arlington Stadium ticket offices. While the trades that landed Palmeiro and Franco started phones ringing, the Ryan signing really lit up the switchboard. "It's been incredible," said John Schriever, who heads the ticket office. "We were getting about twenty calls an hour before the announcement, and [ticket information requests have] gone up to about 125 calls an hour."

After making an unsuccessful run for Cincinnati first baseman Nick Esasky, who Grieve saw as a replacement for Larry Parrish at designated hitter, he returned to Texas feeling every bit the conquering warrior. In three frantic days, he had completed five transactions involving seventeen players, including five former #1 draft choices. "We're a much more competitive team," he said. "We thought we would have to make trades with our pitching staff to help our offense. But as it turned out we're stronger offensively with the addition of Palmeiro and Franco, and we have a stronger starting staff with the addition of Nolan Ryan and Jamie Moyer taking Paul Kilgus's place. Our bullpen is a little shaky without Mitch, but I think our ten-man pitching staff will be at least as good and our offense better next year. Time will tell if that is true."

Grieve's willingness to part with players considered at the forefront of the Rangers' youth movement surprised many teams. "For years, all they said was they would not trade their young players," complained one club executive. "Then they traded three of them in one trade."

Even Grieve seemed surprised by the final body count: seven newcomers including right-hander Darrel Akerfelds, drafted from Cleveland, and ten players traded away, including eight from the forty-man roster. "It is kind of shocking thinking about how many new people there are, how many old guys you like who aren't (here) any more," he said. "There's going to be some shock. But everybody thought we had to make some moves because we had leveled off the last couple of years. We were not making the kind of progress we needed. Hopefully, these moves will make us better.

"You can't run scared. You can't worry about what might happen. I hope Jerry Browne does mature into a good major-league player. That's what we think he will do. I hope Oddibe goes to Cleveland and develops consistency, and that Mitch goes to Chicago and becomes a bullpen stopper who can save twenty-five to thirty games."

Having been outbid for Esasky by the Boston Red Sox, who sent first baseman Todd Benzinger and pitcher Jeff Sellers to Cincinnati in exchange for Esasky and left-hander Rob Murphy, Grieve still needed to address the absence of a designated hitter.

It did not seem to be a major problem, but the market was very soft. For the third consecutive year, Grieve rejected the possibility of signing Irving resident Bob Horner, who was coming off two shoulder surgeries. Grieve could not get excited about available free agents like Larry Herndon, either. There was *one* name on the list that caught his attention: Buddy Bell.

A few years earlier, Grieve had vowed privately that the Rangers were happy to get rid of Bell. Bell had, he said, become too self-involved to mesh with the young team Grieve was building. Some people around the front office had even called Bell a "cancer" because of his beaten-down presence in the clubhouse. But all was forgotten now that Grieve had a need Bell could fill.

"There were circumstances involved that were not ideal for both Buddy and the Rangers," Grieve explained. "But there were no parting salvos, no ill feelings expressed. I think it was a mutual understanding that a trade would be good. But a lot of water has gone under the dam since then, and no bridges were burned."

The well-spoken Grieve must have wanted Bell badly to resort to two clichés in the same sentence. He was not alone in his pursuit of Bell, who was coming off a year in which he had only five more home runs than knee surgeries (seven vs. two) hitting a combined .241 with Cincinnati and Houston. The Astros had not tendered him a contract, making him a free agent, and Milwaukee, Cleveland, San Diego, and the Chicago White Sox joined the Rangers in expressing early interest.

Grieve's first call to Bell came after coach Toby Harrah had passed along a message from Bell indicating his interest. But in the end, it was Grieve who did the pursuing. As he did with Ryan, Grieve paid a surprisingly heavy price to land the thirty-seven-year-old Bell: $530,000 on a one-year contract.

"I'm very excited about coming back," said Bell, who had spent 1979-85 in Texas. "I had high hopes, but I didn't think it would ever happen. My loyalty to that organization was a lot deeper than I ever thought it was."

Valentine would not guarantee Bell a regular spot, saying only that Bell figured to be the designated hitter against left-handed pitchers and add some insurance behind Steve Buechele at third base and Rafael Palmeiro at first. Bell's agent, Ed Keating, said he was sacrificing playing time by not accepting an offer from Milwaukee. The Brewers' sales pitch included calls from owner Bud Selig and former player Sal Bando, a Milwaukee businessman.

"I know I have to make some adjustments at this point in my career," Bell said. "Even though I think I can still play every day, I'm not going to do that. I expect to do exactly what they told me I was going to do. That's OK with me."

Bell's first stint with the Rangers had ended after he closed a hotel door on his thumb and missed the first series Valentine managed. There had been an angry dispute over his contract and what amounted to a cold war with Doug Rader, Valentine's predecessor. When the Rangers could get only Jeff Russell, an eighteen-game loser, and outfielder Duane Walker for him from Cincinnati, even Bell had been puzzled. "Have I got a disease?" he asked.

Now, Bell said, "I'm not going to lie and say I wasn't steamed about the way things went at the last. I was partly to blame for that, and the organization was partly to blame for that. I guess my loyalty to those people is a lot deeper than people realize . . . A leave of absence was probably the best thing for me. I'm excited about coming back. I am really excited.

"The problems I had with Texas were very minimal compared to the good times I had. I don't want people to forget, and more importantly I don't want to forget, the good times I had in Texas. That's why I'm coming back."

"I just think it was the ideal fit," Grieve crowed.

Two weeks later, Grieve also sunk $350,000 into signing left-handed hitter Rick Leach, a thirty-one-year-old free agent whose batting average had declined from .309 to .282 to .276 in recent seasons with the Toronto Blue Jays. Leach figured to be a fourth outfielder and sometime designated hitter. Grieve also orchestrated the re-signing of Ranger free agents Jim Sundberg, Cecilio Guante, and Ed Vande Berg.

Sundberg, who had been signed by Texas after his release from the Chicago Cubs last July, gave Grieve a scare. Sundberg was needed to provide depth behind rookie Chad Kreuter, but he balked after overtures from the Minnesota Twins. Sundberg wanted to stay in Texas, but the Twins were talking about a two-year contract. Given his obsession with catching more games than anyone in history, that was attractive.

But it never came to pass. The Twins offered Sundberg only a one-year contract with an option for 1990, and he accepted the Rangers' guaranteed $275,000 with incentives that could make it worth about $600,000.

"If Chad Kreuter wins the catching job, he'll do most of the catching, with Sunny and Geno [Petralli] pitching in," Grieve said. "If he's not ready, having Sunny as a guy who can do a lot of catching is a comfortable situation. We weren't comfortable going to spring training with Chad, Geno, and Mike Stanley as the catchers."

Nor was Sundberg comfortable going to spring training so much in the background. "I don't by any means look at being a third catcher," said Sundberg, thirty-seven. "I think the whole catching situation is pretty much up in the air."

* * *

The busy off-season had both Grieve and Valentine looking forward to another season. The Rangers had rebuilt a disappointing offense while actually adding to their pitching depth. More important, they had sent a signal that these were different times for the formerly sleepy franchise.

"Probably the most important byproduct of all that change," Oakland General Manager Sandy Alderson said of the Rangers, "is a change in their image and self-image."

Ranger officials had avoided embarrassment by spending $3.9 million to retain shortstop Scott Fletcher, and they struck a major blow by successfully outbidding others for Nolan Ryan. "They had a very aggressive image [during the winter], but when they got everyone's attention was when they signed Nolan Ryan," said Bud Selig, owner of the Brewers. "I think it's quite exciting. I think Mike Stone, Eddie Chiles, Tom Grieve, and Bobby Valentine should all get a pat on the back. Nobody was going to give them anything but an 'A' for effort, but they appear to have done very well besides. I don't think anyone realizes how important Nolan Ryan will be to them."

After the winter meetings, the Rangers had to extend hours at the ticket office to accommodate the sudden surge of interest. There was a run of colds and flu cases among salesmen, who frequently escorted interested fans for a tour of stadium sections in 40 degree weather and rain. "We didn't sign Nolan Ryan as some kind of public relations ploy. I can guarantee that," Stone said. "We signed him because he led the National League in strikeouts last year . . . because Nolan Ryan will make a substantial contribution to our pitching staff. I think it was a very responsible signing."

What Stone was saying was the truth, but there was also truth in the improved image. Richard Justice of *The Washington Post* compared the signing of Ryan to an NBA team's acquiring Magic Johnson. Trades that brought in Julio Franco and Rafael Palmeiro drove home the organization's new commitment to winning now, not next year. The Athletics' Alderson said the Rangers had "become an unknown factor" in the American League West race. What he did not say directly was that before the shake-up they were no threat to Oakland, Kansas City, and Minnesota. Perhaps they had not been a threat even to California, which had surprisingly hired Doug Rader to manage in 1989.

"With Ryan they have not only another quality starter, but they have another anchor to build their starters around," Alderson said. "Offensively, with the addition of Palmeiro and Franco, even though they gave up Pete O'Brien, they improved. They will score more runs."

But as important as anything, in Alderson's eyes, was the simple improvement in self-image. "The way they played last year left a lot of doubt about whether they could be good enough to beat the good teams," he said. "With the changes they have made, I think they are a contender, but nobody knows. I think that is positive. They can look at themselves and think they are good enough, and we as competition have to be concerned about them."

To Valentine, Ryan was the key move.

"We have said we would bid for the right player, but we really haven't been able to go out and compete for a top free agent from another team," he said. "We've tried. We've been competitive with our contracts on a couple of occasions, but we've never been able to land that guy. This time we have. Our fans, players, and [the] people who work for us are saying, 'The Rangers finally did it.' Because of that, I think it's a really big deal for us."

It was the most important deal the Rangers had ever made.

"Come, Gentle Spring!"

For Nolan Ryan, time flew between the December day he signed with the Rangers and the February day he would leave for spring training in Port Charlotte, Florida. Ryan didn't dread the coming season, or the challenge of returning to the American League.

Yet he grew melancholy as the time to leave approached. He wanted to find a house in Arlington and go to the annual cattle sale in Houston, which would delay his arrival in the Rangers' camp by about a week. But mostly he wanted to spend as much time as possible with his family: Ruth, the Alvin High School sweetheart who had kept him from being lonely during his four frightening years with the New York Mets; Reid, a promising high school right-hander; Reese, a thirteen year-old named after ageless California Angels' coach Jimmy Reese; and Wendy, whose twelfth birthday would fall in the middle of spring training.

Family means a lot to Ryan. That's why he's stayed in the town where he was raised, allowing his children to walk the same halls of the same schools he and Ruth attended. The family lives about a mile and a half away from the house Nolan and his father left nightly to work a circulation route for the *Houston Post.*

Until negotiations with Astros owner John McMullen turned bitter— McMullen's first offer was a salary cut, not the way to deal with a man as proud as Ryan—the fireballer had thought he would finish out his Hall of Fame career with the Houston Astros. Now he would have to adjust to a different future. "It's going to be an adjustment," he said on February 12, while the rest of his family was at the Astrodome for the NBA All-Star Game. "I won't be as accessible to a lot of things as I was when I was with Houston, a lot of personal things and my cattle business. But the big thing is, being in Arlington will be less of a handicap for my family than me."

Ryan projects an image of individualism, but enjoys the security that comes from being part of a team. It was more difficult than he'd thought it would be to leave the Astros. "At this time of year, the realization of what is happening to you probably hits you more," Ryan reflected. "As every day goes by, your thoughts are preoccupied with getting ready for a baseball season . . . It's tough to read stories about [the Astros] in the paper, and know it no longer affects me. They had been a big part of me for nine years, and not being there anymore is . . . depressing at times. But the opportunity of going up with Dallas, the Rangers, a club where excitement is running very high, and to be a part of a new group of people coming together, that is exciting in its own."

Bobby Valentine, seldom wanting for energy, practically skipped from field to field when he arrived in Port Charlotte. He had waited impatiently since the winter meetings, perhaps since Tommy Lasorda had told him to forget playing and take steps toward a managerial career. Valentine's goal has always been to participate in a World Series, a goal he failed to reach as a player. He's driven to get there as a manager, and behind the numbing realities of the last two seasons, he hoped–believed–that this would be the year the world discovered he was as smart as he thinks he is.

Two of the biggest reasons for Valentine's optimism reported to Port Charlotte on Friday, February 24. That day they shared one of the back diamonds at the Rangers' complex. They held their own little clinic in hitting, smacking balls all over the field. Some carried beyond the chain-link outfield fences. Valentine was beside himself, like a teenager who'd just picked up his driver's license. "You can't write this," he said, "but there were more line drives hit today than all of last season."

Then he laughed.

Palmeiro and Franco, the two batters, joined in on the high times. "I didn't know it was going to be this loose, this much fun," Palmeiro said. "I'm still meeting some of the guys. It seems like it's going to be a good spring because we have a team here that can win."

Palmeiro came to camp comfortable because he already knew so many Texas players. He had played amateur and winter ball with Pete Incaviglia, Ruben Sierra, Mike Stanley, and Edwin Correa. He had gotten to know Jeff Russell on an All-Star tour of Japan the previous November.

"I didn't really expect to feel like I was left out," Palmeiro said. "I think I'll like it here. They've welcomed me real well. They've joked with me, made me laugh. They've made me feel like I'm one of them."

When Palmeiro arrived in the large clubhouse, he found three boxes of mail which had been forwarded by the Chicago Cubs. There was so much mail it was packed in large boxes that had initially contained color televisions. It was a reminder of an ugly split with the organization that had taken him with its first-round pick in the 1985 draft, after his All-American career at Mississippi State.

Palmeiro seemed bitter about the way the deal was handled by Cubs General Manager Jim Frey and manager Don Zimmer.

Palmeiro loved playing for the Cubs. Not only did he like the city so well that he stayed through the icy winters, but he and his wife, Lynne, named their cocker spaniel Wrigley, in honor of the old ballpark. Palmeiro declined to return reporters' phone calls after the December trade, but later said he was in his Chicago apartment, screening calls over his telephone recorder—waiting for the farewell call from Frey. He'd had to wait a week. "I have no idea why he didn't call earlier," Palmeiro said. "He can't tell me he tried because I was there every day."

By the time Frey called, Palmeiro had blasted the trade in the Chicago papers. "These people don't know what the hell they're doing," he told the *Sun-Times*. "These guys in the front office . . . it's going straight down, it seems like. I don't know what they're doing. It would be fine if you could get someone to win now, but they're not doing it. They're getting rid of their future and screwing up the present.

"That's what happens when you get two guys who don't know what the hell's going on. I just wish Dallas (Green) were back, man. I'd be around if Dallas were here."

Palmeiro had toned down his statements later, but when he reported to camp he was still baffled by the deal that had sent him to Texas along with left-handers Jamie Moyer and Drew Hall for Mitch Williams, Paul Kilgus, Steve Wilson, Curtis Wilkerson, and minor-leaguers Pablo Delgado and Luis Benitez. "I don't know what the trade was about," he said. "I know they wanted pitching, but what they said they wanted was a first-class pitcher, a quality pitcher, a guy who can win twenty games. They didn't get that. They got Mitch Williams, a guy who is a stopper. The bottom line is they didn't get what they were after. The Texas Rangers wanted me, and they [the Cubs] were willing to give me up."

Palmeiro, who didn't turn twenty-four until September, had finished second in the National League in 1988 with a .307 batting average. But after averaging one homer every 15.8 at bats with the Cubs in June 1987, he hit only eight homers and drove in 53 runs in his 580 at bats. He didn't have a single game-winning RBI. It was a disappointing season for a hitter who had already been compared to Don Mattingly and Keith Hernandez.

Palmeiro claimed he got caught up in hitting for an average when he was leading the National League in May and still hitting as high as .335 in June. "I got away from my game, from hitting homers and driving the ball," he said. "I was too interested in the average. I saw myself winning the batting title. I was just happy making contact, going the other way. That's not my game." Palmeiro still managed 41 doubles, which ranked him behind only Andres Galarraga. "I had a lot of doubles, but I think I should have had more doubles and home runs if I wasn't worried about the batting title."

While Grieve touted him as an annual contender for the batting title, Palmeiro came to Florida thinking the Rangers expected more of him. He sensed that they expected him to develop into a complete hitter along the lines of Mattingly or Will Clark, Palmeiro's former Mississippi State teammate.

"They haven't said it, I know they haven't admitted it, but they know I can do it," he said. "I think they expect me to do it. They know it, and I know it. They're expecting it, which is fine because I think I can do it. I don't feel pressure on me at all. There's a lot of talent here. I don't come here trying to do everything. There're players like Ruben Sierra and Pete Incaviglia here. You go down the line and there's a lot of talent. I'm getting a lot of attention, but it's only because of the trade. It seems like everybody here is a good young player."

Palmeiro, mostly a left fielder, was to be moved to first base by the Rangers. "Playing the outfield is pretty easy, but I think playing first is even easier," he said. "You're more in the game, but how hard is it to take a throw from the infield?"

Like Palmeiro, Franco was happy in his new surroundings. He chattered constantly through his first day in a Rangers uniform, meeting new teammates and reacquainting himself with old friends. "I like it here," he said. "I've got confidence I'll do good here. If I stay healthy, I'm going to put some numbers on the scoreboard."

Julio Franco was only twenty-seven but had spent the last six seasons in the major leagues, so he was one of the more experienced Rangers. He'd been known for his selfishness and rapid mood swings in Cleveland, but quickly showed signs of becoming a leader in the Texas clubhouse.

While Franco's image raised doubts after the three-for-one swap that took popular first baseman Pete O'Brien from Texas, he came to Texas with an attitude Valentine had been trying to instill for four seasons. "Winning is what it's all about," Franco said. "That's the way it is with me. You get all or you get nothing. I like guys who play hard. I don't like seeing happy faces on the diamond. I like seeing a guy mad, angry, playing hard. I see guys laughing and I hate it. It's not the place to laugh. It's business. It's only three hours a day. If you can't be serious, concentrate for three hours, you don't deserve to be a big-league ballplayer.

"I hate guys thinking, 'We lost the game but I got three hits.' We're in it together. When I lose a game, I hate to see people laughing in the clubhouse. I hate it."

Valentine's mood was elevated again when Ruben Sierra arrived two days later. Valentine felt like a proud father whose son had come home after boot camp—where did the little kid go?

Sierra showed the effects of a quiet winter spent largely in a San Juan gym. He weighed 204 pounds on the clubhouse scales—sixteen pounds more than at the end of the 1988 season and almost thirty pounds more than when he'd made his major-league debut in 1986. While Sierra felt he should probably get down to 195 for Opening Day, Valentine was genuinely impressed by the change in

Sierra. "It's not fat," said the manager. "He didn't come in overweight; he came in strong. It seems like the fashionable thing to do in baseball, and more often than not the stronger player is the better player."

Sierra, who had always before played a full season of winter ball, had this year begun a weight-lifting program in November. The impetus to stay in the gym came in a discussion with Valentine at the end of last season. "He said I was just going to goof around in Puerto Rico," Sierra said. "He said I wasn't going to do anything all winter. I said, 'You're going to tell the difference when I come to spring training next year.'"

Valentine provided a similar version of that conversation. "I challenged him to be dedicated to whatever he was doing—playing baseball or working out," he said. "I wanted him to make a conscientious effort to feel better about himself when the season started. He said he didn't want to play winter ball, he wanted to get strong. I said, 'It's going to take an effort on your part, it's not just going to happen overnight.' It looks like he put forth an effort."

Sierra repeated as the Rangers' Player of the Year in 1988 despite falling off statistically from 1987. He led the team with 23 homers and 91 RBIs but hit only .254. In his own evaluation, it was a disappointing year.

"This is going to help my power," he said. "It will make me stronger the whole season."

Finally, on Tuesday, February 28, Ryan, arrived. It was definitely not business as usual. Before Ryan could throw his first pitch, he had to endure another news conference—the third since he'd signed his $2 million contract with Texas in December. National reporters joined writers from Texas and Florida in questioning Ryan about his latest career move while television crews rolled film.

When that was done, Ryan joined his new teammates in the clubhouse. He exchanged his dark green Ralph Lauren dress shirt for a blue workout jersey, shook hands with locker partners Bobby Witt and Charlie Hough, and headed out to a back field for the 4 P.M. workout. One comical scene came when he ambled over to introduce himself to Franco. "Nolan Ryan," he said, thrusting his hand out to the man seated in front of Franco's locker. "Bernardo," replied the man. It was Franco's brother and personal valet, not the ballplayer himself.

That's the way it goes on new teams. Once the workout began, things were smoother, but even then Ryan was the center of attention. Hough aimed one of his verbal barrages at Ryan. "Come on, take your hat off," Hough said to the balding hurler. "Let these guys see your head."

Later, Hough jokingly complained about one of the drills. "I don't give a damn if you don't do it," Valentine shot back. "Now we've got someone to replace you."

Ryan headed to a side mound with pitching coach Tom House and catcher Geno Petralli. After a little soft toss, Ryan threw for twenty minutes. He displayed all three of his pitches—fastball, curveball, and changeup. House spoke to him while he threw but declined to make any major changes in the motion Ryan has used for twenty-two major-league seasons.

Thank goodness for small blessings. "He's a treasure," House said later. "It was one of the better experiences of my coaching career."

While Ryan was throwing, Grieve made the long walk from his office to watch him work. He, too, seemed to be enjoying himself. "Sure it's exciting for me," Grieve said. "It was exciting the first time I played against Pete Rose, the first time I played with Fergie Jenkins. That's one of the greatest things about baseball–meeting the people. Having Nolan Ryan in a Ranger uniform is not something I take in stride. If I had to pay to get into his first game, I would."

Ryan seemed to have put his melancholy behind him and appeared to be focused on the job ahead. "I certainly expect us to be a contender," he said of his new team. "It's hard for me to evaluate Oakland because I just saw them in the World Series and playoffs. But I think this ballclub has the potential to give them a run for the division. A lot comes into play, like injuries, but it's also tough for a team to repeat. Maybe that can work against Oakland."

As always, not everything had gone well for the Rangers. Before arriving in Florida, they'd learned that something was amiss with Jose Guzman, who had won thirty-seven games his first three seasons in the majors. Guzman had won only twice after July the previous year, suffering from either a "dead arm" or tendinitis. Wintertime rest had been expected to revive the twenty-five-year-old Puerto Rican, but it had not.

Guzman, who had been out of the States when Tom House assembled his staff for January mini-camps, had trouble throwing in a spring training tune-up at Arlington Stadium. Valentine noticed something strange about his motion, and detected a singular lack of pop on his fastball.

The arm had felt fine when he'd played catch over the winter, but Guzman said he had some pain now. Valentine, concerned, made an appointment for Guzman to see Dr. Frank Jobe in Los Angeles.

Bad reports came back from the examination. Jobe said Guzman's shoulder problems apparently would not require surgery but might put him on the disabled list for awhile, creating more competition for spots on the Rangers' pitching staff.

Jobe diagnosed Guzman as having a slight anterior dislocation on the front side of his shoulder, which he said was causing an impingement on his rotator cuff and biceps tendon, and recommended no baseball, not one toss, for a month. It was an unexpected blow to the Rangers, and put Valentine and House in nasty moods on the first day of spring training.

"This definitely puts him behind schedule," said Grieve. "We just have to wait to see if he can get ready to start the season. I don't know if after two or three times out he can be ready. If he's not, I feel we have some guys who can pick us up without missing a beat."

Guzman's absence left five established starters in Charlie Hough, Nolan Ryan, Bobby Witt, Jamie Moyer, and Jeff Russell, as well as top prospect Kevin Brown and long shots Edwin Correa, Brad Arnsberg, and Ray Hayward. "We're not going to rush him back," said Grieve. "We will give him all the time he needs so we don't wind up right back where we started."

Guzman's injury complicated what appeared to be an easy decision on replacing Mitch Williams in the stopper's role. Russell, an All-Star the previous year after he switched from middle relief to the rotation, had been campaigning to be moved into that job since the Williams trade in December. Valentine now wasn't sure if he could spare Russell in the rotation but wanted to look at him in late relief.

The first opportunity came March 4. Russell was perfect in the eighth and ninth innings as the Rangers lost to the Chicago White Sox 3-2 in the second exhibition game.

"That's what I want to do," Russell said about the switch. "I've got a good feeling about it. We've been looking for a stopper for years, and I seem to be pretty good out of the bullpen."

Had Guzman been healthy, the addition of Ryan would have given the Rangers an extra starter to either trade or move to the bullpen, but now Valentine needed an outside candidate to emerge if he was to have that flexibility again.

"If they want me to be the other starter, I'm not going to tell them I'm not going to do it," Russell said. "I'll go out and do it until Guzie gets healthy, and then go to the bullpen. I feel good as a stopper. I'm not a stopper now, but I am in my mind."

Ruth Ryan had been with Ryan almost as long as his fastball. She was among a record crowd of 5,715 at Charlotte County Stadium, but had barely settled into her seat behind home plate when her husband's debut with the Rangers ended. A tight left hamstring forced Ryan out of an exhibition game against Pittsburgh after one inning. He'd felt the tightness after throwing a 2-2 fastball past Barry Bonds, the Pirates' leadoff hitter, but stayed in the game to give up a two-run homer to Glenn Wilson. .

Ryan did not consider the injury serious, although a muscle problem in the same area had caused him to miss his last two starts with Houston in 1988. "I'll put ice on it," he said, "and continue to work out as I have been. I don't really look at this as a setback. I feel like I came out before I did anything to it."

Ryan, the losing pitcher in a 7-1 defeat, had not even thought of his hamstring all spring. "I had no reason to think about it. What I think it is, I probably extended myself a little more than when I had been throwing batting practice, pitching on the side. It's probably just more a need to stretch it out."

Ryan found similarities between his one-inning stint and his exhibition debut after signing with Houston in 1980. Houston was playing Los Angeles in Vero Beach, and Ryan remembers Dodger hitters depositing about three balls in the palm trees that sit beyond the outfield.

"I remember looking at [Astros owner John] McMullen sitting behind the dugout," Ryan says, "and it looked like he had aged twenty years."

But while Ryan's legs were a new concern, one of the biggest questions of the spring was being answered. It not only looked as if $50,000 pickup Cecil

Espy could play center field, but fading prospect Jeff Kunkel emerged as a decent second-line center fielder. Coming into camp, when Guzman was expected to be healthy, there had been speculation that Grieve would trade for a center fielder, perhaps Willie McGee, Mickey Brantley, or Lloyd Moseby. But Grieve now felt no need to shop around—which was good because he didn't have much to offer.

"I'm happy with what I've seen," he said. "I have not seen anything to make me think that Cecil can't do the job in center field—or Jeff Kunkel, either. Both have shown they're able to swing the bat and have played well defensively out there. But you always have your eyes open on ways to improve the ballclub. You don't say no to trades before they're proposed, but I haven't been making any calls. Nothing has happened to make me get on the phone."

Espy and Kunkel, both former first-round draft choices, had struggled to establish themselves in the major leagues. Between them, they had played fewer than 130 big-league games in center field.

Espy, twenty-six, had played nine professional seasons without establishing himself as a regular. It took him eight seasons to spend a full year in the majors in 1988. His speed had put him in the leadoff spot in the lineup, but he was told all winter that he would have to improve his .288 on-base average from the previous year.

He had done that in spring training, hitting .272 with a .360 on-base percentage. "Having his bat flat on his shoulder has shortened his swing a lot," Valentine said. "I think he's going to drive some balls now instead of just hitting 'em. He's a better hitter than he used to be."

Kunkel, twenty-seven, had spent parts of the last five seasons with Texas, batting .217 in 130 games. He had always been under a cloud, bearing the brunt of Doug Rader's tirades or suffering through a string of injuries. He had also been plagued by a lack of patience at the plate, but had been laying off bad pitches this spring, although he was hitting only .210. Despite Kunkel's soft schedule at Rider College, Grieve had had direct input on the decision to pick Kunkel with the #1 pick in 1983 and had always given the younger player the benefit of the doubt.

But after watching another #1 pick, Oddibe McDowell, go backward for three years, Grieve seemed to think anything would be an improvement. "Neither one of these guys [has] had the reputation that Oddibe McDowell had, but performance-wise I haven't seen anything to think they can't do at least the job Oddibe did," he said. "Oddibe last year was a below-average major-league player at his position."

There was more speculation about who was going to own the Rangers than there was about who would play what position. No one in baseball seemed to think Gaylord Broadcasting's second bid to buy the team would fare any better than its first. Commissioner Peter Ueberroth was personally involved in soliciting alternative ownership groups in the Dallas-Fort Worth area.

While Chiles and others harumphed about the likelihood of turning up a group that had not come forward during the two and a half years since Gaylord's bid was initially rejected, Ueberroth made two trips to the area in February, and held several secret meetings.

At the end of his second visit, he decided to do a favor for the reporters, whom he normally treated like IRS auditors. Pausing in Delta's Crown Club before boarding a February 23 flight back to New York, he named a group headed by George W. Bush, son of President Bush, and Dallas investment banker Edward "Rusty" Rose III as the most viable alternative.

"This will not be a toy for us," Bush told the *Times Herald's* Kurt Iverson. "This will be a serious business venture. [We have] a good group of Texans, but we are not at liberty now to reveal the rest of our members."

Although he was irritated that Ueberroth had not coordinated his efforts through him, Chiles said the Bush group could be acceptable if Gaylord were to be rejected. "I would be delighted if they got the team," he said after a Republican Party dinner in Fort Worth. "I've known George since he was a little boy, and he's an outstanding man."

Ueberroth vowed to stay involved. "We are going to see this new partnership through to completion," he said. "Eddie has complete say-so, and we understand that he is agreeable for this to move forward. We understand his concern is that Mr. Gaylord will be treated equally."

American League owners, meeting on March 9 at Florida's Bonaventure Resort, rejected Gaylord Broadcasting's bid by a 10-4 vote, putting the team back on the open market. The Bush-Rose group now appeared close to striking its own deal with Chiles to purchase his 58 percent interest in the franchise.

"It's no surprise at all," Edward L. Gaylord said of the rejection. "Now we just have to wait and see what Mr. Chiles wants to do. It's his franchise to sell. I imagine if he finds a good buyer and good type of person to sell to, then we'll stay in. I imagine he'll work with us because he's a good partner and he's always kept us in mind when dealing with the team."

Sources indicated that the Bush-Rose group had agreed to match the purchase price of $46.4 million (originally set by the Florida group of Frank Morsani and Bill Mack) for Chiles's share of the team and of Arlington Stadium. Gaylord's blessing was viewed as cement for the deal with the Bush-Rose group, which included participation by Fort Worth investment banker Richard Rainwater.

"In my opinion, it's a done deal," Nashville's Larry Schmittou, who had put together one of the many groups pursuing the team, told the *Times Herald.* "I think they are just going through the proper motions now, and it looks like we're a bridesmaid. We don't plan to do anything more."

Bush, Rose, and Rainwater all declined comment on the negotiations. Several questions remained, including the seventy-eight-year-old Chiles's desire to sell the team. He hinted again at the Bonaventure meeting that he would like to keep the Rangers for one more season.

"The Bushes are very nice people," said Chiles, who had asked President Bush to throw out the first pitch at the Rangers' opener April 4. "But right now I don't know what I'm going to do. I might not sell the team. I might take it off the market. I'm in no hurry. I just want to go home and think about it for awhile by myself."

The next day, after the vote against Gaylord, Ueberroth lashed out at Chiles in a news conference. Angered by Chiles's statements that he might decide to hang onto the Rangers, Ueberroth portrayed Chiles as bordering on senility. "I think the owner of the Texas Rangers currently wants to keep the Texas Rangers," said Ueberroth. "But I must tell you that that thermometer goes up and down fairly regularly. Some things in place have been rejected and Gaylord has been rejected. Nothing is currently on the table. It's a difficult situation. I want it resolved before leaving office, but I don't know what can be done at this time."

Chiles's pride apparently suffered when Ueberroth got involved in the sale, but Chiles could still close a deal quickly if he chose to. Those closest to him, including his wife, Fran, encouraged him to cut a deal quickly. They felt that the threat of a player strike in 1990 left a narrow window of opportunity for the sale.

But Chiles remained noncommittal. "On the way home I'll be doing some thinking," Chiles said before returning to Fort Worth. Ueberroth made no public forecasts. "It's a changing panorama out there," he said. "The principal is Eddie Chiles. I would write as gospel whatever he has to say today. But I would be ready to (then) write what he has to say tomorrow. . . . He thinks that team will be in post-season play, and it may well be."

Eight days later, at a hastily assembled news conference at the Arlington Hilton, Chiles announced that he had agreed in principle to sell controlling interest in the Rangers to the Bush-Rose group.

It was quite an achievement for Bush, who with Ueberroth's help had put together the group largely to prove his acumen as a businessman. His position as managing general partner for the twenty-five limited partners would also give him visibility in case he decided to seek the Republican nomination for Texas governor, as had been rumored.

For Bush, the toughest part of the negotiations was getting Chiles to put his name on a contract that ended his frustrating tenure. "Eddie didn't earn his reputation as a tough trader for nothing," Bush said. "When we were dealing with Eddie, it wasn't negotiation of money. It was negotiation of love because he has cared and nurtured this team and he was selling something he loves. Because of the deal we made with Eddie, he doesn't have to give it up. When we win the World Series, Eddie Chiles, more than anybody else in the world, deserves to be in that clubhouse getting champagne poured on him."

Edward Gaylord attended the news conference, to say he would join with the Bush-Rose group. "I'm glad Eddie finally found somebody from Texas to buy the team," Gaylord said. "All I've wanted all along is local owners. The only reason I intervened was to keep the Tampa people and the New Yorkers out. I'm happier about all this than Eddie Chiles."

The Bush-Rose group would be able to put the club's finances in a stronger position than ever before. Bush vowed that big headaches would not come with the big backing. "We're not going to tell the baseball people how to play baseball," he said. "I think I hit about .316 my last year of Little League. I peaked. They shouldn't be concerned with their jobs. They want a winner just like we want."

Bush told the news conference he'd received a call from his father earlier in the day. "I talked to the President this morning, and he kept talking about wanting to play first base," Bush said. "I told him Rafael Palmeiro is a heck of a player. He just hung up."

At home, on the road, even overseas to the tune of a calypso beat, all the Rangers could do as the spring wound down was win. They won only two of their first nine exhibition games, then reeled off nine straight victories. It was the longest winning streak in the franchise's slowpoke history, either in spring training or in the regular season.

In the second of two games against the Chicago White Sox in Puerto Rico, Kevin Brown and fringe relievers Ed Vande Berg, Paul Wilmet, and Dwayne Henry combined to throw a four-hit shutout as the Rangers won their ninth straight, 8-0. Pete Incaviglia, who had spent the spring working to cut down his stride and strike out less, connected for his second home run in three games, the only homers he would hit all spring.

"It's important to show our guys they can do this," Valentine said. "Doing this means you can put together a streak. Even though it's only spring training, we're putting together a streak. We're also scoring a lot of runs, and have been bunching our hits. That has not been one of our fortes."

Steve Buechele credited the good times to the new mix of players. "Everybody is just gooning out," he said. "We kind of have that feeling that we're going to win. Everyone is talking about winning right now. All of the new guys are good, positive guys to have. They have blended in, creating a good chemistry. But I also think a couple [of] singles, a double, and a home run makes for good chemistry, too."

Ryan had slowly worked his way back into shape from the tight hamstring, making a few appearances in exhibition games, but on March 23 gave the Rangers a real scare. Pitching in a camp game with their Class AA Tulsa club, Ryan pulled his left calf muscle breaking off the mound to cover first base—the third time in five spring outings he had had to leave early because of problems with his left leg.

Trainer Bill Zeigler called the injury a "very mild strain," but Valentine was pessimistic about Ryan's availability for his first start of the season, a much-advertised April 6 date against the Detroit Tigers at Arlington Stadium. "If he can't stay on schedule," Valentine said, "it will throw everything off. It will be very, very difficult to project him opening the season."

Ryan had come out of his previous start early, working only three innings March 19 at Joe Robbie Stadium in Miami because of an especially soft pitching mound. "Pitching on that type of mound, sliding around as much as I did, may have been the start of it," Ryan said. "The last three days I've kind of modified my running because my legs have been tight."

Despite the short-term pessimism, Valentine and House projected long-range confidence about the $2-million investment. "He's had leg troubles before," House said, "and he always gets 200-plus innings and comes to the party."

Valentine agreed. "It would really frighten me if leg injuries hadn't been a simple matter of fact in his past," he said. "He was pulling muscles in his leg in the early '70s when I played with him. When we got Nolan, we got him knowing he's going to pull muscles in his leg. I don't see it as an indication of age as much as just his being. He pulls leg muscles."

It wasn't a very reassuring thought.

In the final cut, Valentine included rookie catcher Chad Kreuter and rookie pitchers Kenny Rogers, Brad Arnsberg, and Brown on his roster for Opening Night, keeping Arnsberg and Rogers at the expense of Drew Hall, the left-hander acquired in the Palmeiro deal, and right-hander Darrel Akerfelds. Vande Berg and infielder Bobby Meacham, acquired in a one-for-one deal for Bob Brower, were released.

Valentine said that the final pitching decisions were the toughest he had faced in his four springs as a manager. "These weren't cut and dried," he said. "There was a whole lot of gray area – on the positive side for the first time. I think Drew Hall can help us, and Akerfelds can help. If I had a bet, I would say they will before the season is over."

There was no question about Brown, the 1986 first-round draft choice from Georgia Tech. He had been the hottest pitcher in camp. His fastball was clocked at 95 MPH two days before the cuts were made, when he extended his streak of scoreless innings to 13 in a loss to the Chicago White Sox. He had a 3.12 earned run average, giving up 19 hits and walking six in 26 innings. He had struck out 14. "Kevin Brown is going to be a big winner in the big leagues," Valentine said. "It is just a matter of when that happens."

No one could accuse Brown of lacking ambition. "If I get the opportunity, keep throwing the ball like I've been, I'm shooting for twenty wins," said Brown. "Some people may think that's out of the question, that it's not being realistic. But I think we've got the kind of team that could give a pitcher a shot at it."

Ryan recovered quickly from his calf problem, which proved to be a strain, rather than a pulled muscle. He prepared for the season with a series of exercises which were not awe-inspiring – on one, he slowly walked up and down the stairs leading to the club's offices – but which did the job. He worked in a simulated game on March 28, and had no problems with his left leg during a final tuneup April 1 against the Astros in Oklahoma City. He pronounced himself ready to open the season, a relief to ticket-holders as well as to Valentine.

A final 10-5 loss to the Astros, managed by former Texas coach Art Howe, did nothing to diminish the Rangers' optimism as they ended a 17-11 spring. They had set a club record for spring victories, scoring an average of 5.6 runs per game and batting .286 as a team. It was an early sign that Grieve made his off-season moves wisely.

"This lineup should be more consistent than we have been," Incaviglia said. "Our lineup last year was pretty good when we were playing good, but it could be real bad if some guys weren't swinging the bat. Now we've got guys like Palmeiro, Franco. They're going to hit .300."

Franco, who seemed never to stop talking, got in the last word. "We are going to score runs," he said. "That is one thing I know about this team. We'll score some runs . . . and we'll have fun doing it."

An April To Remember

Six months and two days after the miserable 1988 season came to an end, Bobby Valentine was back in the spotlight at Arlington Stadium. The opener had seemed a long time coming for the newly reconstituted team—a team that brought back only ten players who had been in uniform for the 1988 opener. Newcomers occupied first base, second base, designated hitter, the bench, and the bullpen. Even the clubhouse had been changed. Valentine had recommended an off-season overhaul, and according to coach Davey Lopes, the new light gray carpet made the place look about as bright "as a prison."

With Detroit in town, the matchup of Jack Morris and Charlie Hough was perhaps the best in the majors on Opening Day. Over the previous seven years, no one had won more games than Morris (126) and Hough (111). Tickets were available only through scalpers, but recently fired Dallas Cowboys coach Tom Landry did not have to scramble for one. With President Bush unavailable, he had been asked to throw out the first pitch.

Before his one-hop toss to Jim Sundberg, the crowd of 40,375 gave Landry what was probably the longest standing ovation in the history of the stadium. It was the third standing O of the night, as Nolan Ryan and Buddy Bell were both greeted with roars during the player introductions.

Once the pomp and circumstance had been observed, Hough and Morris began a fascinating battle between the two most stubborn pitchers in the American League. Hough had been uncharacteristically nervous beforehand, fretting about the first impression the revamped Rangers would make.

But his nerves didn't show on the mound. He got through the first inning with seven pitches. Morris came back with a hitless inning, making a nice play to throw out leadoff man Cecil Espy, who hit a high chopper back to the mound. Hough threw only nine pitches in a perfect second inning, but Morris was equally perfect, building a 1-2-3 inning around strikeouts of Julio Franco and

Geno Petralli. Hough had to work a little in the third, letting runners reach first and third before getting rookie Torey Lovullo to hit a foul pop for the third out. He was rewarded with a 2-0 lead, thanks to consecutive opposite-field doubles by Espy and Scott Fletcher. Espy came into second base with his fists flying after driving a 1-1 pitch into the left-field corner. But Hough struggled in the fourth, walking leadoff man Lou Whitaker and throwing cleanup man Alan Trammell a 2-0 fastball that was sent into the left-field corner for a double, moving Whitaker to third with no outs. Hough fought back, getting Fred Lynn to hit a foul pop to Petralli on a 1-1 knuckleball, striking out Matt Nokes with a 2-2 knuckler, and getting Chris Brown to ground out on a 2-0 knuckleball. The Rangers still led 2-0, and Hough had survived his biggest crisis of the night. "That's when he threw me his best knuckler," Lynn said afterward. "I did hit it straight up in the air, but I was lucky to get wood on it. Tonight, he was in charge."

Hough retired 18 of 21 hitters after giving up the double to Trammell in the fourth inning, recording the Rangers' first-ever complete game shutout on Opening Day. But his pitching wasn't the only thing for the crowd to applaud. Rafael Palmeiro drilled another opposite-field double over the head of third baseman Brown in the fifth inning, producing another run. Espy shoved a fist into the air and did a little Super Bowl Shuffle on the warning track after leaping to catch a drive by Whitaker in the sixth inning. Bell singled into center off Morris to lead off the seventh inning, causing an interruption in play as the ball was retrieved. It was his 2,500th career hit. Then Fletcher provided the final 4-0 margin with a single up the middle to score Bell.

It had been, in many ways, a good start to the season. "What a great way to open," said Valentine. "I was thinking before the game we have three sure standing O's—Tom Landry's throwing out the ball, so you got to figure Texans are going to give him a standing ovation. I figured Nolan Ryan would get one when he was introduced, and I expected Buddy would get his 2,500th hit. Then Charlie got a fourth for finishing up Opening Day with a win. It was all even more than I expected."

Hough had allowed five hits and walked two, drawing praise from Morris. "He's my idol," Morris said. "My goal is to pitch one game like he does. Just one game. How can he pitch that good and never break a sweat?"

Morris also praised the Rangers' new-look attack, which had turned six hits into four runs. "The balls they hit were timely," said Morris. "They got the key hits with men on base. They were things of beauty—this line, that line, this line, that line. I can't pitch a whole lot better."

Hough saw himself riding a wave that had begun when the Rangers won fifteen of their last nineteen preseason games.

"Tonight's game was a lot like we played in spring training," he said. "It was a very well played ball game. I don't think we made a mistake in the whole ball game."

After a day off, the Rangers returned for Game 2 against Detroit. It was

Ryan's debut, which made the atmosphere like Opening Day, Part II. The media showing was as strong as it had been two days earlier, which forced club publicist John Blake to assign seats in the tiny press box. Two went to Houston columnists Dale Robertson and Ed Fowler, who had come to write about the Hall of Famer who got away from the Astros. One went to Ken Picking, who covers the American League for *USA Today*. His newspaper had had its own phone in the Arlington Stadium press box for two years but had a reporter there to use it only when the visiting team commanded attention. Today was different.

But good seats were available in the stands, as a quirk in scheduling forced Texas to start the game at 5 P.M. The stadium was barely half full when Alvin mayor Allen Gray threw out the first pitch. Ryan's first pitch was an outside fastball to Tigers leadoff hitter Ken Williams. Ryan went three-and-oh to Williams, but then came back to strike him out with the next three pitches. The third was the Ryan Express, a heat-seeking missile of a fastball that was past Williams while he was still trying to get his bat in motion. Ryan struck out the next hitter, the rookie Lovullo, on three pitches. But Whitaker dinked a 1-2 fastball into center for a single. No problem. Ryan reared back and struck out Trammell on four pitches—the fourth of which was a curveball that paralyzed the hapless batter.

The first inning was not an indication of things to come for Ryan, however. He struggled mightily to get through just five innings. At times it was a fright show for the 330 fans who had bussed up from Alvin to watch Ryan's first American League outing since 1979. He showed his age when he was twice forced to cover first base. While his fastball was clocked at 96 MPH on the Rangers' radar gun, he did not have command. He struck out eight but gave up four runs and seven hits in five innings.

Ryan hadn't wanted to disappoint the Alvin contingent, which had purchased tickets long ago. But when the 107-pitch ordeal ended, both Valentine and Ryan admitted they had taken a risk starting Ryan so quickly after the leg problems he had suffered in the spring. Valentine also revealed that allergies had forced Ryan to make an emergency trip to the doctor's office the previous day.

"We rushed this start . . . he rushed this start," Valentine said. "He wanted to get out there tonight, but his spring training wasn't quite what it should have been. This was really extended spring training."

Valentine hadn't really minded the experience, however, as the Rangers scored four runs in five innings against Detroit starter Jeff Robinson, tying the game 4-4 when it was turned over to the bullpens. Espy's speed made the difference for Texas. With one out in the seventh inning, he barrelled around third base to score from second on an infield dribbler by Palmeiro. First baseman Billy Bean fielded the roller, then turned to toss it to pitcher Frank Williams. Espy committed himself when he saw Bean's back and scored so quickly Williams didn't even bother with a throw to home plate. "There were forty cameras here, and I bet none of them caught Cecil coming across the plate," Valentine said. "Twenty thousand people . . . probably were wondering why the bases weren't loaded."

Jeff Russell retired five straight to get the save as Texas won 5-4 to sweep the two-game series. The last out came on a diving catch by Franco after Lynn centered a 3-2 fastball. "I was nervous, very nervous," Russell said. "I was sweating when I came off the field. I was eating pizza [afterward] and still sweating. I'm glad I got this one out of the way."

Russell was also glad Lynn did not get some loft on the 3-2 fastball he threw with the bases empty in the ninth. "That pitch to Lynn was right down the pipe," he said. "I didn't want to walk him. Luckily, it had some movement on it and he just missed the sweet spot. Julio made a great play."

Including spring training, Russell had finished all thirteen of his appearances and was three-for-three in save opportunities. It made for a good sidebar. But it was Espy who was surrounded by reporters afterward for the second time in two games. "I was thinking about (scoring) when I was running," said Espy, who had scored four of the Rangers' nine runs in the two victories. "I saw the ball chopped on the ground, and I thought if he [Bean] turns his back, I'm going to keep running. It was a tough decision for him to make."

Third-base coach Dave Oliver said there was nothing tough about his decision. "I couldn't have tackled him if I wanted to," Oliver said. "He can fly."

On a team built around Clydesdales like Steve Buechele, Petralli, Bell, and Palmeiro, Espy's speed was a subtle key. He ran like a thoroughbred. In the minor leagues, he once stole 74 bases in 131 games. First-base coach Toby Harrah felt you had to go back to the Rangers' original third baseman to find a comparable player in Texas.

"He is right there with Davey Nelson," said Harrah. "He's a real, real aggressive base runner. To me, that's as important as having speed. I've seen a lot of guys who have great speed who don't take advantage of it. He takes advantage of it."

Valentine and Tom Grieve were giddy as they reviewed the game in Valentine's office. Reporters filtered in and out, and Valentine called one back to make a private observation.

"You can't write this," he said, "but there was one thing about that game I really loved. Did you see when Franco walked with two men on base? He turned to Inky and told him, okay, go get him. I loved that. We've had guys here the last few years that would have been so upset about being walked that they wouldn't have even known who was on deck."

Grieve chimed in on the same note—their shared perception of Pete O'Brien and Larry Parrish as selfish players. It seemed the better Valentine and Grieve felt about the 1989 Rangers, the deeper their bitterness grew regarding the earlier teams.

Bobby Witt stank in his first start, and the Rangers lost to the Toronto Blue Jays, 10-9. The Blue Jays scored the winning run when Kelly Gruber hit a solo homer off Cecilio Guante in the seventh inning. Guante hit the next batter, Tony Fernandez, in the face with an 0-2 fastball. The pitch put Fernandez in the hospital with a broken cheekbone, taking him out of the lineup for six weeks. But it was an expensive night for the Rangers, too, as Bell felt something strange in his left knee after trying to beat out a double play. The knee locked on him the next morning, sending him to Cincinnati for the seventh knee surgery of his career. He was expected back before Fernandez, but not much earlier.

It was jacket weather at Arlington Stadium for the first day game of the season that Sunday. Jamie Moyer's 13-strikeout debut on Saturday night had put spring in the Rangers' stride, but Texas hitters couldn't do much with Toronto's John Cerutti, a left-hander they thought they should hammer.

Kevin Brown came out strong in his debut as the Rangers' fifth starter, retiring eight straight to start the game. But he gave up a cheap run when Chad Kreuter's passed ball negated a strikeout in the seventh, and trailed 2-1 when Valentine took him out of the game in the eighth. It seemed that would be the final score, but Palmeiro woke up the crowd when he jerked the ball over first baseman Fred McGriff's head for a one-out double in the ninth. Jays manager Jimy Williams called for Tom Henke, the right-handed reliever almost ruined by Doug Rader. He had saved eleven games against Texas since the Rangers had lost him in the compensation draft in 1984.

But Henke was no mystery this time. Ruben Sierra hit a 1-2 fastball into the right-field bleachers to give the Rangers a 3-2 victory. The crowd brought back Sierra for a curtain call while replays of the game-winning homer ran on the Diamond Vision screen.

That's not all that went right for Texas that day. Oakland, Minnesota, and the Chicago White Sox, who had shared first place in the American League West, all lost. The Rangers' 4-1 start put them in first place for the first time since the 1986 magic ended on June 25.

The Rangers hit the road, but the road did nothing to slow their momentum. Game-time temperature in Milwaukee for the Brewers' home opener was 33 degrees, but the Rangers stayed hot. It was a well-timed trip, as Milwaukee had an overloaded disabled list, playing without Paul Molitor, Ted Higuera, Juan Nieves, Greg Brock, and Dale Sveum. But circumstances conspired against the visitors. A rain-out Sunday in Detroit allowed Brewers manager Tom Trebelhorn to start Chris Bosio, who had a lifetime 2.37 ERA against Texas, instead of Mike Birkbeck, and Charlie Hough had never won at Milwaukee's County Stadium. There was concern.

It seemed justified as Hough got shelled in the second inning. Rob Deer led off the inning with a homer to left field. Hough walked three of the next six hitters and failed to get out of the second, leaving with two men out and Texas behind 4-2. It was a quick hook for Hough, who had always gotten the benefit of the doubt from Valentine.

But it proved to be a game-saving move. Brad Arnsberg, Kenny Rogers, Guante, and Russell teamed up to throw 8⅓ innings of shutout relief. Incaviglia, who had been a basket case since the first week of spring training, tied the score 4-4 with a 430-foot homer off Bosio in the sixth inning, his first of the year, and Sierra again put Texas ahead. This time it was a tenth-inning double to left-center off reliever Chuck Crim that scored Palmeiro with the winning run.

"This is a fun club," said Russell, who got the win by retiring all four Brewers hitters he faced. "During the tenth inning, a song comes on the speakers, and we're all in the dugout singing it. It's like we know we're going to score a run this inning regardless."

The clubhouse theme of the moment was relief pitching—the bullpen had gone 3-1 with two saves and a 1.23 ERA during the Rangers' 5-1 start. Despite the presence of Williams, the bullpen had often been a black hole in 1988, with the fewest victories (ten) and the highest ERA (4.48) in the major leagues. But the new season had brought a new feeling.

"That's a pretty good offensive team, and the bullpen came in, got me out of an inning and shut them down for the rest of the game. That's about as good as it gets," Hough said after the game. "I think Bobby has a lot of confidence in them to take me out when he did. There have been times in the past when the bullpen hasn't been as solid and I would have stayed in there. I wouldn't have minded staying in there."

Arnsberg, who replaced Hough in the second inning, gave up three hits and no runs in 4⅔ innings. He embodied the new spirit among relief pitchers. He had been the comeback story of the spring, returning to the majors less than one year after undergoing the "Tommy John surgery," in which a tendon was transplanted from his left wrist into his right elbow. Now even the cold did not bother him. He did not even wear an undershirt this day.

"When I had sleeves on after the surgery, it would irritate the scar and bring back bad memories," Arnsberg said. "I don't think I'll ever wear sleeves again."

The bullpen had been rewarded for a newly efficient defense. With Espy setting the tone, Texas' offense had averaged 5.3 runs in its first six games, scoring 32 runs on only 47 hits. It took 1,378 hits for the Rangers to score 637 runs in 1988. "We're scoring runs like the ones we used to give up all the time," Valentine said. "Bobby (Witt) couldn't hold 'em on, so he'd walk 'em, they'd steal second, move to third on a ground ball and score on something else weak."

Espy and the others at the top of the order, Fletcher and Palmeiro, led the way. Between them, they scored 14 of the first 32 runs, producing many in simple ways. Having Espy on base had been a plus for Fletcher and Palmeiro. Both received more fastballs with pitchers worried about Espy stealing a base. "I dare say some teams have had meetings where they've said, 'We can't let him get on base,' " Valentine said. "Scotty makes things work, too, because he is so unselfish. He has taken an awfully lot of good pitches to hit, working the pitcher."

With Espy on base, Fletcher (five-for-eight) and Palmeiro (three-for-five) had gone a combined eight-for-thirteen. "Pitchers do pitch differently with Cecil on base," said Fletcher. "They tend to give you a lot of fastballs, good pitches to hit. That's the advantage of having a guy with good speed on base."

Espy had been something of an enigma in his first two years in the Texas organization. He kept to himself much of the time and could be moody. But now he seemed to revel in the attention. "I feel good, mainly because we're winning. That's the best thing," he said. "We played well in spring training, but it's good to see it carrying over into the season. I've been doing what I have to do—putting the ball in play and getting on base. This team believes in itself. We have to do the little things to win games, but we believe we can do them."

A day off in Milwaukee might be the greatest misnomer in the American League, comparable to a vacation in Afghanistan. Cleveland's bad, but at least there's always the chance that the river will catch on fire. In Milwaukee, where the Rangers had a day to burn after the Brewers' home opener, the activities choice was between TV game shows and walking the streets downtown.

Tracy Ringolsby, who covered the team for *The Dallas Morning News*, suggested a trip to Wrigley Field for an afternoon Cardinals-Cubs game. Three other reporters, including the *Fort Worth Star-Telegram*'s Jim Reeves and Tony DeMarco, took him up on it. First the group stopped by the Pfister Hotel for a morning briefing with Valentine.

When Valentine heard of the trip, he invited himself along. So four reporters, public relations man John Blake, and Valentine piled into a rented Cadillac for the ninety-minute trip to Chicago. Valentine sat up front, squeezed between Ringolsby and DeMarco, and appeared as relaxed as he had been in a long time. There's nothing he looks forward to more than watching baseball, and this trip would give him a chance to watch some of his former players.

Four of the six players sent to Chicago for Palmeiro, Moyer, and left-hander Drew Hall had opened the season on the Cubs' roster, including, of course, Mitch Williams.

The wild left-hander was already on his way to folk-hero status in Chicago, having protected a one-run lead over Philadelphia on Opening Day by first loading the bases with three singles and then striking out Mike Schmidt, Chris James, and Mark Ryal. "This is a key day," Valentine said. "Mitch hasn't pitched for three days. If he doesn't get in the game today, he'll go crazy."

Valentine recounted how he hadn't really wanted to give up Williams, how the Cubs trade was originally fronted by Jose Guzman instead of Williams.

Once at Wrigley, Valentine and the other weren't disappointed. Don Zimmer called on Williams in the ninth inning, and he deliverd a vintage performance. After starting him out with two strikes, Williams walked Jim Lindeman. But he came back to strike out Jose Oquendo, who chased a high fastball, and retire Tony Pena on a weak grounder, earning his third save in three chances.

Williams, known for quick exits in Texas, likes to hang around the Cubs clubhouse after the game. He talks with reporters and teammates, acting like the model team player. Curtis Wilkerson had noticed a change in Williams.

"He's been acting different," said Wilkerson. "He knows that there are players here who won't let him get away with the stuff he did in Texas. The big pitcher keeps him straight." It was a reference to Rick Sutcliffe.

While Valentine had looked forward to seeing his former players, he chose not to visit the Chicago clubhouse. It was a disappointment to Williams, Wilkerson, and Paul Kilgus, all of whom asked about Valentine. "Is he afraid of us?" Williams asked. In truth, Valentine simply decided against intruding. "I've never seen another manager in my clubhouse," he said. "I don't know that I'd want to, either."

On the way back, Valentine was again wedged between Ringolsby and DeMarco. When talk turned to Toronto manager, Jimy Williams, Valentine admitted lingering concern about Cecilio Guante's beaning of Tony Fernandez in Texas. "It's hard for me to like him," he said of Williams, "when I know he is going to try to hurt my shortstop."

There was no retaliation the night of the errant fastball from Guante, who like Fernandez is from the Dominican Republic, but Valentine was worried after a tense conversation with Williams. Now he was afraid that Fletcher, Fernandez's counterpart at second, would have some trouble when the Rangers travelled to Toronto the next week. But that was a worry for another day.

On the 44 degree night of April 12, the Ryan Express rolled down the tracks at County Stadium. Through six innings Ryan had not allowed even one base runner while the Rangers took a 4-0 lead. His fastball was at its most impressive since he'd donned a Texas uniform, and the depleted Brewers hitters couldn't catch up to it. The Milwaukee lineup was still without several starters, and their replacements scored moral victories by simply putting the ball in play.

Ryan struck out 12 of the first 18 hitters, including B.J. Surhoff, Robin Yount, Rob Deer, Glenn Braggs, Terry Francona, and Joey Meyer in order the first time through the order. He started out the seventh by fanning Jim Gantner with a screaming fastball on the inside corner, then retired Surhoff when catcher Chad Kreuter made a terrific play on a dribbler down the first-base line. Yount lifted a high pop into foul territory behind first for what should have been the third out, but Franco called for Palmeiro to make the play, and Palmeiro thought Franco was saying he had it.

Ryan resumed the battle with Yount. The veteran center fielder extended him to 3-2, then took a borderline pitch at the knees that umpire Al Clark called ball four, ending the bid at perfection. Ryan struck out Deer to end the seventh, but threw 12 pitches he wouldn't have had to if the foul pop had been caught.

It showed in the next inning. After the Rangers scored four more runs in the top of the eighth, Ryan came out without his best velocity. He walked Braggs to start the inning, then lost a chance to pick up his sixth career no-hitter when Terry Francona, a left-handed hitter, lined a fastball over Steve Buechele's head for a single. Ryan then retired three straight to preserve the shutout before he and Valentine agreed to call it a night. Milwaukee scored a run against reliever Craig McMurtry in the ninth, but Texas still took an 8-1 victory.

Afterward, in a dingy meeting room in the bowels of County Stadium, Ryan spoke at an impromptu news conference. "I think I've had better stuff," said Ryan. "I think the big thing tonight was getting ahead of hitters. I had a good change-up, and they haven't seen me. I think that was to my advantage. Later in the game, they got a little more selective, stopped swinging at pitches. I was fortunate to get as far as I did without my curveball."

Ryan had thrown 134 pitches, including ninety-five fastballs. The best of those had registered at 97-98 MPH on the radar gun. He had gotten only one strike on the 11 curveballs he'd tried, but had had good control of his change-up. "What's amazing is he had no curveball all night," said Milwaukee right fielder Rob Deer, who struck out twice. "He couldn't get his curveball over. When he does, I hear he's really unhittable."

For Ryan, there was no great disappointment about losing the chance at a no-hitter. "As many times as I've been in that situation, I'm realistic enough to not get too caught up in it," he said. "The last six outs are the toughest outs."

Bobby Witt prolonged the winning streak with a 6-1 victory over the Brewers the next day. Finding his fastball, he struck out eight in eight innings to finish the three-game sweep–quite a change from the previous two years, when the Rangers went a combined 0-5 on their first trip to County Stadium.

That wasn't the only change. Sierra had become a cold-weather hitting fool. He was known for his slow starts, hitting .167 with only five RBIs the previous April and .214 in April 1987. But with high winds and temperatures dropping fast from 50 degrees, Franco hit a three-run homer and drove in four runs while Sierra kept swinging his hot bat. He was two-for-three with a sacrifice fly and two runs batted in, raising his batting average to .419.

"Julio has been talking to me a lot," Sierra said. "He's been saying I've got to hit in cold weather if I'm going to hit .300. I've been swinging the bat good, so I don't worry about cold weather. I just worry about swinging the bat good."

Franco did more than talk. His ninth-inning homer off reliever Paul Mirabella broke open a game that stood at 2-1 through eight innings and raised his RBI total to twelve, which led the American League. It was his second straight four-RBI game, his third of the season. But his message to Sierra was on his mind afterward. "He told me he was scared to hit the ball hard when it's cold," Franco said. "I said, 'If you'll get that out of your mind, you'll swing the bat hard. Try to hit the ball on the fat part of the bat, then it won't hurt.' That problem is all mental."

How cold was it? "I mean really cold," Sierra said. "You can't feel the bat. Your hands are freezing, your feet are freezing." Franco saw things differently. "It's not cold," he said. "Just wait till we get to Toronto and Cleveland."

Something very weird kept happening to the Rangers–a phenomenon rarely seen during their stay in Texas. Every time they did something, even when Valentine chose to do nothing special, things worked out. As the Rangers went on to Detroit, it was becoming routine.

For the second night in a row, an eighth-inning move considered but not made by Valentine weighed heavily in a tough victory—this one by a 4-2 score over the Tigers. Former University of Michigan quarterback Rick Leach broke a 2-2 tie with a pinch-hit single off reliever Frank Williams in the eighth inning as Texas won its fifth in a row, including four straight on what normally had been a depressing first trip to the East. Leach's game-winning hit brought some cheers from the Tiger Stadium crowd of 12,384 and caused Valentine to don a Michigan football helmet for his post-game press conference.

A man can get giddy when he's managing a team that puts together an 0-1 start, unprecedented in that team's eighteen-year history. "It was a tough one," Valentine said. "But when guys are playing good, everybody looks good."

Even the manager.

It had been Valentine's decision to let Witt take care of a 2-1 lead with the bases loaded in the eighth inning that was the turning point in Thursday's win in Milwaukee. The next night, Valentine played his cards exactly right in not pinch-hitting for .172 hitter Steve Buechele with the game on the line.

A nice recovery by Texas starter Jamie Moyer had left the scored tied 2-2 through the seventh inning. The unfortunate Williams, a right-hander who wasn't offered a contract by Cincinnati, appeared to have things under control in the eighth.

Franco reached second base, but there were two outs for Geno Petralli, who was one-for-three and had been robbed of another hit on a nice play by first baseman Torey Lovullo. Sparky Anderson ordered an intentional walk to bring up Buechele, who had apparently left his hitting shoes in Port Charlotte. He had struck out weakly in all three at bats against starter Doyle Alexander.

Valentine considered using Leach to hit for Buechele, even sending infielder Jeff Kunkel out to warm up, but let Buechele hit. "He's going to get a lot of big hits for us," Valentine said later. "He got a lot last year and he'll get a lot this year. If he's not seeing the ball or wasn't swinging good, he's usually honest about that. Doyle just had him tied up in knots. This was a different pitcher."

Williams jumped out ahead of Buechele 1-2, but then threw three straight balls to walk him and load the bases. Valentine called for Leach to bat for catcher Jim Sundberg, who was oh-for-two and had earlier cut himself above his left eye bouncing a helmet off the concrete dugout floor. Leach pulled a 1-1 fastball into right-center to score Franco and Petralli, providing a two-run cushion for Jeff Russell to protect.

Valentine said he never thought about possible second guesses when he saved Leach to hit for Sundberg instead of Buechele. "You'll have a long time before you see me pinch hit for Boo," Valentine said. "I'll be second-guessed for that for a long time."

With his 92 MPH sinker making its jet fighter dips and dives, Kevin Brown had the Tigers in his hands the next day. He was overpowering, leaving little doubt about another Texas victory. He allowed seven hits and would have had a shutout except for an error by Fletcher. He was clearly riding a wave.

"You walk out on the field and everybody knows you are going to win unless something really unusual happens," Brown said. "That has to have a positive effect on everybody. I don't think anybody isn't feeling it."

Alan Trammell's eighth-inning double was the only extra-base hit off Brown, who lowered his own ERA to 0.55 and the staff ERA to 2.08, which led the majors. He got 17 outs on ground balls and five with strikeouts, dropping Detroit's early-season batting average to .210. "We're not swinging the bats well but you have to call that performance pitching," Trammell said. "They've got some good arms over there."

Tigers manager Sparky Anderson was impressed with Brown. "There's a lot of life in that kid's arm," Anderson said. "The ball moves for him."

Pitching coach Tom House couldn't agree more. "I think," House said, "he's turned what they call the corner. Nobody can be perfect all year long, but I think we've got ourselves a pretty good little pitcher."

Sundberg had been around for some good starts in his eleven years in Texas. He was a rookie with Billy Martin's "Turn-Around Gang" in 1974 and a senior spokesman with Doug Rader's fast-out-of-the-gate team in 1983. But he sensed something different, something a little more tangible, about this team.

Standing around Rip Collins' visiting clubhouse in Detroit, Sundberg was talking about that difference. It lay in spring training, which the Rangers finished with wins in fifteen of their last nineteen games. "I've seen enough springs to know that how you do then doesn't always have much meaning for you. But what it shows this year is that this team is not a fluke," said Sundberg. "You don't go 15-4 at the end of the spring and then go 9-1 to start the season because of a fluke. It shows this team has the ability to contend."

Charlie Hough came out without control of his knuckleball on the Sunday getaway game in Detroit, but it didn't matter. Two-run homers by Buechele and Incaviglia and a solo shot into the upper deck in right by Palmeiro carried the Rangers past Jack Morris and the Tigers 9-6, finishing off a perfect 6-0 road trip— only the second perfect trip of at least six games in club history. It was the eighth straight win, and sent Valentine's team back to Arlington with a 10-1 record.

For many in the clubhouse, those numbers recalled 1987, when Texas had a 1-10 record after eleven games. "We just reversed it," said Buechele. "You look around the clubhouse now and everybody is taking it in stride. We expect to win every game, and we're doing it in a variety of ways. We lost in some pretty incredible ways (two years ago). We knew that had to end sooner or later."

As much as he enjoyed the new high, Valentine admitted to distinct memories of the 1-10 start two years ago. "I'd like to say I forgot about that but I didn't," Valentine said. "That was a lousy time. We couldn't do anything right, and the other teams wouldn't do anything wrong. We're doing some things wrong now, but the other teams aren't taking advantage of them."

* * *

The Dallas-Fort Worth area was practically drooling over Ryan and the Rangers. Television cameras and a few fans greeted the team when it arrived back at Dallas-Fort Worth Airport, and ticket lines began forming early the next morning at Arlington Stadium. Ryan was to start for the first time since Milwaukee.

Valentine recounted a story he had been told by a neighbor who was driving along Interstate 30 when Ryan took the mound for his Texas debut April 6. When Ryan struck out the side in the first inning against Detroit, cars on the highway started flashing their headlights. "Isn't that great?" asked Valentine.

Prospective owner George W. Bush spent time in the dugout before the game, telling reporters and anyone else who would listen about the direction he intended to take the Rangers after he got approval to purchase the club. His first priority, he said, was to cash in on the winning streak. "I manage to get around and make five or six speeches a week," Bush said. "Now all anybody ever wants me to talk about is the Rangers. I go to my local drugstore and I can't get out the door because everybody is talking baseball."

Greatness escaped Ryan again before the home folks. Watched by a Monday-night stadium record crowd of 38,274, the Express clanked to a stop without getting anyone out in the sixth inning. Robin Yount, the fourth batter of the game, had ended all thoughts of a no-hitter in the first inning. The shutout was gone in a two-run, three-hit second inning. Only stubbornness let Ryan escape trailing only 2-1 in the sixth inning. He gave up seven hits and walked six suddenly patient Brewers hitters in a five-inning outing. Pitching coach Tom House suspected the 134-pitch night in Milwaukee had taken its toll on Ryan. "He was a true veteran," House said. "He didn't feel real good about anything but stayed out there and gave it everything he had."

Texas could not mount an attack against Bill Wegman and lost 8-1, with rookie Bill Spiers inflicting much of the damage with an eighth-inning grand slam off Arnsberg. The Rangers' winning streak had been stopped at eight games.

"You're going to have games like that sometimes," Incaviglia said. "You play 162, and you're going to lose a few. We aren't going to worry about it. We have to keep doing what we've been doing. Nolan didn't have his best stuff tonight, but he'll be back and pitching in five days or so."

Valentine also shrugged off the disappointment. "Any baseball fan knows there's 162 games, and we're still off to a good start," Valentine said. "That's the most excitement I've seen in these fans for a baseball game here. We'll bring them back."

Bush and his group received unanimous approval from major league owners the next day, April 19, officially ending the Eddie Chiles era in Arlington. "The first time," quipped George W., "a Bush ever won an election unanimously."

Back on the road, the Rangers did not enjoy their final visit to Toronto's Exhibition Stadium. Fletcher was not knocked down by Blue Jays pitchers, but did go one-for-seven as Toronto scored 6-3 and 4-2 victories—the Rangers' first back-to-back losses of the season. Mike Flanagan shut down Texas Saturday, dropping its record to 12-4 overall and 0-2 on the road trip.

Valentine was still in a good mood. "This is pretty disastrous," he said after the second loss. "We'll have to call a team meeting tomorrow to make sure everybody has their wits about them."

Valentine was joking, but Ryan was all business as he prepared for his fourth start with the Rangers. After he had warmed up in the bullpen, taking longer than usual because the thermometer read forty-four degrees, he walked down to the dugout and delivered a short message to his teammates. "This," said Ryan, "ends today."

Sierra hit a high homer to right off Todd Stottlemyre, giving Ryan a 2-0 lead to take to the mound in the first inning. He ran into a little trouble, walking Nelson Liriano with one out and then failing to keep him close enough to first to spoil a steal attempt. But he blew a fastball past George Bell to end the inning. Then he struck out the side in the second, getting Fred McGriff, Jesse Barfield, and Ernie Whitt in order to show how seriously he took the proceedings.

Rafael Palmeiro made a nice catch on a blooped foul by Bell in the fourth inning, but Ryan needed little help. Walks of Lloyd Moseby in the third and sixth innings gave the Blue Jays their only base runners between the second and eighth innings, as Ryan again closed in on his sixth career no-hitter. He had all three pitches—fastball, curveball, and change-up—working, and was in complete control. Ryan rarely lets himself think about a no-hitter, but he thought of nothing else as he took a 4-0 lead to the mound in the ninth.

Ryan got the first out when Moseby hit a foul pop run down by Steve Buechele. Liriano, batting .208, came up for his fourth plate appearance. Ryan went 1-1 on him with two fastballs, then fired another. It was supposed to be on the outside corner, at the knees, but drifted to the middle of the plate. Liriano pulled it over Palmeiro's head and into the right-field corner for a triple.

Ryan was caught by the television cameras shouting a string of expletives on the mound, and shock set in on the Rangers' bench. "I felt like throwing my chair at him when he ran down the baseline," coach Davey Lopes said later about Liriano. Ryan lost his shutout when Kelly Gruber grounded out to Buechele, scoring Liriano from third, then closed out a 4-1 victory by getting Bell to hit a fly to Espy in center. It raised the Rangers' record to 13-4, but felt like a defeat in the clubhouse. "It's depressing, really," Lopes said. "Emotionally, it was a downer. I don't know about anybody else, but I think it felt secondary to win the game."

Even Ryan admitted to a strange feeling of defeat. "I'm more disappointed about that than [pleased] about winning the ball game," he said about the Liriano triple. "I generally just go out to try and win the ball game, but to get that close, it's disappointing."

Ryan seemed more befuddled than crushed when he lost a no-hit try on an eighth-inning single by Terry Francona April 12 in Milwaukee. He threw only one of 11 curveballs for strikes that night, relying almost entirely on his fastball to strike out a club-record fifteen Brewers. But this was different. His fastball may not have been as good as it had been in Milwaukee, but he had kept hitters guessing by throwing it only 70 percent of the time. Included in his 128 pitches were 23 curveballs, 12 for strikes, and 16 change-ups, 10 for strikes. "I thought I had better stuff today. I had the pitches to do it," said Ryan. "In Milwaukee, their guys hadn't seen me. It was cold, and I didn't feel that good. It was one of those games where you wonder how you got where you were at with the stuff you have."

Toronto hitters were amazed by what they'd seen. "I've seen him throw a lot harder before," said catcher Bob Brenly, who had played for San Francisco through the 1988 season. "He had a game at Candlestick [Park] where he was clocked over 100 [MPH]. I've seen him when he's had a better curveball. But I've never seen him when he had all three pitches working so well and was getting them over the plate."

As he walked to the team bus, Charlie Hough was still shaking his head. "This is as depressed as you can be over a victory," Hough said. "He was throwing so well . . . I really thought he was going to get it."

Bush's first move as the Rangers' managing general partner was a sign of support for the Grieve-Valentine regime. After Grieve and club president Mike Stone approached him on the subject, Bush received authority from his fellow owners to extend the contract of scouting director Sandy Johnson through the 1992 season. It not only eased concerns in Johnson's scouting department but also provided some assurance that the transition between owners might actually be as orderly as Bush and Rose had vowed.

"It really sends a message out," Johnson said. "Mike [Stone] and Tom [Grieve] have been talking scouting and development all along, and we're on a roll right now. You can see results."

Johnson admitted there had been some concern from scouts and minor-league personnel about the club's continued commitment to player development. Under Johnson's direction, the scouting department's budget had been more than doubled, and was well into the upper half among major league teams.

"When you go through changes in ownership, you're always concerned about the philosophy–do you have to operate any differently?" Johnson said. "This says I'll be able to keep doing my thing."

During Johnson's four years in Texas, the Rangers had added a sixth minor-league team and had stepped up their scouting in Latin America. Johnson's four drafts with the Rangers had produced Bobby Witt, Kevin Brown, Chad Kreuter, and Mike Stanley, in addition to top prospects Monty Farris, Dean Palmer, and Brian Bohanon.

Also, Johnson was instrumental in acquiring Incaviglia after Montreal had failed to sign him, and had taken a $50,000 gamble on Espy in the draft of unprotected minor-leaguers before the 1987 season. His push into Latin America had yielded prospects Juan Gonzalez, Sammy Sosa, Wilson Alvarez, and Jose Oliva.

"Sandy Johnson has been one of the most important people in our baseball operation," Grieve said. "Based on our philosophy, what we're trying to accomplish, Sandy has always been an important person in our franchise. Based on his performance in the last four years, I had a strong desire to keep him in the franchise."

With Johnson's contract out of the way, Stone and Grieve were the only members of the management team not under contract beyond the end of the season. Bush denied he'd had contract talks with either of them, but hoped Johnson's contract would also signify his confidence in them. "I don't sense any nervousness whatsoever," Bush said. "In discussions regarding Sandy, their opinions were well received. That should be a clear signal that we value their opinions."

Contract extensions would make a clearer signal. But for now, Bush's stance made it seem that at least one of the two executives was in danger of losing his job–and Stone appeared the more vulnerable.

While Julio Franco was off to a great start with Texas, he apparently was not missed in Cleveland. There were only 6,585 fans at Cleveland Stadium for Franco's first game back there with the Rangers, but they booed Franco relentlessly throughout an 11-7 victory for the Rangers. "They're great," Franco said of the fans. "I love them, they love me."

At least they knew he was there. In Cleveland, Franco was still remembered for his two disappearances as well as his erratic behavior in the clubhouse. It was quite a contrast with his image in Texas, where Franco was showing leadership skills in the clubhouse. *Cleveland Plain Dealer* columnist Bill Livingston wrote about the difference, saying that "next we'll hear that Margo Adams is giving marital counseling."

Franco remained oblivious to his reception. "I don't care what they do," he said. "We won the game, that's all that matters."

Pete O'Brien, Oddibe McDowell, and Jerry Browne had two hits apiece in the first game against their old team. But behind a four-RBI night for Buechele, the Rangers pounded out 19 hits against Rich Yett and relievers Scott Bailes and Brad Havens.

The big story of the next day was *Sports Illustrated*, which featured Ryan and the Rangers on its cover. The Rangers paused from their reading to take a 3-2, ten-inning victory over Indians left-hander Greg Swindell on a bloop double by Geno Petralli. That ended a 3-2 road trip and raised the team's record to 9-2 on the road and 15-4 overall.

"This was a big game because we started off the road trip 0-2 but came back to win three games," said Moyer, who stayed at 3-0 with a no-decision. "This could have been the kind of trip where we went 1-4 or 2-3. Three-and-two is a great way to go back."

While the Rangers led the American League West, they were impressed by the way Oakland and Kansas City had started the season. Texas led the Athletics by only one game and the Royals by three games. "We're off to a record start, and the A's are right there," Moyer said. "In any other division in baseball we would be four or six games in front."

Still, they were in first place and heading home to set a weekend attendance record in a scintillating series against the Red Sox. Friday night's game drew a crowd of 35,440, including about ten thousand who stuck around through a two-hour, two-minute rain delay to see the game eventually suspended at 1:21 A.M. because of the American League's curfew. A sellout crowd of 41,050 packed the park Saturday night, watching the Rangers win the suspended game 7-6 on Franco's twelfth-inning homer, then lose the regular game 8-5 on two homers by Boston's Ellis Burks, a native of nearby Everman.

Tickets for the Sunday finale had begun selling about ten days earlier when it became apparent that Ryan and Roger Clemens were on a collision course. They had never pitched against each other before, but would in the final contest of the three-game series. The last tickets were sold by 10 A.M. for the afternoon game, giving the Rangers back-to-back sellouts for the first time ever.

For the Yankees, Red Sox, Cubs, or Dodgers, that might not be an accomplishment, but this was the Rangers. The team was playing baseball, and scalpers were turning a profit.

Times were changing.

The Ryan-Clemens matchup disappointed only Clemens. History prevailed for seven innings, but in the end gave way to the spirit of the moment at Arlington Stadium. Another year, another month, and Palmeiro's long drive to right field would have been nothing but a memento for one of the fans jammed into the bleacher seats in foul territory. But, befitting the best month of baseball ever in North Texas, Palmeiro's drive stayed true. It struck a screen on the foul pole for a two-run homer in the eighth inning, turning a 1-0 loss to Clemens into a 2-1 victory for Ryan. One day's history was rewritten, as the Rangers escaped from their bumbling past.

Palmeiro's third home run brought Ryan to his feet in the dugout and began a massive celebration in the stands, filled by a sell-out crowd of 40,429. "I think the fans got their money's worth today," Ryan said. "They came out with the expectation of seeing a good game, and they did."

By winning two of three games against Boston, Texas finished April 17-5. The .773 winning percentage was its best ever for a month, but even at twelve games over .500 they were a mere one game ahead of Oakland. Without Jose Canseco and Mark McGwire for most of the month, the A's had gone 18-8 in April.

For seven innings, the showdown between the forty-two-year-old Ryan and twenty-six-year-old Clemens had provided abridged versions of their careers. Ryan was winning the K-count, but in the process losing to Clemens because he, and not the younger fireballer, was beating himself. Ryan's command of pitches had been similar to the April 23rd game in Toronto, when he came within two outs of his sixth career no-hitter. For the third time in his five starts in Texas, he had worked through the fourth inning without allowing a hit.

But this time he trailed 1-0. Boston scored a first-inning run when Danny

Heep trotted home after an 0-2 fastball from Ryan to Jim Rice sailed past Petralli. "I was setting up for a fastball in," Petralli said. "I felt like I should have caught it. I just didn't get it. I would have felt bad if we didn't score."

A 1-0 Texas loss would have focused attention on first-base umpire Durwood Merrill. His call on a close play kept Heep out of a double play in the first inning. But this day there were no villains – only heroes.

It was a fitting end to the month.

14

"If You Can't Stand the Heat..."

There was going to be little room for error in the American League West. This had been obvious since the World Series, when the Athletics' surprising five-game loss to Los Angeles had ended any thoughts of complacency by Oakland. That singular lack of complacency became apparent when, after compiling the league's lowest earned run average in 1988, the A's added wandering Mariner Mike Moore.

It would take a sustained effort to stay with Oakland, and five days into May the Rangers buckled under the chore of matching the A's victories. Five days after the best month in its history, Texas slipped out of the lead in the American League West. The Rangers lost six of their first seven games in May.

Cleveland started the slide, scoring 19 runs in two nights at Arlington Stadium, and pounding Bobby Witt and Jamie Moyer. Kevin Brown answered those losses with a two-hitter against New York, but Charlie Hough failed to make it out of the first inning in an 11-7 loss the next night, cutting the division lead to only percentage points and giving the Rangers a 3-4 record on the homestand that included the victory of Nolan Ryan over Roger Clemens.

Needing a lift, the Rangers ran into trouble in Boston, where Clemens, the Red Sox, and an excited city awaited Clemens-Ryan II. Fenway Park was buzzing at game time. Boston papers contributed to what passes as baseball hysteria in May, writing all week about the feud between Ryan and the Red Sox.

Ellis Burks was still angry about being hit on the shoulder and earflap of his helmet by a Ryan fastball in Arlington, and Clemens had not backed off the stance that he had to make certain "adjustments" to his pitching style to protect his hitters. It all gave a Wrestle Mania-like air to the proceedings.

But there was not much comparison between this game and their previous match-up. Five days after a dominating shutdown by Ryan, Mike Greenwell twice wrapped fastballs around the right-field foul pole for home runs–the first giving Boston a 1-0 lead, the second tying the score 3-3 in the sixth inning. And things really got out of hand in the seventh inning.

Jody Reed led off with a double to left field and was bunted to third base by Marty Barrett. Up came Burks. Ryan jumped ahead of him with two balls and two strikes, then buzzed a fastball high and inside. Burks ducked out of the way, then dropped his bat and began berating Ryan. He took a few steps toward the mound before Geno Petralli intervened. While this was going on, Jim Rice lumbered out of the dugout carrying his bat and both benches and bullpens emptied onto the field.

"I was making a statement," Burks said later. "I told him he can't throw any more like that."

But Burks's reaction seemed more like an overreaction to Ryan and Valentine. After all, if a pitcher wants to throw at a hitter, he's probably not going to do it with the game tied and a runner on third base.

"I think that's just a reflection of what's built up," Ryan said. "I can't believe if he had given it any thought at all he would think anybody is throwing at him in that situation." Valentine agreed. "It's absolutely impossible for a pitcher to be trying to throw at a hitter with a 2-2 pitch and the winning run on third," he said. "He's just a little shaky from the other day. I don't blame him."

Burks eventually won the confrontation, regrouping and grounding a single through the left side. It opened the door to a four-run inning, putting Boston ahead 7-3. With the crowd of 32,555 roaring, Valentine came out of the dugout to relieve Ryan after the RBI single by Burks. In a sarcastic moment, Ryan tipped his hat to the crowd as he left the mound. "I just wanted to acknowledge the fact that I heard them," Ryan said. "They're fans. They're entitled to do whatever they want. I expected the reaction I got tonight with everything that had been said and written."

Ryan then walked with his head down into the dugout and up the tunnel to the quirky old visiting clubhouse. He didn't even seem to notice when one Boston fanatic showered him with beer. "It's not the first time," he said, "and I'm sure it won't be the last. Fans are fans."

What stuck with Valentine afterward was the memory of an aborted rally in the eighth inning. Doubles by Ruben Sierra and Franco off Clemens and Lee Smith, respectively, led a comeback that brought the Rangers within 7-6, with runners on first and second for Cecil Espy with two outs. Espy hit a routine grounder to Reed at short, but somehow Jeff Stone had gotten into second base ahead of Reed's flip to Barrett. That's the way it looked but umpire Rich Garcia called Stone out, sealing a 7-6 loss.

"I was calling safe myself because I knew I was safe," said Stone, a twenty-eight-year-old journeyman passing through the Rangers on his way out of base-ball. "It was just an unbelievable call. He took us out of the inning. We had him on the ropes. Bases loaded, anything could happen—wild pitch, error. That was a big blow. Everybody got so quiet in the dugout after that . . . I told myself if there's a grounder I'm going to beat the throw. I bust my butt getting down there and beat the throw, but get called out. It's a little frustrating."

Coupled with Dave Stewart's 5-3 win in Detroit, the loss dropped Texas into second place in the American League West, one full game behind Oakland. While the second Ryan-Clemens match-up was memorable, it was hardly how the Rangers had hoped to begin their ten-game road trip.

Things never got much better on the trip. They were swept in three games by the Boston Red Sox. In New York, the Rangers won one, lost one, and had one game rained out. They also lost a player, as Rick Leach simply vanished between Boston and New York. There was an irony to the disappearance, as Leach had spoken for the team after the last of three losses at Fenway Park.

"As hot as we were early in the season, I don't think anybody thought we were going to keep playing that way for a long time," Leach said. "It just doesn't work that way in this game. But the same ingredients are there. We just have to put a cork in the dam and get back on a winning streak. There's no need to panic. We're right in the thick of things. We just have to be man enough as individuals to keep fighting."

The next day, his name was on the Yankee Stadium lineup card but he was elsewhere in the city. General Manager Tom Grieve filed a missing persons report with the New York Police Department, and teammates feared he had been mugged on the subway. Leach's absence became a full-scale police matter when he still had not contacted anyone by the next morning. A search was underway by New York police, Yankees security, and the security staff from Commissioner Bart Giamatti's office. It led the police, along with hotel security and Valentine, to inspect Leach's room at Manhattan's Grand Hyatt Hotel. They were looking for a name, an address, anything that could lead them to Leach, but instead found something that shouldn't have shocked Valentine but did.

Valentine was not without his own vices, but had a baseball man's perspective of the world. There was nothing more important to him than the game, and he believed nothing should prevent a player from being in condition to play it. But Leach apparently had a problem. The police found a cellophane bag containing less than one ounce of marijuana—proof perhaps of a bigger problem. While this was hardly headline news, it drew a police citation—called a desk appearance ticket—for misdemeanor possession.

About the same time this was happening, Leach called Grieve. He was all right, and wanted to meet Grieve somewhere away from the hotel. Grieve told no one but Valentine and walked across Manhattan to meet Leach while the team continued to worry.

Grieve and Leach arrived at Yankee Stadium shortly before 7 P.M. Leach made a brief apology to his teammates—tearful at one point—then went with Grieve to a press workroom for a news conference.

Leach clearly had not seen a razor since leaving Boston forty-eight hours before. He looked tired and sounded sorry about the whole affair. "There's no way you can put it that will say anything good about what happened," he said. "I don't feel good about it. I'm going to be man enough to face up to what happened."

Leach would be lost to the Rangers for three games, as Giamatti's office ordered him to stay in New York for drug testing. He was allowed to rejoin the team only on the condition that he submit to regular drug counseling and testing.

It was an unsettling incident that contributed to a 2-7 road trip which ended with three losses in four games at Kansas City. Two were sure signs of a team heading in the wrong direction.

A late rally fizzled Friday. Texas trailed 4-2 in a game started by Bobby Witt and Kansas City's Charlie Leibrandt before awakening with two outs in the bottom of the ninth inning. Palmeiro got things going with his second double of the game (his eleventh of the year). Ruben Sierra followed with an RBI single through the right side of the infield.

Royals reliever Steve Farr then threw an outside fastball to Julio Franco, who lined it down the right-field foul line. As surely as Palmeiro's dramatic game-winner against Clemens two weeks earlier, it was heading for the foul pole. But this one kept slicing until it dove into the seats just to the right of the pole. Foul ball. Franco then hit a routine fly to end another loss.

What happened to destiny's team? "When Julio hits one that way, it's a different spin," Palmeiro said, "The ball spins away. I hit it, and the ball stays straight going that way. That's the only difference."

Franco sat in front of his locker for a long time afterward, shouting obscenities at the baseball gods. "I can't believe that ball went foul," he said. "I hit the ball ten feet inside the foul line. It was tailing like crazy. That's the game right there. When I hit it, I said, 'Home run, home run.' "

Before returning to Texas Sunday, the Rangers had to suffer through both a two-hour, eleven-minute rain delay and a 3-2, ten-inning loss. The Royals scored one run when Sierra and Cecil Espy let a liner by rookie Luis de los Santos fall between them, then got the winning run when Espy's throw from shallow center pulled catcher Geno Petralli up the baseline. Valentine still thought Petralli made a swipe tag on Willie Wilson. He briefly argued the call with umpire Derryl Cousins on the field and let fly a string of expletives in the clubhouse.

It was an appropriate end to a trip that dropped Texas to 20-15 and all the way from first place in the West to fourth, behind Oakland, Kansas City, and California. The Rangers didn't know it then, but they would stay in the same position most of the season.

How does the song go?

Riding high in April, shot down in May.

Yeah, that's it.

* * *

Torrential rains postponed the opener of a nine-game homestand before the first pitch was thrown. It was still pouring when Valentine arrived at his twenty-three-acre spread in east Fort Worth the night of May 16. As he did every night when the team was at home, Valentine walked to his barn to move the horses that are such a joy to his wife, Mary. He rotated some into the barn and let some outside to roam the property in the night. It was a mindless chore.

But the next morning, Valentine awoke late, at almost eight A.M. He knew something was wrong when Mary looked out the window and saw the neighbor's pasture under water. What once had been Valentine's pasture had also become a mighty river. Nearby Village Creek had overflowed after a tremendous rush of water from Lake Arlington.

Valentine had known his property was in a flood plain when he bought it in 1986, but neighbors said there hadn't been a flood in a hundred years. They called it the hundred-year flood plain, and they were right.

This certainly was a flood. The house was safe on high ground, but somewhere in the water were three horses including Bobby Jr.'s Welsh pony, Cinnamon Stitch.

Valentine pulled on bright green running shorts and dashed out the back door. In the distance, atop a tiny knoll that had become an island, he could see two of the horses. He ran to the barn for harness and lead ropes and tried to make his way to them. For thirty minutes he looked for a way through the water, but everywhere he turned the water was too deep and too swift. He noticed traffic helicopters circling overhead, and went to call the stations. Maybe they have seen a way to get to the horses.

The KVIL copter swooped down to pick up Valentine and a neighbor's son. It airlifted them to the horses, dropping them in waist-deep water.

They put harnesses and lead ropes on the horses, then started a roundabout route back to the house. As before, it seemed, the water was too deep to walk the horses through. Finally they settled on a back way out through the four-foot stream. It took them almost an hour.

Valentine watched for the pony the whole way, but never spotted her. When he got back to the house, he saw Mary and two friends, Zack Minasian and Pat Martchenke, in the middle of the flood waters. He yelled at them to get back, and saw that they were trying to get to the pony. They were too late, however, and the pony disappeared into the water.

With Bobby, Jr. expected home soon, Valentine took it upon himself to locate the pony's body and get it buried – fast. With the help of Minasian, Martchenke, and *Star-Telegram* columnist Jim Reeves – an intrepid reporter, always on the scene – he managed it. It didn't feel much like a victory.

By the time the ordeal was finished, it was time to leave for the ballpark. Much of Valentine's time before the game was spent recounting his adventures, which had been broadcast live by KVIL radio. "We were trying to get out of there because we thought the water was going to get higher. I'm thinking it's going to get two-three feet higher any minute," Valentine said. "They had told me the lake was going to open and the skies were going to open. Finally, we got back to the road and an hour, forty-five minutes after I started, we were out of there."

Valentine admitted to being legitimately scared. "It was honest-to-goodness scary," he said. "It wasn't so bad when we could see the house, but when we got about fifty acres away, in the middle of the woods where we couldn't see anything, and the water was moving, it got real serious."

The only good news for Valentine came when he went to the bullpen that night. Jose Guzman, out since the beginning of spring training, had gotten the go-ahead from Dr. Frank Jobe to begin throwing off a mound. He had a good workout, and said he was pain-free. Guzman was considered about a month away from beginning a rehab stint in the minor leagues.

But things were not to be that simple. Guzman came out for his second session throwing off the mound two days later. He loosened up, threw a few pitches, then called pitching coach Tom House over. He was having more pain in his shoulder, and could not complete the workout.

Guzman's future had appeared unlimited, but on May 22 he walked away from Arlington Memorial Hospital feeling a new kinship with teammate and countryman Edwin Correa. Like Correa, Guzman would have to cope with an injury that could end his pitching career. He had been out all season with a subluxation of the shoulder, but now an arthrogram and Magnetic Resonance Imaging exam revealed what Dr. Mike Mycoskie, the Rangers' orthopedic specialist, called a partially torn rotator cuff.

Mycoskie made no promises. "A lot of guys who have had this type thing have come back," Mycoskie said. "It doesn't have to be career-threatening. But no matter what happens, he's not going to pitch this year."

Guzman would have his shoulder examined by Jobe, who was expected to recommend arthroscopic surgery. Mycoskie said that Jobe might find more than a partial tear. "We've had people who have had complete tears that didn't show up on X-rays," Mycoskie said. "When you go in, it is a complete tear. But there's definitely some kind of tear, without any question."

When House got the news, he walked away from the clubhouse, heading up the tunnel to the dugout. He was angry. Mycoskie had said the tear must have happened in the most recent throwing session, but House wasn't so sure. Guzman had never before been given an MRI test or arthrogram, so it was impossible to know if he'd had this tear since August, when he'd first complained of shoulder pain. House, on the verge of tears, vented his frustration for reporters. "I am sick of this," House said. "I am sick of pitchers having a look on their face like the one I just saw on Guzie's face."

Since the June night in 1987 when Correa had almost become a side-armer to get through five innings of a game against Minnesota, the careers of four other promising young pitchers had been careers interrupted for at least one year apiece.

A roll call:

• Correa, then twenty-one, had won sixteen games in the major leagues when a stress fracture was diagnosed in his shoulder. He was now twenty-three, had undergone one arthroscopic surgery to remove torn cartilage from his shoulder and seemed on the verge of complete recovery twice, but hadn't pitched in a game since July 5, 1987. He was attempting another comeback under House's supervision, lifting weights to strengthen the shoulder as a last-ditch alternative to major surgery.

• Arnsberg had been the top pitcher in the International League at age twenty-four with Columbus in 1987, but what was called a strained elbow ended his brief stay with the New York Yankees later that year. One trade and seven months later, it was found he had a torn ligament in his elbow, and he missed the entire 1988 season.

• Ray Hayward, drafted ahead of Roger Clemens in 1983, had just turned twenty-seven when he threw a six-hit shutout in Toronto last May. But by June he was experiencing serious pain in his shoulder and his 1988 season was finished in August. He tried a comeback in spring training but underwent rotator cuff surgery May 2.

• Jose Cecena possessed both a nasty screwball and Valentine's confidence in spring training, 1988. He was twenty-four when he earned his first save in the major leagues but by June went on the disabled list with what was originally considered a minor inflammation. Surgery to remove bone chips was performed in August, and he was back in Jobe's office in March for the same "Tommy John" surgery that Arnsberg had needed one year earlier.

With Guzman included, that was four starting pitchers and one potential stopper sidelined at the average age of twenty-four, when they should have been coming into bloom. It was an unprecedented run of pitching injuries for the Texas organization–but management was showing no great alarm.

"I don't think it's an inordinate amount [of injuries] for a major league team," said Rangers president Mike Stone. "The old adage that you can never have enough pitchers is based on the fact that injuries to throwing arms are fairly commonplace."

Mycoskie, part of the Arlington family of physicians which had worked for the team since the Rangers' arrival, also saw the string of injuries as unavoidable for pitchers. "I've spent a lot of time thinking about this, talking to people in the organization, and there's really nothing to pinpoint other than a bad rash of problems," Mycoskie said. "There's no pattern to the injuries. I wish there [were], so we could take a look at something we're doing and try to stop it. I don't think we can put the blame on anything. It's just bad luck. That's what it boils down to."

Texas was hardly the only team with this problem. St. Louis had been without Danny Cox and Greg Mathews for most of the last two years, and in San Francisco, Atlee Hammaker, Mike Krukow, and Dave Dravecky had undergone surgery in recent years. There were many other cases.

"It's probably just our turn," Mycoskie said. "Some of those guys are just getting to the age where pitchers start to have problems. Three or four years ago we had (Bobby) Witt, Guzman, Correa, Mitch Williams, and those guys.

Real young pitchers are not going to have that many problems. Now we're getting to point they've put on all those innings. We're starting to get to the point where you see wear and tear. Some of their shoulders just aren't up to it. All the good high school pitchers don't make it. Their arms wear out. Maybe we're starting to see some of our arms wear out."

A sad assessment.

On the field, the Rangers could not get out of their funk. They went 4-4 for the rain-soaked homestand, then took a schizophrenic road trip during which they swept a three-game series in Minnesota, only to lose all three games in Baltimore. The Orioles, a surprising early leader in the American League East after winning fifty-four games in 1988, finished a sweep against Texas with an 8-5 victory over Witt. Baltimore had beaten Ryan and Moyer 6-1 and 6-2, respectively, the previous two nights.

The three games were not the only losses in Baltimore. Pitchers kept falling, too. Middle reliever Craig McMurtry went on the fifteen-day disabled list with tendinitis in his shoulder Monday, the same day Charlie Hough got two cortisone shots in his aching shoulder. Left-hander Jamie Moyer came out of his Memorial Stadium start clutching his shoulder in the fourth inning and joined McMurtry, Guzman, Correa, et al., on the disabled list. He was flown back to Arlington, where Mycoskie diagnosed the injury as a strained triceps muscle.

The Rangers expected Moyer to miss at least a month, leaving the organization with only four of its top eight starters. "The rotator is clean, and it's not ligament tears," Valentine said. "It is muscular. I'm not looking at it as real short term, but I don't think he's going to need an operation or be permanently disabled." Mike Jeffcoat, a disaster when given an opportunity in previous seasons, was recalled to replace Moyer in the starting rotation.

Then there was Witt. He was healthy but had gone 2-5 with a 7.97 earned run average in his last seven starts, sending his season ERA to 6.25. It had been only 1.43 higher when he'd been packed off for Class AAA Oklahoma City on May 10, 1988, but now the Rangers' brass claimed he was on the way to solving his problems. Baltimore manager Frank Robinson differed. "He's not the same pitcher he used to be," Robinson said. "He had that real hard breaking ball and the ninety-plus fastball. He was devastating before."

This was not how the team that went 17-5 figured to be coming out of May—27-22 and struggling to stay in contact with California and Oakland at the top of the division. Its distance behind the first-place Angels had grown to 5½ games.

"If I'm going to look back, I'm going to look all the way back to April," Valentine said. "I want to remember April, not May. There wasn't much that happened in May I want to remember."

Valentine's team could still look ahead to the Arlington Stadium series against Oakland and California June 9-14. It had not played the two teams at the top of the West all year. Things seemed to be breaking right, despite a strange thing Ryan said after a June 6 White Sox game. "Maybe," he said, "the next time I pitch they should have helmet night in the bleachers."

The future Hall of Famer was having his best season in a decade, but his comment was prophetic. On the eve of the Oakland series, a strange thing happened. Ryan gave up four homers in a game for the first time in his 690 appearances in the major leagues—and he won.

Ryan hung on to get the victory as the Rangers beat the White Sox 11-7. He allowed six runs in eight innings, the most runs he had given up in a victory since 1976. He picked up his seventh victory earlier than any season since 1977, as the Rangers took three of four from Chicago. They moved back to seven games over .500 (32-25), 5½ games behind first-place Oakland, and one game behind third-place Kansas City. They were entering a stretch of six games against the Athletics and the second-place Angels.

"We're playing good," Valentine said. "We're swinging the bats good. We're playing good defense. The guys who were struggling are swinging the bats better and the guys who were swinging 'em well have maintained it. We're feeling good."

Sierra got four hits in the victory over the White Sox, including homers from both sides of the plate—a three-run shot and a solo homer—and a double. He drove in five runs and scored three himself, moving within four of teammate Julio Franco in the league's RBI race, 50-46. The three-run homer came off reliever Ken Patterson in the ninth, when Sierra tried to hit a gap to finish off the cycle. Instead he hit his ninth homer.

"I've never hit for the cycle, so that's what I was thinking about," Sierra said. "I was trying to hit the ball in the gap and I hit it good. It went a long way."

Sierra continued to show the effects of a winter spent pumping iron in a Puerto Rico gym. He had his fourth four-hit game of the year and raised his RBI total to a level he had never before reached in June.

"He felt in stature he didn't really measure up to the big boys," Valentine said of the twenty-three-year-old Sierra. "He wasn't grown up physically. He's grown up physically now. I think Julio has helped him grow up mentally."

Sierra demonstrated his new strength with a 401-foot homer to right field off Eric King. "He let the ball get in on him, and was still strong enough to put the ball out of the park," Ryan said.

White Sox manager Jeff Torborg knew he was in for a long night. "I couldn't believe it," he said. "It was chin-high and (Sierra) just muscled it out of there."

With Rafael Palmeiro and Pete Incaviglia driving in two runs apiece, it marked the third time in Ryan's twelve starts that his Texas teammates had scored at least eight runs, and the seventh time they had scored at least six. The Rangers were averaging 5.5 runs behind Ryan—quite an improvement from 1987, when he had led the National League with a 2.76 earned-run average but had won only eight of thirty-four starts.

"He's accomplished many feats," said Buddy Bell, who had his second consecutive two-hit night. "I think that's probably the least explainable."

The support doesn't surprise Ryan.

"This is a good offensive ball club," Ryan said. "When you have a ball club
that is as good offensively as this one, you're going to have nights when you
don't deserve to win but still win. You get a few extra wins like that." Even on
helmet night.

It was a good way to go into the first series of the year against Oakland,
which continued to amaze by winning without Jose Canseco. He had been out
all season with a bad wrist (and would not play until after the All-Star break).
The Rangers had Charlie Hough, Bobby Witt, and hot rookie Kevin Brown facing Oakland's Dave Stewart, Storm Davis, and Mike Moore.

Just when it looked like the Rangers were going to tilt in the opener, left-
handed rookie Kenny Rogers came in to unplug the Arlington Stadium pinball
machine before Mark McGwire hit another quadruple bonus. Instead of a free
game, Rogers and tag-team partner Jeff Russell gave Texas a confidence-
building 11-8 victory before a Friday-night crowd of 35,799.

There had been six lead changes before Rogers bailed Cecilio Guante out of
a two-on, no-out jam to protect a two-run lead in the eighth. Russell then
pitched a perfect ninth for his fourth save in a week as the Rangers raised their
record to 4-1 on the homestand, moving within 4½ games of Oakland.

"Kenny was unbelievable," Russell said. "The job he did was a key to the
game. He got us out of a big inning and really picked us up. I think that let a lot
of wind out of their sails."

On a night when Hough again struggled and Stewart had his shortest outing in two seasons, there was a long roll call of offensive contributors. Incaviglia had the most timely hit – a two-run double off Eric Plunk to break an
8-8 tie in the sixth inning. Franco had a solo homer and drove in runs in four
different rallies, raising his American League-high RBI total to 54 and equalling his 1988 total. Sierra had his second straight four-hit night, Bell got his
first RBI in seventy-four plate appearances with a bases-loaded walk against
Gene Nelson, and Cecil Espy drove in a run by surprising the A's with a two-out
bunt single.

It all added up to make McGwire's first-inning grand slam off Hough a moot
point as the Rangers won their first game of the year against the defending
American League champs. "That was an exciting game to watch," Valentine
said. "It was probably as exciting a game as we've played in Arlington. People
say (the A's) aren't at full strength, but the guys they have playing are doing an
outstanding job."

The Rangers hoped the game sent a message. "It's got to be a plus," said
Russell, who earned his fourteenth save in sixteen chances. "It's got to show,
especially to them, what this ball club is made of. We're a ball club to be reck-
oned with, not a ball club that's going to fall over if someone scores a few runs.
We're going to play tough."

Leads were especially cheap in the first four innings of the opener. Stewart and the A's failed to hang onto 4-0 and 6-5 leads, while Hough and reliever Gary Mielke couldn't maintain a 5-4 lead.

"We added on but they added on, too," said A's designated hitter Dave Parker. "It felt like a basketball game out there with all those lead changes."

The game was decided in the Oakland eighth inning. Texas led 10-8, but an error by Palmeiro and Guante's walk of Dave Henderson put two on with no outs. Valentine called for Rogers to face Parker. He hit Rogers' first pitch, an inside fastball, right to Franco, starting a double play. "Sometimes you give up hits, but this time I got a ground ball," Rogers said. "I was going to stay in on him. I was just happy he hit the first pitch."

Texas went into the tank the next night against arch-enemy Storm Davis, who—inexplicably—had baffled the Rangers since his "Cy Clone" days in Baltimore. Davis was 10-0 against Texas until losing to Russell in June 1988, and raised his career record against the Rangers to 12-1 with a 5-1 victory to even the series. He gave up two hits and one walk in five innings before Tony La Russa turned to the bullpen combination of Todd Burns and Rick Honeycutt to close it out.

Witt walked three of the game's first four hitters in allowing four runs in the first inning. There was no getting out of that hole, so the Rangers began play on Sunday needing a victory to win the series and get back within 4½ games. But while many of the faces were new, the team's performance in its biggest series to date was all too familiar. Bats went dead when they should have rung.

Moore and two relievers combined on a three-hitter to beat Texas by a 5-1 score for the second consecutive game, giving the A's a split-decision victory in the series. The autopsy was easy.

"We just didn't do our job," Franco said. "It's as simple as that. Last night we didn't put enough hits together. Tonight, the same thing."

Six different Oakland pitchers held Texas to two runs and seven hits. Oakland had recovered from its 11-8 loss Friday night to win two out of three, moving three games in front of second-place California in the American League West. This was the A's biggest lead of the year, and 6½ games ahead of fourth-place Texas.

Moore, pursued by Texas in the winter before signing as a free agent with Oakland, raised both his record this year and his lifetime mark against Texas to 8-4 while lowering his earned run average to 1.91, behind only California left-hander Chuck Finley among American League pitchers.

Moore gave up three hits and allowed only an unearned run in 6⅓ innings, striking out three and walking only one.

"I knew he would help them," Valentine said. "He's a good pitcher. He pitched different tonight. He came up with an overhand curveball, and pitched away most of the night. He was like seeing a new guy for the first time for a lot of our hitters."

Texas hitters could not afford to continue their two-game letdown the next night, when the Angels followed the A's into town. The California pitching staff led the American League with a 2.82 ERA.

"You've got to beat these guys," Franco said. "These are the guys we have to beat–Oakland, Kansas City, and California. You know they're going to be up there when September comes around. We have to be there, too. We have to start now."

A surprising shutout by Mike Jeffcoat, who had replaced Jamie Moyer in the starting rotation, and a doubleheader sweep keyed by Ryan and Hough gave the Rangers a three-game sweep of the Angels. It spoiled the return of Doug Rader, who had been hired to manage California.

Rader, back in the big leagues, was *in control*. That was what everybody said, hard as it was for long-time Rader-watchers to believe. But times change, and sometimes people change, too. Maybe Douglas Lee Rader had.

Rader didn't want to talk about it, but there was a certain symmetry in his return to Arlington with the Angels. They were baseball's most surprising team, just as his Rangers had been the biggest surprise in the American League in the first half of 1983, their first season under Rader's control. The Angels had gone from 75-87 disappointments the previous two seasons to a team that thus far had been alone in persistently pressing the Oakland Athletics.

With a pitching staff that had already thrown eleven shutouts, California looked superior to the Texas team he took from sixth-place in 1982 into first place at the All-Star break in 1983. But had Rader himself really changed? He certainly wanted everyone to think so, and some people did.

"It seems like he's stepped back and looked at what happened," said Baltimore right-hander Dave Schmidt, a member of the '83 Rangers. "It's a sign of a mature individual to admit mistakes, and I read stories all winter where he said he made mistakes in Texas. I think that's good."

Rader–and almost everyone else associated with the Rangers' quick start after he replaced Darrell Johnson–remembers the '83 season as an incredible struggle. At times that year, according to Charlie Hough, Rader's managerial style teetered on the brink of insanity.

"He was driving himself crazy with what he was doing," Hough said, "and he was driving the ball club. He just thought he was going to change everything in the organization by being tougher."

Rader finished his tenure in Texas with a 155-200 record as manager, including a 111-167 record after the '83 team got off to a 44-33 start. There was no way to avoid an ugly crash when Rader's train jumped the tracks after the All-Star break that first season. It did enough destruction along the way to leave Rader out of the circle of major league managers for 3½ years after Texas president Mike Stone fired him in May of 1985. The time away gave Rader a chance for introspection. He arrived at many of the same conclusions others had reached years before.

"There's no question I was overbearing," Rader said. "I tried to get more out of us, pushed people harder than I should, and wound up frustrating a lot of people. Looking back on it, you wish you hadn't done it that way, but what is the right way to do it? It's well documented that I put too much emotion into what I did. It affected a lot of people. I'd be silly to do it again. Not that losses don't affect me now, but I don't carry them with me the next day. I'm just lightening up."

Still, there was skepticism in the Texas clubhouse about the "new" Rader. One player called him a "wolf in sheep's clothing."

Rader had taken a Texas team that had gone 64-98 under Don Zimmer and Johnson and turned it into a world-beater for two of the first three months of 1983. A 12-9 April was followed by a 10-15 May, then everything came together in June. With Mike Smithson and Frank Tanana carrying the starting rotation, Buddy Bell hitting six homers, Billy Sample batting .309, and George Wright driving in 23 runs, the Rangers went 19-9 to move into first place in the West. The spirit of that team was personified by a brawl that started when Wayne Tolleson took exception to a cheap shot at second base from California's Bobby Grich.

Rader held frequent meetings trying to mold the team in his own macho image. He shouted at opposing pitchers from the dugout, exploded into rages during post-game interview sessions, and generally kept everyone on edge. At the time, Jim Sundberg had described his style as MBI: "managing by intimidation."

"He wanted us to do real well badly, and as is the case players were over-trying a little bit, pressing," Schmidt said. "That doesn't work for players. It doesn't work for anybody in sports. It was all right when the team was playing well. When a team plays as well as we played in the first half of 1983 you just feel great going out there. But when things start to go bad it's a test of a manager's true feelings, true skills. It seemed like we all tried to do a little too much. We kept being pushed, and the results showed [in] the way the year turned out."

Rader has similar memories of a year which ended with the Rangers 77-85 and in third place, twenty-two games behind the Chicago White Sox. "Not to blow smoke in my direction, but in '83 it was really a matter of pulling and pushing," Rader said. "It took an enormous amount of energy . . . It wore me out, it wore my coaches out, and it wore my players out. It just wasn't meant to be maintained."

Rader now claimed that he'd realized all along that his first Rangers team was on borrowed time at the top. "I saw how we were winning. I saw our bull-pen. I saw every time there was a chance to score a two-out run, usually the run scored," Rader said. "It wasn't as though we just went out and won ball games. The truth is we really did get a lot of breaks. You hate to talk about it's being a matter of breaks because there were an awful lot of good guys on that team, and they were giving everything they had. I don't mean to make less of it than what it was—a real nice three months . . . But when you really look carefully at that ballclub, it was very fragile."

Sundberg still called 1983 his most difficult year, largely because of a personality difference with Rader, but he agreed with Rader's assessment of the team. "We really were overachievers," he said. "We hung together in that first half . . . somehow."

Hough also agreed. "He (Rader) didn't have a good enough ballclub here," he said. "We played well at times, but it was obvious with our depth and talent level we couldn't compete for that length of time. I think it got to him. It made him less of a manager. He couldn't accept our talent level and manage that talent level to maybe raise it a bit."

While Angels GM Mike Port had raved about the way Rader worked with a coaching staff he'd inherited, Hough remembered the lack of communication between Rader and his coaching staff in Texas. It had included Dick Such, Merv Rettenmund, Rich Donnelly, Glenn Ezell, and Wayne Terwilliger, all of whom were back in the big leagues under different managers by 1989.

"More than anything, we had no coaches . . . not to say the guys we had weren't good coaches," Hough said. "But they were no factor. There was no hitting coach, no pitching coach, no defense coach. It was Doug. Doggone it, managing in the big leagues is way too tough for you to be a coach, too."

Rader said failure had taught him a lesson. "I thought a lot of the people we had in Texas," Rader said. "I really think they were good people, but for some reason or another I didn't want to let go. I didn't know how to. When I came [to California], I was very fortunate in having people who were already here. I knew I wasn't successful the other way, and I ended up frustrating everybody, including myself, so the only logical conclusion was to try another way."

The new style seemed to be working. Angels pitching coach Marcel Lachemann had been given much of the credit for an amazing turnaround by Kirk McCaskill and the Angels' pitching staff. But focusing on any change in Rader's style risked overlooking both the basic reason for the Angels' success thus far and the reason why others in the West had grown genuinely wary of California: They were deep in talent.

"The way we arrived at this point is a much more graceful one [than in Texas]," Rader said. "It took a lot less effort, a lot less pushing, a lot less of me. Because of that, I think it has a chance to perpetuate itself."

Time would judge the Angels, as well as their manager. In baseball, there's no hiding a fraud.

Kansas City emerged the big winner in the first round of games between the top four teams in the West. The Royals went 5-1 against California and Oakland while the Rangers were 4-2 against Oakland (which went 3-3) and California (which was 0-6).

"Things get interesting when the top teams start playing each other," Ryan said. "I think this goes to show that there's no real clear-cut favorite in the division. I think all four teams are going to be in it. It's going to stay that way."

That was the Rangers' hope.

* * *

Nine days after the Angels left town, Buddy Bell gave in to the voices that had been haunting him for weeks, deciding after a 4-0 victory over Cleveland June 23 that he would retire the following day. He could never grow accustomed to a seat on the bench, and after the April knee surgery he was unable to force his way into the playing situations that had marked his previous seventeen major league seasons.

" . . . I think it's all I can do," Bell said. "Based on my performance, based on what I've done in the past, I just couldn't adjust to the role that I will have here. After playing every day it seems like it's just doesn't work to sit on the bench."

Bell, thirty-seven, said he'd asked Tom Grieve and Valentine for his release before calling Valentine Friday afternoon to tell him he had decided to retire.

"We didn't want to release him," Grieve said. "You only release players you don't want. We had a role for Buddy to fill on this team. We never considered (a release). I liked having him in a Rangers uniform, even if he's not the player he used to be. I think it would have been best for Buddy to play until the end of the year, but we understand his decision and respect his decision."

There was no formal press conference to announce Bell's retirement. He prefered to handle it quietly, talking with reporters in trainer Bill Zeigler's office late at night. His eyes brimmed with tears, and he occasionally stopped to collect his thoughts.

"Everybody wants to play forever," Bell said. "It's been a tough day today. There's one reason for this—I couldn't handle my role. I wish to hell I could, but I'm too locked into playing every day, playing both sides of the game."

Bell was hitting .183 with no homers and three RBIs in eighty-two at bats after missing sixteen games to have arthroscopic knee surgery in April. It was unfamiliar territory for a player who had won six consecutive Gold Gloves and was a .279 career hitter in eighteen seasons.

Bell hoped to remain with the Rangers in another capacity, possibly as a scout or instructor. "I want to stay in this organization somehow," he said. "I'm going to talk to (Grieve) next week about that. I'm sure we'll work something out so I can stay here. It's a lot easier for me to work when I know people and care about the organization."

Although Bell had gone seven-for-twenty-two in his final ten games, he had started five times in an eighteen-game span. He might have sensed how far he had dropped out of Valentine's plans when he was not in the lineup against New York left-hander Dave LaPoint.

"This is not an impulsive decision," Bell said. "Because of the way I've been hitting, I've been thinking about this for quite some time. The only way I could really come out of something like this is to play on an everyday basis, and that wasn't possible here."

Bell had gotten only seventy-five at bats in fifty-two games since being activated April 28. He had started back-to-back games only eight times, and had never started more than three in a row. "I couldn't deal with it," Bell said.

"That's not Bobby's fault, Tom's fault, and it's not my fault. I'm used to playing every day. I just couldn't adjust. I couldn't do that."

When Bell signed with the Rangers in January, he'd claimed he was not doing it for the money. He had proved that by walking away from almost $300,000 of his $530,000 contract.

Valentine applauded Bell's effort. "I thought he made every physical effort that a man can do," he said. "But the mental part of it was the toughest. To change your whole mind-set, or how you perceive yourself as a player, was the difficult thing. Since he's retired, I guess it was the impossible thing for him to do."

When Bell officially went into retirement, there were no speeches and no news conference. There was just Bell, the one-time cover boy for two of baseball's worst franchises, making the rounds, shaking hands, and saying his farewells.

"My career has been pretty much of a secret," Bell said. "That's the way I wanted to go out, too."

"You think of Buddy as a fan favorite, a favorite among his teammates and one of the best all-around players who played the last twenty-five years," said Grieve. "He was a fine fielder, had 2,500 hits, was a role model, and never had the luxury of playing on a really good team. As good a player as he was, he probably was underrated, because he never got to play on a great team or in a major media market."

After being drafted by Cleveland in the sixteenth round of the 1969 draft, Bell was always the big fish in a small pond. While peers George Brett and Mike Schmidt will be remembered for their actions in pennant races, Bell's heroism was in trying to keep his teams out of the cellar.

In the spring of 1982, Bell called the Rangers the best team he had ever been on. Then he suffered through a 64-98 season that got Don Zimmer fired. That was one of ten second-division finishes for Bell from 1972 through 1988. The teams he had played on in Cleveland, Texas, Cincinnati, and Houston compiled a 1309-1440 record, including a 466-517 record with the Rangers.

Bell had played on one runnerup in Texas (1981) and three in Cincinnati (1985-87), but before retiring he had played in more games without getting into a post-season game than any other active player in the majors. He beat out Rangers' coach Toby Harrah for that distinction.

The lack of a championship ring would not be a source of great disappointment to Bell in future years. "I've always said the only thing I could ask for was the opportunity to get there," he said. "There are so many good things that happened to me. I couldn't ask for anything else."

Valentine sympathized with Bell's having never had the chance to play in a league championship series, much less a World Series. "It's a damn shame," he said. "I was hoping this was going to be the year for it to happen."

15

No Playoffs, Please—We're the Texas Rangers

By July, April seemed a long way back, like the last service station you passed before noticing you were almost out of gas. Nolan Ryan's starts were awaited anxiously by those following the team, as there was little else to get worked up about. Ruben Sierra and Julio Franco continued to hit the ball hard, but Rafael Palmeiro had begun a death spiral at the plate after leading the league with a .361 average on May 28. The fabulous April had been followed by a 10-17 May and a 16-13 June that ended with the Rangers being unable to get on a roll despite a stretch against Cleveland, Chicago, and Seattle.

But things seemed different with Ryan pitching. There was always a sense that this could be the night he threw his sixth no-hitter; after all, he had trounced Seattle with a one-hitter June 3, then had lost another bid when Sierra lost a gap shot by Brook Jacoby in the Arlington Stadium lights during the eighth inning on June 25. It was also relief from the inconsistencies of Bobby Witt and Charlie Hough, who was trying to pitch his way through pain in his shoulder.

With the season approaching its mid-point, Ryan and rookie Kevin Brown were the reliable hurlers in the rotation. Ryan appeared on his way to a seventh selection for the All-Star Game, but the prospect didn't thrill him. He winced

172

whenever the subject came up, and honest as always, told reporters he would rather have the three days to spend with his family in Alvin. But the game was being played in Anaheim, and Ryan still had a soft spot for the Angels. Though he had left there on shaky terms with then-GM Buzzie Bavasi, his relationship with the Angel fans was special.

That became apparent on July 6, when Ryan made his first appearance at Anaheim Stadium since 1979. His return was something of an event in trendy Southern California–though a showing of old loyalties rather than a fad.

When the Angels had made their off-season pitch to re-sign Ryan for 1989, Fountain Valley restaurateur Bill Madden had shipped Ryan a petition bearing nearly ten thousand signatures. Madden also had sent a videotape of Ryan's milestones with the Angels, interspersed among personal pleas from other Ryan diehard fans.

"It made me feel good that so many people wanted me to come back and play here," Ryan said. "A lot of time had elapsed, you know."

Madden told the *Orange-County Register*'s Randy Youngman that he would be at the game, although it would be strange to see Ryan pitching in the Rangers' gray road uniforms instead of the Angels' home whites. "It feels a little bit like an old girlfriend's coming back to town," he said. "You still like her, but you know things could have worked out better. Seeing how the Angels are ahead of the Rangers [in the standings], I think it would have been better if Nolan would have come back here. Just think how strong the Angels would have been with him on their staff."

The first of three standing ovations for Ryan began when he walked in from the bullpen before the game. Bob Hope had just given a short speech as part of the pre-game ceremonies, and received polite applause from the crowd. But the response didn't compare to what greeted Ryan as he entered from left field. Sensing the uniqueness of the moment, pitching coach Tom House and catcher Chad Kreuter peeled off into foul territory, allowing Ryan to walk alone in the applause.

"It was a special feeling," Ryan said later. "Coming out of the bullpen, I don't think I've ever had a reception like that. It was one of the highlights of my career. I'll always remember it."

Ryan turned in a vintage performance, which was a relief for the Rangers. They had lost five of their last six games, including three straight in the four-game series with California. Ryan threw a three-hitter, beating the Angels 3-0. "The key to the game was that I had the best curveball I've had all year. I think I established it and they were looking for it. That made my fastball as good as it was."

Ryan struck out twelve in what was only his second complete-game shut-out since 1984. He left to the same kind of standing ovation that had greeted him. "The fans here have always treated me special," Ryan said. "But for an opposing player to be treated like that means a lot to me."

Homers by Steve Buechele and Sierra had provided Ryan with all the support necessary in his tenth win, knocking California out of the West lead it had taken from Oakland. The victory let the Rangers take a five-game deficit to Oakland for a weekend series just before the three-day All-Star break.

Ryan appeared to be softening his stance on the All-Star Game. He'd said earlier that he'd prefer to spend the days off with his family, and that it made "no difference" that the game would be played where he had pitched in 1972-79 and had thrown four of his no-hitters. But back in his old home territory, he amended that position.

"If I get selected for it, coming to Anaheim would make it special," Ryan said. "I have nothing but good memories from my years here, in this stadium." Ryan's lone lament was the new look Anaheim Stadium had been given when it was enclosed as an incentive to the Los Angeles Rams.

"It's disapointing to me to see this stadium the way it is now," he said. "When I left, they hadn't closed it in. I thought it was the best stadium in baseball. Now it's just another big stadium."

Texas closed the first half strong, winning two of three at the Oakland Coliseum to finish 47-39, its best record at the break since 1983. It trailed California by 5½ games and Oakland by four.

Sierra's three-run homer and one of Witt's best performances carried the Rangers to a 6-3 victory in the Friday night opener. The play of the game was made by Rick Leach, who knocked himself unconscious when he ran into the left-field wall while catching a Mark McGwire drive.

The Saturday game was the best effort Valentine's team would give all season. It was just one game in a six-month schedule, but it looked different—like a battle between two tired armies whose generals had a score to settle.

After both bullpens blew leads in the last two innings, the conflict ended when the Rangers' phalanx of Palmeiro, Sierra, and Franco strung together tenth-inning singles against Oakland relievers Matt Young and Gene Nelson. (Dennis Eckersley was on the disabled list with a strained rotator cuff.) Jeff Russell then got McGwire to hit into a game-ending double play, putting a 5-4 final score on a game that had stood 2-1 when Valentine pulled an exhausted Brown at the start of the eighth inning.

Afterward, the Texas clubhouse looked like an NFL locker room. Everyone moved slowly except the trainers. Gary Mielke, one of only eight Rangers who didn't play, had his arm wrapped in ice just from getting ready in the bullpen. Leach, who had made a pinch-hit appearance despite the whiplash he'd suffered the night before, got more treatment for his stiff neck. Valentine talked about how he had considered using Ryan as a defensive replacement.

"First base," Ryan said.

No, it was not a normal mid-season game. For the Rangers, it was a fight for survival. They had started the West Coast road trip with three losses at Anaheim Stadium that helped catapult California into the division lead, and they knew how tenuous was their claim to being part of the American League West race.

"That's why I felt I could play today," said Leach. "Looking at the situation with California and Oakland, we have to hang in there. If we come in and lose these three games, it's going to do nothing but dig us a deeper hole for the second half."

Russell made his earliest appearance with a lead since April 14. He bounced back after giving up a two-run homer to Rickey Henderson in Oakland's three-run eighth to get the victory as the Rangers raised their record to 3-3 on the trip. Valentine had downplayed the trip's significance, but he certainly wasn't managing like it was any other series. Late-inning moves by both Valentine and Tony La Russa set this season series apart from the rest. Valentine used four different pitchers in the eighth inning Friday; La Russa had made ten moves in an 11-8 loss June 9 at Arlington Stadium.

"They're sporting their studs out there, and both teams have a lot of studs," Russell said. "All players like to play in these games. We get high from it."

Texas closed the road trip 3-4, losing 7-1 to Bob Welch the next day. "This was just a tough stretch," Valentine said. "But they've got three days to rejuvenate. Pitchers came on real strong. We battled through some injuries. I think we're in good shape."

Tom Grieve didn't entirely agree. Pete Incaviglia, Steve Buechele, and Scott Fletcher had been major disappointments in the first half of the season. Grieve also saw a glaring weakness at designated hitter, where the lack of productivity that led Buddy Bell to retire had contributed to Valentine's trying twenty-five different players since releasing Larry Parrish one year earlier.

While his players made the franchise's best-ever showing at the All-Star Game—Ryan became the oldest pitcher ever to win, while Sierra and Franco combined for three hits and Russell pitched an inning—Grieve was talking with Chicago White Sox General Manager Larry Himes about Harold Baines, who was on the trading block despite an All-Star season. Typically, Grieve declined to confirm what he was working on, but addressed the situation in generalities.

"We need," Grieve said, "to find someone who can provide offense somewhere in our lineup. Now we're trying to find any way to improve our offense."

Grieve continued to pursue the Baines trade through some different avenues —the Rangers began by offering Incaviglia, but Himes' interest lay largely in top minor-league prospects—and sweated when it looked like Baines would go to the Baltimore Orioles. New Baltimore General Manager Roland Hemond had been with the White Sox when they drafted Baines with the first pick in the country, and the addition of Baines to a thin lineup figured to give the Orioles a realistic shot in the second half.

But while Grieve and Himes continued to talk, the Rangers came back from the break with a thud. The Indians took three of four at Cleveland Stadium, beating both Ryan and Brown; the Rangers then returned to Arlington for the longest homestand of the year—thirteen games in fourteen days against Boston, New York, Toronto, and Milwaukee. It took a four-game sweep of the crumbling Yankees to go 8-5 during those two weeks. The final weekend of the homestand, Jeffcoat was bombed in a 15-3 loss to the Brewers that dropped Texas seven games behind the first-place Angels.

But the Rangers had been in their biggest hole of the season for less than twelve hours when Grieve got what he'd wanted–Baines.

Grieve again showed a preference for productivity over sentimentality. He sent shortstop Scott Fletcher and top prospects Wilson Alvarez (a nineteen-year-old left-hander) and Sammy Sosa (a twenty-year-old outfielder) to the White Sox for Baines and infielder Fred Manrique.

Grieve denied looking for a quick fix for the growing deficit, saying that the deal would help Texas in years to come. But everyone knew it was also designed to light the retro rockets on a team that had played three games under .500 since April.

"For the last few years we've been trying very hard to fill the designated hitter's spot," Grieve said. "We think we filled it with the best designated hitter in baseball. It was a good step for our offense, which was already a good offense. But you don't make a trade for the last two months of the season. Harold Baines is thirty years old, and we think he can help for who knows how long–four, five, or six years."

Baines, pleased to be with a winning team, hopped a flight and was in the lineup Saturday night. Valentine had the luxury of batting three of the American League's All-Star starters–Baines, Ruben Sierra, and Julio Franco–in succession.

And he still lost–9-2 to the Brewers.

Still, combined with Palmeiro and Incaviglia, that nucleus commanded attention. "Texas did a pretty good job," Minnesota manager Tom Kelly said. "Palmeiro, Franco, Sierra, and Harold Baines batting together sounds pretty impressive."

Baines had been voted the American League's top designated hitter both of the last two seasons. He was one of only four major-leaguers with at least 50 extra-base hits in each of the last seven seasons, and had been undergoing a renaissance with help from White Sox hitting instructor Walt Hriniak. Baines came to Texas batting .321 with 13 homers and 56 runs batted in. Even Fletcher admitted he'd probably help a slumping lineup that was sixth in the American League with an average of 4.51 runs per game.

"I think Harold will help," said Fletcher. "Harold is a person who takes care of himself, plays hard all the time, and works hard. He loves to play, loves to hit. He's a top quality player."

When Fletcher became the Rangers' first millionaire during the winter, most people thought he would be wearing a Texas uniform until they tore down Arlington Stadium and built another ballpark. But Fletcher's tenure with the Rangers ended after only 3½ years. His popularity in the clubhouse was un-paralleled, and his trade to the Chicago White Sox reminded his teammates just how uncertain baseball careers can be.

"Here today, gone tomorrow," Russell said. "I had no idea this could happen. Scott was a leader around here. But we traded away a good player and got a good player."

A desire to stay in Arlington, where he recently had bought a home, was one of the reasons Fletcher gave for re-signing with Texas in November, when he was pursued by the White Sox and six other teams. "I didn't know about the rest of my career," said Fletcher, who was hitting .239 with 22 RBIs in eighty-three games. "Texas is a place I enjoyed playing. I enjoyed the area and the people. I enjoyed playing for Bobby. That went into my decision. But I went into this game knowing nothing is guaranteed. No matter what you sign, anything can happen."

There was a quiet feeling that Fletcher's performance had declined as a result of his record contract. "I think he put a lot on himself because of his contract, to perform up to the contract," Hough reflected. "He seemed to be under a lot of tension inside. It's understandable, and he's going to get over it, too. Scotty is going to be a good player."

In hindsight, Grieve also saw the contract as an impediment to Fletcher's performance. He had led the Rangers in hitting three consecutive years to merit an increase from his $575,000 salary last year.

"My guess would be it [affected him]," Grieve said. "As proud as he is, I think he was trying to be a better player than he has been. He'll try to scale new heights, and maybe put too much pressure on himself."

Baines didn't seem thrilled about the trade to Texas. Then again, he seldom seemed thrilled about anything. Three weeks after the trade, White Sox co-owner Jerry Reinsdorf decided to retire the # 3 he had worn in Chicago. Baines's reaction: "I can take it or leave it."

Excitable guy, huh?

Well, everyone said Baines was a nice guy, but he was about as outgoing as a potted plant. He had played with the White Sox since 1980, and had developed a reputation for quiet toughness. He'd undergone arthroscopic surgery on his right knee in 1986 and again in 1987, but hadn't played fewer than 132 games since 1981.

Baines had had no problems with his knee in 1989, and was available for duty in the outfield. But he knew the Rangers saw him almost exclusively as a DH, and that was okay with him. "I know my role," Baines said. "It's to be the best hitter I can be."

Baines had never caused waves. He said little other than "yes, sir" when the White Sox offered him a minor-league contract, then headed straight for Appleton, Wisconsin. He went from there to Knoxville, Tennessee, and then to Des Moines, Iowa. Three weeks after turning twenty-one he was in the White Sox lineup for Opening Day, 1980.

By age twenty-four, Baines had led Tony La Russa's White Sox to a division championship in 1983. Baines's sacrifice fly had clinched Chicago's first baseball title since 1959. He was a two-time All-Star outfielder by the age of twenty-seven, before his two knee surgeries. His answer: Working hard to get his knee back into condition, and become the best DH in the business. His reward: Combined salaries of $3,539,751 the last five years, including a $1,189,751 salary this year. He expected at least five more years of increasing earnings.

For all his material success, Baines and his wife continued to raise their three children (ages five, three, and nineteen months) in the small Maryland town of St. Michaels, only nine miles from Baines's hometown, Easton. "I'll probably always be there," Baines said. "It's so peaceful there."

While Baines had been in the major leagues longer than any Rangers except Ryan, Hough, and Sundberg, his collected quotes wouldn't have filled an index card. "You don't open up *Sports Illustrated* and see Harold Baines in the 'They Said It' column very often," Grieve said. "It seems like all anybody knows about him is that he's a great hitter." Baines earned his teammates' respect by letting a lifetime .465 slugging percentage represent him in the clubhouse.

"There's two types of players—one who is quiet and one who is screaming," said Manrique. "Harold's a great player, but the only screaming he does is inside him. Sometimes players try to be political, go around screaming too much. I have problems with that. Harold's not like that."

Baines agreed with that assessment. "I'm not a rah-rah guy," Baines said. "I'm pulling for the guys, but I'm not shouting. I just try to bust my butt on the field. It pays off."

Both Alvarez and Sosa had spent time with the Rangers. Grieve conceded they were top prospects but cited depth in the farm system as a key to trading them. He claimed the Rangers had six minor-league outfielders "comparable" to Sosa, most notably nineteen-year-old Juan Gonzalez, who was hitting .293 with nine homers and 53 RBIs at Class AA Tulsa, and 1989 draft choices Donald Harris and Dan Peltier. He cited a similar stock of left-handed pitchers, with 1987 #1 draft choice Brian Bohanon and eighteen-year-old Darren Oliver chief among them.

Texas had gotten burned in the past by trading youth for veteran players, but neither Valentine nor Grieve seemed too concerned about history's repeating itself. "The player we're getting," Valentine said, "is not Lee Mazzilli."

Following the trade, Valentine installed Jeff Kunkel as his everyday shortstop, but it didn't take long for Kunkel's erratic play to give Manrique a chance to work at the position. Neither was steady, and their play showed that the team was still going in the wrong direction, despite Grieve's best efforts.

The Rangers were 55-46 before acquiring Baines, but lost seven of the first ten after the trade. It wasn't Baines's fault. After an 0-for-4 debut in that anticlimactic 9-2 beating, he had three hits his second night in town, including two doubles. His homer with two outs in the ninth gave Texas a 4-3 victory at Tiger Stadium in the opener of a nine-game road trip.

But not much else was going right. Detroit, suffering through its first losing season in more than a decade, recovered to take two out of three. Then the Rangers dropped two of three in Baltimore, where the Rangers lineup put only two runs on the Memorial Stadium scoreboard in consecutive losses to rookies Bob Milacki and Pete Harnisch (who took a combined record of 6-14 into their starts).

In Toronto's new SkyDome, the Blue Jays were handed a 2-1 victory over the surprising Jeffcoat. Back-to-back throwing errors by Manrique in the sixth inning allowed both runs to score. The Rangers hit rock bottom the next night, looking pathetic against a neophyte named Mauro "Goose" Gozzo. A long reliever in the Class AA Southern League when the season began, he sent Texas tumbling to its fourth consecutive loss, this one by a 7-0 score. The Rangers' plight was epitomized by Rick Leach's oversliding third base and being tagged out after going from first to third base on a ninth-inning passed ball.

This was ugly.

Texas managed only five hits in Gozzo's debut in the major leagues. The meager hitting by a lineup which included three All-Star starters had finally ensured that Valentine's fifth season in Texas would end like those before it—on the outside looking in at the American League West race.

Valentine insisted that August 8 was far too early for a postmortem, but the facts pointed toward another dull September. Having scored five runs on twenty-four hits in the last four games, the Rangers were five games over 500 and nine games behind California. "It's called baseball," Valentine said. "Sometimes they fall in, sometimes they don't. You've got to battle through it."

Along with the slim hope of a Rangers resurrection, one more Ryan sideshow kept the interest of fans. He was closing in on his 5,000th career strikeout, a milestone which focused national attention on Arlington. He had entered the season needing 225 to reach 5,000, and that had seemed no sure bet. He had struck out that many only three times in the ten previous seasons.

But he approached the total inexorably. As the season went on, the question became *when* Ryan would get the milestone strikeout, and even that became fairly easy to figure as it approached. There was little doubt it would be in Arlington Stadium, as the schedule allowed him to pitch at home five times in a stretch of six starts. But it seemed he might reach it too quickly, as he started at the Kingdome in Seattle August 16 with 4,986 career strikeouts.

Ryan struck out eight in a routine 3-1 victory, making it almost a lock that the 5,000th strikeout would come on August 22, when the Rangers opened an absolutely-last-chance homestand against Oakland and California. They trailed the Athletics by 9½ games, meaning a sweep would bring them back within only 6½. Not a bright prospect.

But Ryan's quest for 5,000 made it the Rangers earliest sellout ever. Long lines formed at the ticket office the morning after Ryan's start in Seattle, and by noon that day all the tickets were gone.

On a beautiful North Texas night, Ryan disappointed no one, striking out thirteen when six would have been enough to satisfy the crowd of 42,869. He had been uncharacteristically nervous. In fact, he had been so preoccupied that it had taken some extra navigation even to reach the stadium. "Coming to the ballpark," Ryan said, "I missed the road to the stadium and had to turn around and come back. That shows where my mind was."

Ryan made Rickey Henderson his 5,000th strikeout victim, blazing a 3-2 fastball past him after five others had avoided becoming a footnote to history. But he was given the kind of support that has too often characterized his twenty-three seasons with the New York Mets, California Angels, Houston Astros, and Rangers. The Rangers lost 2-0, largely because of some lackadaisical plays in the outfield.

Welch and Dennis Eckersley matched Ryan's five-hitter, sending away the second-largest Arlington crowd ever to marvel at Ryan's feat and say last rites for the Rangers.

"The game tonight was probably a reflection of why Oakland was where they were all year," said Ryan after the game. "They got good pitching, and they're a good ball club. Hopefully tomorrow we'll come out and get headed in the right direction. It's a big week for us."

It was actually a fatal week. The Rangers lost two out of three to both Oakland and California.

Despite the addition of Baines, things never did get much better. There was an interesting pennant race in the American League West, but it was between Oakland, California, and Kansas City. In the end, Oakland's addition of Rickey Henderson gave the Athletics what they needed to repeat with a pitching staff that again had the lowest ERA in the AL. The Rangers were not a factor, finishing 83-79 and in fourth place. Amazingly, that represented their second-highest victory total in the 1980s. It was not the season Valentine had dreamed about after the successful winter, but it was a step in the right direction.

Ruben Sierra finished with a .306 average, 29 homers, and 119 runs batted in, but was beaten out for the American League MVP award by Milwaukee's Robin Yount. He scored 101 runs and set club records with 78 extra-base hits and 344 total bases. Jeff Russell led the league with 38 saves, earning the Rolaids Relief Man award in his first year as a stopper. Kevin Brown pitched well enough (12-9, 3.35) to receive a few Rookie of the Year votes. But only Ryan was amazing.

He maintained his magic all the way through his final start of the year, a near no-hitter at Anaheim Stadium. Returning to the scene of his only shutout of the season and a victory in the All-Star Game, Ryan actually flirted with perfection for eight innings. He sat down the first 22 California hitters before a single by Brian Downing broke the spell. From there, he finished off a three-hit, 2-0 victory. He also struck out 13, giving him 301 for the season—the first 300-strikeout season in the AL since Ryan had done it before in 1977.

The morning after that masterpiece, he sat in a booth at the Anaheim Marriott and told reporters that he had decided to return, at the age of forty-three, for the 1990 season—a decision based on two things, his family and his arm.

His wife, Ruth, and his children had all enjoyed the summer in Arlington and wanted to see him pitch some more. His arm seemed to be ageless. He was eleven victories shy of the three hundred plateau, and there seemed little doubt he would reach that in 1990. Ryan not only had made each of his thirty-two scheduled starts, but for the first time had pitched through the fifth inning every time. Among his other 1989 accomplishments:

• He'd won 16 games, equalling his best total since 1977. He'd also become the oldest pitcher to ever get a win in the All-Star Game.

• He'd flirted with his sixth career no-hitter five times, taking two into the ninth inning and three others into the eighth. He'd also pitched a one-hitter, giving up only a single to Seattle's Harold Reynolds.

• He'd set a club record for strikeouts, averaging 9.4 per start and 11.3 per nine innings, the third-best ratio ever (he had averaged 11.5 in 1987 and Dwight Gooden had averaged 11.4 in 1984). It was the twenty-second 300-strikeout season in the majors—he had done it five times previously—and the first in the American League since he had done it himself in 1977. He had become the oldest pitcher, by eleven years, to fan 300. He had also raised his record strikeout total to 5,076, 940 more than Steve Carlton's runner-up total.

• He'd held the opposition to a .187 batting average, the best in the major leagues, by allowing 162 hits in 239⅓ innings.

"If this year was different than any other year, it was probably because of my consistency," Ryan said. "I was probably more consistent. I didn't have a week or ten days when I had a bad spell, some bad games."

He credited Rangers pitching coach Tom House with improving Ryan's already successful conditioning program.

While Ryan's age caused Houston to offer him a pay cut after last season, Grieve found no need to set limits. Ryan now talked about being physically capable of pitching until age forty-five.

"I guess I was programmed for so long with Houston about my age," he said. "Houston was always thinking I was in my last year. I went through a month of May last year where I didn't know if I could pitch any more, and (Astros General Manager) Bill Wood told me in the negotiations last winter he thought I was done in May. He was thinking I was a risk.

"The Rangers' attitude is completely opposite. They feel, 'If he wants to pitch until he's forty-five, he probably can.' My age has affected my attitude about what to expect, but the longer I go, the more convinced I am that if I keep myself in good shape, I should be able to continue to perform."

Despite Ryan, inconsistent starting pitching again was the Rangers' cause of death. Charlie Hough had slumped to 10-13 and Bobby Witt had regressed, finishing 13-13 with a 5.14 ERA in thirty-one starts. They were the two best answers to the question of why Valentine couldn't squeeze more victories from his revamped team.

Valentine seemed to understand this, and as the season wound down he did not sink to the emotional lows of the two previous Septembers. He accepted the team's fate with more ease than before, looking to the bright side of another season of unfulfilled dreams.

"Other than the fact we were 17-5 at the beginning, it was satisfying because of the things we accomplished and the growth that we've made individually," Valentine said. "Our future is in place, defined. From where we came, from last year, the feeling of almost despair we had at the end of last year, to the feeling I have right now, it is satisfying."

Grieve shared the frustration of losing the magical start, but cited the club record attendance of 2,043,993 as a measure of public approval for the Rangers' direction.

"Your imagination wanders a little bit when you're 17-5," he said, "You say, 'Wow,' but on the other hand you look at all the indicators that go into good teams, and there were still some question marks at that time. I still judge the season a success. I define our success in the fact we drew two million people. We had never done that before, so evidently we've never put that kind of product on the field before. We went from twenty-one games under .500 to where we are, which is a sign of a successful year. Also, now we have a solid nucleus of players, All-Star players, that we've never had before. But it's not a success in the most important way – we didn't win a pennant. That's what it's all about."

Maybe someday they will. At the end of 1989, George W. Bush seemed to think so. The Rangers' managing general partner indicated confidence in the club's management, saying he planned to keep it on the developmental path Grieve had put it on under Eddie Chiles.

No one, it seemed, enjoyed the franchise's third winning season in the '80s more than Bush. "It was a great season," Bush said. "There were a lot of thrills – Nolan's 5,000th strikeout, the Ryan-Clemens game, Sierra's homer with two outs in the ninth to help sweep the Yankees. There were just a lot of exciting plays from a team that was fun to watch."

Bush let his thoughts wander.

"I see the nucleus there," he said. "I think this team's mission is to be a contender. Next year is a year for us to contend. Hopefully for the next decade, every year we're in contention. Just like the season is long, my tenure in baseball is going to be long, and I'm a patient guy. I want to win, but if we're in contention we'll have done what we should do for our fans. And if you're in contention long enough, good things will happen."

There were changes to be made over the winter, and questions to address. Valentine wanted another starting pitcher from somewhere, as well as help in the bullpen. Cecil Espy, Grieve admitted, looked like "the center fielder of the future half the time and a minor-leaguer the other half . . . " It was that characterization that led to the signing of Gold Glover Gary Pettis. There were also holes at catcher, where Chad Kreuter's rookie season had ended with a .152 batting average and a league-high twenty-one passed balls, and perhaps at shortstop, where both Kunkel and Manrique were struggling.

But with the Rangers, there had always been holes. Now there was hope to go with the holes – a strength for every weakness. That may not have been much of a legacy for 4½ years of building by the Grieve-Valentine regime, but at least they were managing to roll the rock uphill, even if it was an inch at a time. Not even they knew how far they were from the top.

But the sun was breaking through from time to time. Maybe, just maybe, the black cloud was lifting.

The memory will always be sharp. It was June, 1984, and my first road trip with the Texas Rangers. The team was traveling to Seattle for a series with the woeful Mariners, and my eyes were open wide to everything that went on around me.

Baseball had always seemed the toughest yet purest sport of all. I had always wanted to cover a major-league team, and now I had gotten the chance. Randy Youngman had left the *Times Herald* to cover the Dodgers for *The Orange County Register,* and our new sports editor, Mike Bevans, had called me at the Indianapolis 500 to ask if I wanted the beat. You bet I did.

Many at my paper would have passed on the assignment. Not only was it demanding, but at the time it could be very unrewarding. As prestige went, the Rangers couldn't touch the Cowboys or Mavericks. Tom Landry was at the crest of his popularity in the NFL, and Dallas-Fort Worth sports fans had just discovered the NBA. The Mavs had somehow beaten the Seattle Supersonics in their first-ever playoff series—the Miracle at Moody—and were on their way to what many figured would be the top of the Western Division once Kareem got too old to bury that skyhook at Crunch Time.

While Doug Rader's team was coming off a honeymoon season, it had already started slowly in '84 and was on its way to drawing a mere 1.1 million fans. An old team, it wasn't going to get much better without major changes. Even I could see that. But the job still grabbed me. This was the major leagues, and I was along for a ride. I could relate.

In keeping with the times, though, the Rangers struggled during my baptismal series at the Kingdome. Rader was wound tight, and after one game he and the *Fort Worth Star-Telegram*'s Jim Reeves got into a shouting match over something that was asked or had been written. Maybe it was the tone of somebody's voice, or the color of someone's socks. I'm not exactly sure and it doesn't really matter. All I knew was that the scene was ugly.

The tension in Rader's office hit you like the first wave of heat from a car that had sat for hours in the August sun. Reeves did not back down to Rader, but there clearly wasn't much pleasure in standing up to him. It was a no-win proposition.

That night, Reeves and I sat in a quiet bar at the Seattle Sheraton and talked about the job I had just begun. I was excited. Reeves had been doing it for at least ten years, and was one of the best anywhere. His even personality, combined with a willingness to work and his love of a good time, made him the perfect baseball writer. He was at the top of his game.

He was also depressed.

Very depressed.

Reeves stared down into his drink and wondered aloud how he was going to make it through the season. I would come to know that feeling, but it shocked me coming from Revo. He explained that the job just wasn't fun for him anymore. There were two reasons: Rader and losing, in either order.

Sports reporters are expected to be objective, and as a group those around the Rangers always have been. But no matter what a journalism professor tells you, a reporter's sharpest instinct is survival. Life is a lot easier covering a team that is winning at least every other night. Nobody likes to walk into a small room filled with large men and, night after night, ask just how they could have screwed up another game. Players and managers certainly don't like dealing with those questions. What they may not realize is how little pleasure asking them gives.

Well, times changed. Rader went the way of all the managers who had preceded him in Arlington. Reeves hung around to cover the team's promising first full season under Bobby Valentine's direction, then was kicked upstairs as a columnist for the *Star-Telegram*. Tim Kurkjian, who had covered the team for *The Dallas Morning News*, went to cover the Orioles for *The Baltimore Sun*, and Paul Hagen, Reeves' colleague at the *Star-Telegram* (and another *Times Herald* alum), went to cover the Phillies for the *Philadelphia Daily News*. I stayed. So, too, did the image of Revo at that Sheraton bar.

To me, that always seemed like a sign that the Rangers had sunk to record depths. They had managed to take all the pleasure out of a game that is the best one we have yet invented. Baseball has only one unforgivable sin, and that is it—to be played without joy.

This is the prelude to a difficult judgment. Five and a half seasons later, the Rangers were still trying to break from their losing script. Despite a 17-5 April in 1989, they had not come closer to an American League West title under Valentine than they did in that magical season of '86. That year, they improved twenty-five games in the final standings and finished five games behind Gene Mauch's California Angels. It was supposed to be the start of something big.

But after three more long seasons, they had not produced results. Many people thought it was time for a change of direction. Valentine had become an amazingly popular whipping boy throughout the major leagues. One September day in '89, at least three players who knew Valentine asked me if I thought he should get fired. They clearly thought so. Two American League scouts echoed the sentiment. One of those rated Valentine thirteenth among the league's managers that year, ahead of only Cleveland's Doc Edwards, who had already been fired.

Not many people in baseball like Valentine. That's clear. He has a way of irritating people. Mostly he does it with the way he carries himself. He walks with a strut. He talks with a strut. He struts when he wins, and he evens manages the appearance of a strut when he loses. The one thing he has yet to do is back it up with enduring success. No one knows that better than Valentine.

When the Baltimore Orioles came to Arlington Stadium leading the American League East in September '89, one Baltimore reporter asked Valentine to talk about what a team in the O's position goes through as the 162-game season is cut down to one or two dozen games. Valentine smiled for a second, then told a painful truth. "You're asking the wrong person," he said. "I've never been in that position."

I have always considered Valentine seriously intelligent and sincere about wanting to do the best job possible. Not many people love the game more, and few work harder. While most managers retreat to homes in Florida or California for the winter, Valentine moved to North Texas when he joined with the Rangers. He stays at the Arlington Stadium batting cage during the off-season, throwing batting practice to whatever players care enough to work out. It's grunt work, yet Valentine never complains.

But in baseball you aren't judged by your qualities. The won-loss record is usually all anyone wants to know. Valentine's record stood at 368-408 after 1989, and because of that he became a regular target on the radio talk shows. People wanted him out of town. There was an irony to this, of course. The Rangers had always been blasted—inside baseball and out—for their lack of stability. It was the single biggest reason they went through their first eighteen seasons in Texas without a division title. What would have happened if they had stuck with Whitey Herzog back in 1973? You get the point. Now they were finally giving one man a real chance to succeed, and their adherence to the status quo came under question.

But at least people were calling the talk shows. Even into football season, people were talking about the Rangers. No matter what they were saying, this was a milepost which showed just how far the franchise had come since gambling on Tom Grieve as the general manager and then, after severing ties with Rader, letting Grieve pick his own manager.

Despite the downward spiral after April, the club set an attendance record in '89, topping the two-million mark for the first time. On one amazing Saturday night in September, when the Cowboys were playing the Houston Oilers at Texas Stadium and SMU was playing the first game after its football program was given the death penalty by the NCAA, more than thirty thousand went to Arlington Stadium to watch the Rangers beat Kansas City.

Talk about a change of managers overlooks just how much progress has been made in five years. Through a combination of player development, shrewd trades and roll-the-dice spending, Grieve collected five of the AL's twenty-eight All-Star players—18 percent—in '89. Ruben Sierra, Julio Franco, and Harold Baines figure to be the backbone of the attack for years to come. Jeff Russell should be among the league's top stoppers for five to ten years, providing he remains healthy. Even though he turned forty-three in 1990, Nolan Ryan appears to have one or two more strong years left in his remarkable body.

A commitment to scouting and player development puts the club in position to compete long-term with the best organizations in baseball—the New York Mets, Toronto Blue Jays, St. Louis Cardinals, and Oakland Athletics. There are more players who may follow the paths of Sierra and Kevin Brown. Keep these names in mind: Juan Gonzalez, Robb Nen, Dean Palmer, Mark Petkovsek, Monty Fariss, Kevin Belcher, Donald Harris, Dan Peltier, and Darren Oliver. It was no fluke that the Rangers' farm teams combined to have their best record ever in 1989. Given enough time, talent will produce results.

I grew up in Dallas in the '60s, when the Cowboys were still trying to make a name for themselves. The success that would put them in the NFL playoffs seventeen times in eighteen years was hardly overnight. There was a time when fans wanted Tom Landry on the streets. He came to the job without a reputation, like Valentine, and lost big-time before teasing the population with gradual improvement. The team that would go to five Super Bowls was known only as "Next Year's Champions."

But eventually the Cowboys broke through and won, then kept winning. Call me crazy, but I believe the same thing can happen with the Rangers. Finally, the foundation has been laid. Now it's just a matter of catching some clear weather and good breaks to finish the project. One of these seasons, hopefully in our lifetimes, there will be baseball after September in Arlington. Book it.

Bruce Springsteen said it best: *Show a little faith, there's magic in the night.* Even at Arlington Stadium.

Phil Rogers, October 1989

Index